BEYOND THE GREEN GATE

A MEMOIR OF FAITH, FAMILY AND THE FAR SIDE OF HOME

SHERYL ROBERTS

SACRA DOMUS PUBLISHING

For my patient, adventure-loving husband, John

For my ten children and my in-loves who married into our family and the growing brood of grandchildren that keep me young and ready for the next adventure

For our dear Khmer friends, our rocks in a hard place

DISCLOSURE

These are my memories taken from my letters home, my ministry updates written to supporters, interviews with family and friends, and my pages and pages of personal journals. Some memories are clear as day, others are vague and cloudy. I tried to stay true to the events, but this is only my perspective, and I do not presume upon others' experiences named in this story.

Some names of people and places have been changed to protect privacy. Some scene elements and character descriptions have been fictionalized to protect privacy. Some timelines have been compressed, and some characters have been composited. Dialogue has been recreated.

The author assumes full responsibility for the content while acknowledging the subjective nature of personal memory and narrative storytelling. This memoir is a truthful account as I lived it, understood it, and remember it.

FOREWORD

I never set out to write a memoir. Many years ago, when I started writing my stories in long-winded emails or handwritten letters from Cambodia, it was to share my life with family and friends far away in America.

I was told numerous times over the years that I should write a book. But raising ten children was task enough for me for the past thirty years. I was content with journal entries and emails.

But here, over two decades later, I now attempt to put into words not only the small details but also the big picture of what Cambodia taught me.

So why now? I've become increasingly aware of a new breed of maternal anxiety uniquely tied to contemporary pressures and expectations—maybe due to the proliferation of information on the internet, or the temptation to peek into sanitized versions of other moms' lives, or the rash of school shootings, viruses, and vaccination propaganda. I found that mothers are no longer peaceful within their God-given mission.

I am writing this book for them. I want them to know that they can do hard things, overcome illnesses and accidents, have less-than-ideal births, and suffer miscarriages and still find joy, peace, and home. Mothers, around the world, this book is for you.

PROLOGUE

D on't walk off the path. Land mines." Her black hair
bobbed in front of me. I stopped halfway down the path
as my flip-flops stuck in dark brown silky sludge leftover
from the monsoon rains earlier in the day. *They told me they had
cleared all the land mines.*

Pulling my foot free, I followed Sopheap hesitantly toward the
goat barn at the far end of the property. She gestured proudly at their
new goat herd. Some lounged in the shade, others nibbled on weeds
creeping over the gate, and a couple of young bucks butted heads in
the muddy corner. Two inexperienced does, with their heavy udders,
pressed close to the gate waiting to be milked. They struggled with
nursing, so Sopheap made a trip twice a day to bottle-feed the young
kids and milk the mothers. This evening, the young kids leaped playfully between their mothers' legs, full of energy despite the day's heat.

I turned to look back at John carrying Malachi, three years old, on
his shoulders while Mary, six years old, dawdled behind me. I
grabbed her hand to make sure she stayed on the muddy path, though
she would rather scamper barefoot in the tall grass with the land
mines.

It was our two youngest children's special trip to our community
service project in Som Pov Loon in northeast Cambodia one kilo-

meter from the Thai border. The village lay within the world's most heavily mined areas, a stark reminder that this was one of the Khmer Rouge strongholds during the civil war which waged through Cambodia beginning in the late seventies. A few years earlier, we had started a community center there, now run by a Khmer couple who were full of ideas and zeal. Goats were one of them.

"They're cute," I said, pulling my other foot out of the mud, and, thinking of land mines, didn't desire to go any further. "I can see from here."

Sopheap opened the gate with one hand while tucking the baby bottles full of goat's milk in the other. I stood still. John went around me, winking as he passed. "Don't stray off the path."

"I know." I weighed my options—continue down the path or return up the hill to the community center. "I'm going back to hang out with the chickens," I said. John waved and continued down to the goat pen with Malachi.

Mary and I turned and worked our way back up the path, picking our way through the mud until we reached the gate. Pushing it aside, we entered the yard.

"Can I hold a baby chick, Momma?" Mary's dark eyes pleaded with me.

"Let's go see." I hustled her into the yard, which was trilling with the soft clucks of the mother hens. Dozens of them fluttered about with their broods of fluffy chicks.

I scooped up a downy yellow chick. The mother hen squawked, and the chick peeped with distress. "Just hold it a minute, Mary. The momma wants her baby back." We rarely got out of the chaos of Phnom Penh. I was happy to give Mary a taste of farm life given what we left behind in America.

Minutes later the mother hen and her chicks sidled away. Mary, still caressing the baby chick, found me. She lifted him up. "He wants his mommy."

Handing the chick to me, she bounced away to play on the rusted iron swing set in the corner of the dirt driveway. I looked around at dozens of hens and their broods bedding down for the night. Some were under the front deck, others behind the well, more in crevices beyond the shadows. So many hens, but where was this chick's mother?

I felt a prickling unease at the lengthening shadows and the sudden quiet of the barnyard. As I searched for the mother hen, the group came back from the goat pen, the sun setting behind them. There was not much time before we had to head back to the guest house before it got dark.

After pacing and searching, and not having success, I found the closest brood, and as an anxious hen tried to peck my hand, I rested the baby chick in her care, hoping she would scoop it under her wing and nurture it with her warm body.

But instead, deep in her throat, I heard a rumble, then a squawk. Within seconds, she flapped her wings and pecked. Peck, peck, peck. Her beak whipped upon the helpless chick. I gasped, straining to grab the chick back. Too late. It lay bloody and lifeless in my hand.

As the sky grew orange and then red, Mary and Malachi chased the feral cat which hid behind the bags of rice on the porch, John talked with Sopheap about selling goat milk and the recent youth event they'd held in the community center, and I held a dead chick.

HOMELESS

I n 2003, President George W. Bush invaded Iraq; SARS spread across the world, creating panic; the space shuttle *Columbia* disintegrated while reentering the earth's atmosphere; Dan Brown published *The DaVinci Code* in a world divided on biblical interpretation; and I, a simple homeschooling, homesteading mother of seven, found myself homeless.

Time zones tapped the airplane tail, propelling us forward to a place I both longed for and feared. In my arms, ten-month-old Olivia murmured in her sleep. I raised the armrest, moved her into the empty seat next to me, and let her settle for a few more hours of rest on our flight across the Pacific Ocean. I needed to move, stretch, wander. My lithe body was not used to sitting still. Nine hours in, and it cried out for movement. I got up and tapped John on the shoulder to let me out.

He didn't look up at first. My husband, his dark hair streaked with gray, engrossed himself in a pile of passports, immigration forms, and customs papers. Each document had to be filled out before we landed —each document times nine. Nine of us were suspended in space, hurtling toward a foreign and distant land, Cambodia. Without looking up, he shifted his legs and grabbed the pile of papers while I tilted the dull cream-colored tray up enough to inch by.

I glanced at the pile of documents in his hands as I passed, and a question caught my eye. "Home address?"

Home. What an interesting question when you are in no-man's-land 30,000 feet above the surface of the earth. I'd left all that was home.

Home. We had no home, no physical address, no bed to sleep on, no place to wash dishes or dirty fingers and toes. No place to rest after a long day of play or work. Nothing to call our own except for twenty-three pieces of luggage under our feet, which were being flung through space.

Somehow, this question did not move anyone but me. John wrote in my parents' home address in Boulder, Colorado. A legal address to accept tax documents, social security updates, and the occasional personal letter.

I wondered if our not-yet-seen rented house in Phnom Penh would ever feel like home. Did I even want it to? Could I ever replicate the years it took to feather my nest in Colorado in this hot, dusty, dangerous new place?

I passed John as he wrote my parents' Boulder address on each document and wandered to check on the children hunkered down in their private enclaves scattered about the identical blue rows. The hum of the plane engines could not drown out the strange empty echo of the cabin. This was the height of the SARS epidemic, and no one but us was crazy enough to travel, let alone move, to Asia. The plane was deserted.

I found Clara, three years old, curled up in a ball and sleeping with a flat plane pillow and thin blanket resting on her childish form. Her soft, stuffed bear, given to her by her grandmother before we left America, had fallen to the cabin floor to wait until she woke to search for him. Her travel buddy and the oldest brother, Joe, took his job of caring for his sister with stern determination, even at thirteen. With his arm placed on Clara's back, he watched a new movie playing on the screen. His third soda, half drunk, sat on the airplane table.

Next to Joe was eleven-year-old Tim, eyes glued to the movie screen while his left hand perched above a tattered sketchbook. With pencil poised on paper and a half-drawn face grimacing, he was mesmerized by the flickering scene of a movie he had already watched one hundred times at home.

Emma, age five, in the next row didn't need a travel buddy. In her words, she could "do it herself." She sat alone with her Jesse doll given to her by her closest cousin, Erica, at the airport before we boarded the plane. Emma floated between the airplane window, watching the clouds move and shift, holding us aloft, and the aisle where she explored the empty plane under the watchful, kind eyes of the Taiwanese flight attendants.

A few rows further up were Stephen, seven, and Seth, nine, playing computer games on their TV screens. One empty and another half-full cup of ramen noodles sat on their trays while the boys cheered and argued about the marching infantry men pixilated on the screen in front of them. Their backpacks strewn about the cabin floor spilled baseball cards, tattered books, army men, and superheroes who lay forgotten under darkened airplane seats.

I stooped down and scooped up their belongings while muttering that they must keep their things contained. Standing, I gathered their empty ramen containers and walked back to the flight attendants' station in the middle of the plane, where I placed them on the hostess counter.

Turning, the hostesses looked up. The older muttered something to the younger, who grabbed a plastic bag and hurried about the cabin, collecting empty drink cups and ramen containers. The older hostess looked at me, and her face changed in an instant from a frown to a smile. "Thank you. We will take care of you all now."

Something as natural as breathing to me—the constant tidying, organizing, clearing away of daily life—had become a transgression. I had crossed some invisible line, stepped into territory that wasn't mine to claim, and the shame of it settled over me like an unexpected weight. In trying to help, I had somehow violated an unspoken rule.

I wandered back to my seat, sat down with a sigh, and pulled Olivia's blanket up to her shoulders. Well, I could still nurture if I couldn't tidy. I kissed her downy head.

I grabbed a tattered travel magazine and flipped through its glossy advertisements for duty-free liquor and sparkling diamonds, when my eyes rested on a full-paged, color picture of Angkor Wat, the famed ancient temple buried deep in the jungles of Cambodia. So beloved by the Khmer people, they had placed its towering silhouette in the center of their national flag.

I tilted my head to look at its deep, red shadows ablaze in an early sunrise. Its craggy, man-made obelisks loomed over the dense tropical foliage. I thought of Colorado's peaks and pinnacles seen from the picture windows in the home we sold on her fertile plains. The peaks and crags of the Rocky Mountains had sustained and comforted us for decades while we built our serene life among fields of corn and sugar beets.

Resting my head back on the headrest, I closed the magazine. As the world turned beneath me from West to East, the Rocky Mountains behind and Angkor Wat looming ahead, I heard the call to adventure.

In this moment, without children to care for, meals to prepare, or laundry to fold, I pondered our journey to this primitive, troubled, and forgotten place. A place called a missionary graveyard. A place described by one expatriate as apocalyptic, dismal, and in a state of chronic, collective grief. A place called the Land of Smiles. Cambodia.

MISSION TALK

Eighteen months earlier, my head throbbed. Propped up on the couch, I waited for John and the kids to return from Boulder. I had stayed home and nursed my cold with chicken soup, vitamin C tablets, and hours of extra sleep while John and the kids went to church and to lunch at my parents' lake house for the day.

Wrapped in a crocheted blanket with a remote in my hand, I clicked through the channels on TV, waiting for something to catch my eye. I landed on an Animal Planet show, and, between a howling yellow-cheeked gibbon and an African elephant, I drifted in and out of sleep.

John and the kids arrived home late. He got them ready for bed and then came to sit next to me on the couch.

"How are you feeling?"

"Bleh." My head felt like lead, but my fever had broken. "How was your day?"

"Remember Matt and Jean?" John asked.

"Yeah. What about them?" We had known them through mutual friends. They attended a church in another state until Matt felt his family called to go to Cambodia as missionaries. They had moved there a few years earlier.

"Matt is back from Cambodia touring the country to raise money.

He gave a talk at church about their work." John stared at the TV but muted the sound. "I've been thinking since I returned from that trip to Nepal a couple of years ago that . . . well, we should go to the mission field as well."

My heart stopped, and despite the pain in my head, I sat straight up. My eyes were glued to the African elephants forming a circle around their young while I watched the lions pace.

"Seriously?" My voice sounded hoarse. "I thought we might go someday, but . . ."

John leaned over. "I did too. My plan, for two years now, was post-retirement mission work, once the children are grown. But, now, I feel pulled to at least look at this possibility. Maybe even sell some things. Rick would buy my new truck . . ."

"You mean leave Colorado . . . like now?" I heard my voice echo off the ceiling as if detached from me.

"Yeah, now. If you are game?" His voice softened.

Stunned by his urgency and shocked at what this would mean for our family and for me as a mother, I looked up. "Why now?"

"I love my job," he began, looking out at the dark night. "It has been an adventure, and I've spent years training. Now, after all those years, I get to do the fun stuff." John, a police officer for the last twelve years with the Greeley Police Department, a SWAT team member, and an undercover narcotics officer, lived for the adventure and adrenaline rush. "I can't imagine not being a cop. It is who I am. But I also know that I want to be a good father and husband . . ." He paused and looked at his hands. "And I haven't been doing this as well as I could."

I shifted in my seat, waiting. He looked out the window. "I need to get out of police work for this to happen. I need to have a mission bigger than myself."

I brushed some crumbs off the couch cushion and reached down into the overflowing laundry basket. Pulling a stack of clean cloth diapers and caressing them with my thumb, I asked, "What am I going to do? I can't be a missionary. I have six kids."

John reached over. "You're a mom. That's your mission field. You will keep doing what you are doing. You are just going to move your home to Asia."

The sun setting on our farmland framed my mood, and I sagged back into the couch. For years, we had built this life for our children. We would have to give it all up. We would leave behind our farm, church, friends, family, and our homeland, America.

As if reading my mind, John looked up. "I'm not talking about a short-term trip. I mean selling our belongings and moving there . . . and I don't know when or if we'd ever return here to live."

"Okay" was all I could muster though my heart pounded in my chest. "I need to sleep on this."

He nodded, and we moved off to the bedroom in silence. My head hit the pillow, but my feverish brain had not laid the weighty question to rest. Being a missionary had been my lifelong dream and prayer, but the sudden reality of it caught me off guard. Dreams feel different when they are no longer distant.

The next morning, amid the playful chaos of our home, I slipped away to my room. I thumbed through pictures in my photo album tucked in a box under my king-sized bed. Did this adventure feel like me? I needed to be sure.

The old pictures, distinctive in their soft, warm orange and brown tones and grainy texture, stirred my girlish soul. I had been the child with dreams of adventure and heroism—like my determined plot to escape to an imaginary farm with my little sister in tow. There I stood, all of eight years old, stumbling past our driveway, watching Mom wave from the porch. Later, she confessed she'd known all along we wouldn't venture beyond the neighbor's juniper tree. She was right.

More memories flooded as I thumbed through the album. As a young adult, I had escaped from Southern California with its traffic and smog to attend college in the small, hippy town of Boulder, Colorado, snuggled under the Rocky Mountains.

From the bedroom floor, I leaned up to look out the large picture window. The kids, taking a break from their homeschooling, jumped on the trampoline with our Rottweiler puppy, Annabelle, barking and nipping at their heels. I smiled and gazed over them to the barnyard beyond to watch my chickens peck and scratch in the garden soil.

Our life on the farm had been an adventure. Our whole gaggle of children ran feral in the brown fields under the cavernous, blue Colorado sky. Home birthing, homeschooling, homesteading. Maybe caravanning off to an exotic, developing country halfway around the world with my husband and six children was the next logical step in our unconventional journey.

After all, wasn't I the woman who'd shot a skunk between the eyes that threatened our chickens? The same woman who'd taught our eldest to read by candlelight during a week-long power outage? Who'd learned to preserve vegetables and butcher chickens?

But I knew that something more than a sense of adventure lurked underneath. An underlying element of faith, commitment, and responsibility pulsed. Not because I knew how the future was going to turn out, but because I, from a young age, had learned to trust that God held the future.

My faith was basic, comforting, not encumbered by volumes of theological tomes to weigh down the simplicity of it. I lived my spirituality simply, day by day. Churches and denominations had come and gone in my thirty-five years of life, and they shaped me, each one a twist of the kaleidoscope, the same colored bits of glass, but different perspectives with each revolution.

I sat back to remember my spiritual growth as a child.

Fresh out of the womb, an elderly priest baptized me into the Episcopal Church, whetting my love for liturgy. In my middle school years, confirmed in the Lutheran Church, I had my first taste of theology and creeds and service to my community. In high school, I embraced edgy evangelical churches with Pentecostal flavors, complete with raised hands and speaking in tongues. But, in my college years, when my bearded professors locked in their rooms with dusty works by Marx and Nietzsche tried to break my idealistic faith on the altar of their atheistic teachings, my childlike faith almost did not stand up.

The rapid-fire existential questions posited by those professors hell-bent on destroying the faith of fresh-faced freshman at the University of Colorado led me into despair until one night my sophomore year, on the top floor of my ancient sorority house on University Avenue, I heard God ask me, "Will you leave me also?"

Without a beat, I replied with a scripture: "Lord, to whom shall I go? You have the words of eternal life."

A switch flickered on in a dark and cold room of my heart, and peace and light and warmth flooded through my body. I knew God was real, present, and loved me. I could never leave him again.

The next few years, I sought Jesus in every place he could be found. Campus Crusade for Christ, the Vineyard Pentecostal Church, the occasional liturgy at Saint Aidan's Episcopal Church, even Second Baptist African American Church on Baseline Road tickled my fancy when I craved their vibrancy and energy.

After much searching, I settled into the campus faith group Fellowship of Christian Athletes, which met at the break of dawn in the old field house resting behind the red sandstone football stadium. We were a small, intimate group of athletes and non-athletes, like me, who met for early morning Bible study led by local Christian leaders and professors at the university.

One dreary morning in the middle of January 1987, John Roberts, son of Dr. Roberts, a brilliant electrical engineering professor at the university's acclaimed engineering school, slipped into the 7 a.m. meeting. His large hands, rugged from years of milking on a farm, unbuttoned his black trench coat, threadbare and too thin for the winter cold.

I walked up to him after the announcements, cocked my head, and introduced myself. "Hi, I'm Sheryl."

He turned, his brown eyes piercing mine. "John."

I gestured to the overhead projector, blinking at the front of the room with the upcoming retreat details. "You going?"

He cocked his head and shrugged. "We will see."

He made it.

At that retreat high in the Rocky Mountains in that snowy February, John and I spent all our free time together. By the end of the weekend, I knew I had found my life partner. We were engaged in October 1988 and married in May 1989.

Our spiritual journey walked hand in hand with our romantic one. We sought a spiritual home together. There were moments of novelty in Pentecostalism, cultural diversity at Second Baptist, and sacredness in Episcopalism, but our final landing place was a conservative, evangelical, fundamental start-up church that met in the cafeteria of John's old high school. That is where we put down our roots.

Grace Community Church prided itself on being countercultural to all other denominations. It felt like we were pioneering something profoundly important. We cut our spiritual teeth on this flavor of church life and, by default, family life.

The movement's foundation centered on a quiet retreat to home and hearth. The path embraced large families, education at home, natural births, self-sufficient living, and, for the devoted few, mission work abroad. We lived by faith, commitment, and responsibility. It was intoxicating after years of floating between lackluster and nominal churches.

Over the next fourteen years, we walked this road step by step, ticking every box along the way. It was here that I grew to love the simple role of mother, wife, homemaker, and homesteader, the peace that came every day with constructing my world framed in simplicity: God, family, and self-sufficiency. I thrived here. This was my place, my home, and my identity.

I closed my eyes and leaned my head back on the side of the bed. My hands grazed the soft carpet, plucking the piles and twisting, then floating my fingers over the plush breadth. The conversation the night before echoed. It wasn't until that moment that I realized John was not thriving as much as I'd thought he was. As much as I was. He desired to be the perfect Christian man, husband, and father, but he felt shackled by his troubling past with a harsh, unloving father and his profession as a police officer, which kept him in a continual loop of cynicism.

It was not working for him to live this double life. He had been considering mission work since his trip to Nepal in 1999 to visit his missionary sister, Michele. That is where he saw enormous needs and suffering. He witnessed the missionaries serving the "least of these." He ached to live with that kind of purpose. It wasn't until the previous night, September 9, 2001, that he revealed to me this deep yearning.

What was missing from John's work life was serving "the least of these," a foundational teaching of Jesus on mercy and love for the most vulnerable. He had worked for years on the justice side of society—police, SWAT team, lengthy court cases where he served as a witness for the prosecution. Justice. But what about mercy? Mercy was to the least of these. Mission, he believed, was merciful.

I knew John was a fighter for the oppressed. Early in his career as a police officer, he had brought home a young, pregnant, homeless woman and asked if we could give her a place to live for a while. As idealists, we thought this was a good idea. But we were too young and naïve for this venture. She moved out months later.

But this would not be the last time John's compassion would surface. Stray dogs, lost goats, a college student who was fighting with her roommates, a divorced young professional. These all found their place under our roof.

For John, Cambodia was a call to leave a career that was at once full of camaraderie, "the blue brotherhood," while also a stumbling block to growing as a Christian husband and father. No matter how much he loved the work, he yearned to fulfill his true purpose to be completely present for the family who needed him most and to be part of something bigger, something merciful.

I stood, stretched, and curled my toes into the soft carpet. Time to make lunch and bake the rising dough that grew plump in the terracotta bowl. I tucked the photo album back under my bed and, before I left the room, I knew what my answer was going to be.

Mission was going to be our next adventure, the last box to check, the ultimate step of being a worthy Christian. It was in both of our stories. It was going to be another revolution in my spiritual kaleidoscope.

TWO RIVERS

One afternoon, weeks after our talk, John got off the phone and found me canning tomatoes in the kitchen. I was waiting to tell him some news I had found out that morning after spending a week fretting over queasiness and exhaustion.

John leaned in to smell the bubbling tomatoes. "I'm considering going with a few of the guys from the mission team at church to visit Matt in Cambodia. They're leaving in a couple of months, and we'll be gone for about a week total. We can see how things will shape up after we get back."

I backed away from the counter, wiping my hands on my apron. Nodding, but not listening because of the hum in my head.

"Guess what?" I knew I was about to drop a bombshell on him. But I also knew it would not derail him or me. He looked at me, his dark brown eyes curious.

I lifted my green eyes to his. "I'm pregnant. Due next summer. I guess that means we are taking a newborn on the mission field." I steadied myself on the counter.

"I guess it does." His eyes sparkled with excitement. "Babies haven't stopped our plans before. Can't do it now. Shall I plan to go with the mission team in October?"

"That will be a good way to see if it is the right place for us." I paused and stopped stirring, hesitant to bring up things I had heard that day from Beth. "There is some talk . . . about Matt."

John paused. "I have been hearing the same things. That he is a loose cannon, irresponsible. But we won't be working with him directly. They will be our friends, not our colleagues. We will need people there."

"I hope it will be okay. I don't want to get wrapped up in anything that can jeopardize our life there." I stopped.

The kettle was hissing, and the cooked tomatoes were turning into paste. Remembering his phone call, I looked up. "Yes, you need to go to visit Cambodia. I'll be here holding down the fort. I'll gather some gifts for you to take to Jean."

The fort was my home on five acres in rural Colorado. My large home, above the South Platte River graced with large cottonwood trees and ample pastureland for our two Scottish Highland cows, was my sanctuary. Chicken and geese ambled in our flourishing vegetable garden, which fed our growing family throughout the summer and fall.

The children spent mornings and evenings doing farm chores, middays making forts or burying their heads in books, and late afternoons meandering the careening riverbank for hours of unsupervised play. We lived a charmed life: fulfilling, nurturing, and safe.

After John left the room, I looked at the mason jars lining the counter and wondered when we would eat the freshly canned tomatoes. As fast as things were going, we might be long gone before we needed them.

Gone. A chill stirred from a hidden place in my core. Still staring at my gleaming jars of tomatoes, my breath became shallow and weak. My outstretched fingers found the edge of the cluttered counter, and I steadied myself. I had two choices: Run back to John and tell him I had changed my mind or move forward silent and steady. I chose the latter.

I silently stacked the cans in the back of the pantry, placing them next to rows of other canned goods I had preserved over the summer.

Glancing at all my gleaming handiwork, I knew failure was not an option.

I didn't want to return to America in shame. I didn't want to be seen as irresponsible like Matt. At that moment, I knew my old life was dead, and I was losing control of the narrative of the new one.

A few months later, after John returned from his trip to Cambodia, we found ourselves with bowls of ice cream on the leather couch in our living room, chatting about his trip. He shared a story that happened towards the end of the trip when he found himself on a small boat on the swollen waters of the Tonlé Sap River in rural Cambodia. The boat carried five men through a flooded, provincial village on the outskirts of Phnom Penh, at the end of rainy season. In front, chatting with the rest of the men, sat Panha, a Khmer national Christian pastor. It was his habit to visit the small churches that met in their outlying villages.

This time of year, the water was high. Each home tottered on legs planted deep in the riverbed, and the swollen river taunted them with licking waves rising almost to the floorboards. Today, the men buzzed along as young children and adolescents stared at them wide-eyed. It was uncommon to see Caucasian men in their little floating village.

Panha steered the boat to the home of Navin, the only Christian woman in the village. She waited outside for Panha and the foreigners to arrive. Normally, only a handful of villagers attended meetings—for gossip, not the teaching—but today her simple home was bursting with curious villagers eager to meet the foreigners from America.

The men shuffled into her home as she ushered them to pillows placed in a circle in the center of the room. After greetings and an offer of fresh fruit and an assortment of sodas, the men settled in to listen to Panha teach the villagers from his battered, black Khmer Bible.

John mentioned the language being so unfamiliar—nothing like anything he had ever heard before. The heat and droning of Panha's voice in the strange language cast a spell on the men. And then, "Amen," the villagers said in unison.

The villagers stood, bowed towards Navin, Panha, and the foreigners, and then one by one descended the steep wooden steps and floated away in their boats.

John turned to find Panha talking in a low voice to Navin as she rocked and cried. Her face contorted from the nods and feigned smiles.

His hand patted hers as he murmured, "*Baat . . . baat . . .*" (Yes . . yes . . .) He turned to the men and told them her tragic story.

"Her two-year-old son was lost last week." Panha waved his hand outside the hut. The men looked at him in surprise.

"Lost?" John asked.

"Drowned . . . in the river."

At this, my hand trembled and I put my bowl on the oak table next to me. My worst nightmare—losing a child, especially to a drowning.

John described Panha's stoic face and his distant eyes. Panha told the men, "He climbed up on that cooler," motioning to the orange box in the corner by the back window. Every village home had one. It held a block of ice and stored the meat, eggs, and vegetables bought at the market that day.

"She was at the market when he climbed up there and fell out the window. They found him face down in the water an hour later." Panha stood and rested his hand on Navin's shoulder. "We need to go, Ming (young aunt). I'll ask the Phnom Penh church to pray for you. See you next week."

John noticed Navin sniffling and wiping her nose on her sleeve. She stood and, with teary eyes and a stiff smile, bade the men good-bye. John said the story struck him with sadness and horror as they piled back into the boat and headed back to the hotel in Phnom Penh. They needed a shower, a nap, and a substantial dinner before going to sleep. They were leaving on an early morning flight, but John confessed he found it difficult to settle the rest of the day and into the evening.

He ruminated on Navin's story, thinking of his own two-year-old Clara at home. That week, he'd also heard of children whose parents had died of AIDS and were living out their childhoods in over-crowded orphanages; of girls sent from the provinces to work in the garment factories, who then were intercepted along the way and freighted away to brothels to serve rich men from foreign countries; of dying children whose parents paid Buddhist monks to chant prayers instead of finding them hospital care. Each of his own children had come to his mind as he imagined the horror those Cambodian children must face every day.

Looking at him stare out the darkened window, I knew in that moment that Cambodia had entered his bones and lodged in his marrow. Across the Pacific, somewhere over the Aleutian Islands, he must have set his face like flint. He needed to return and bring his family with him. His face said it all.

MAPS

I did not know where Cambodia was. I thought I had a pretty good grasp of geography, a subject I excelled in as a child. Maps had been a passion of mine: I loved reading them, creating maps of imaginary worlds, and dreaming of faraway journeys while flipping through our world atlas in my parents' den. Cambodia, buried somewhere in Southeast Asia, was unfamiliar, strange, exotic.

I had asked John to buy me some maps while he was in Cambodia. I wanted a wall map of the country and another of the capital city, Phnom Penh. He brought home two beautiful maps which I hung in the dining room near the kitchen.

I saw those maps first thing in the morning as the sun lit up my front room with its pale glow. I saw those maps as I taught multiplication tables or waited for a child to finish a spelling test. During dinner, with the loud din of excited children's voices discussing their days, I peered over at Phnom Penh with its streets laced like spokes on a wheel, a city designed by the French.

Before bed, after washing the last dish, with the shadows of night casting eerie images on the maps, I glanced and sighed. Lines on paper, colors and shapes, words in a foreign script that were undecipherable. We were giving up our lives for those lines, shapes, and colors.

It was late one night, after putting the kids to bed, that I leaned back on my worn couch and cracked open *Survival in the Killing Fields* by Dr. Haing Ngor and Roger Warner. Hours later, after the sun had long since disappeared behind the Rocky Mountains, I learned of a history I never knew could happen. I learned that within four years, from 1975 to 1979, the Khmer Rouge (Communist Party of Kampuchea) committed a horrific mass genocide, one of the most heinous crimes of the twentieth century. Two million people died.

Clad in black pajamas, red checkered scarves, and sandals made from car tires, the Communist Khmer Rouge soldiers, peasants, and teenagers moved as one across the countryside of Cambodia, starting in the north, and gained momentum until they drove out everyone from the capital city, Phnom Penh. In three days, this city of 2.5 million people became a ghost town.

Soon, corpses littered the roads, trust evaporated, and fear and suspicion tore apart communities. The regime separated families and sent them to labor camps deep in the jungles.

In 1977, the Khmer Rouge's reign of terror was at its peak. Their reign transformed fields, once lush with rice and teeming with life, into eerie graveyards. Haing Ngor and his wife were stripped of their identities, trudged in line to labor in fields from dawn till dusk, their bodies emaciated, and spirits crushed under the weight of their appalling existence.

As the years dragged on, Pol Pot, the communist dictator, and his Khmer Rouge cadres grew more cruel and more paranoid, determined to transform the country into an agrarian paradise.

I looked out my window at my darkened garden and the neighbor's corn fields beyond, lit by the moon. We were growing food to feed our families, our community, our state, our nation. But none of our labor was on the backs of slaves.

I kept reading. Despite it all, the people tried to cling to their traditions and culture, finding solace in quiet moments. Though food was scarce, they shared what little they had. At night, families huddled close, whispering folk tales, singing traditional songs, and passing on their spiritual beliefs despite the great dangers this presented.

The religious persecution was heavy. The regime either murdered or drove into exile every Buddhist monk and destroyed nearly every Buddhist *wat* (temple) and library and demolished most of the Christian churches, both Protestant and Catholic.

The Cham Muslims recounted the horrors of living under the Khmer Rouge, describing how regime cadres burned their Qurans, forced them to eat pork, and murdered them en masse. To be religious was to be dead.

I had to stop reading. I found my enthusiasm to leave on this mission waning. *What kind of mother takes her children to a place like this?* I closed the book and slid it under a pile of magazines. Flipped off the light switch and went to bed under the shadow of the moon.

I woke the next day; Cambodia's history still haunted me. I went about my duties in a daze, picturing teenagers shrouded in black, armed with AK-47s, and slinking around in jungles. After everyone was asleep that night, I slid the book back out and picked up where I left off.

In January 1979, the Vietnamese-backed Cambodian resistance drove the Khmer Rouge out of power. KR soldiers and leaders fled into the surrounding villages to blend in and try to regroup. They continued to wage war against the prevailing government from their bases along the Thai border.

After the book ended, I turned on my computer and searched for what happened next. Haing Ngor's tragic story whetted my appetite for more. I learned that over the next ten years, Cambodia was in shambles. In 1990, Christian relief, development agencies, and missionaries trickled back into the country. By 1993, the parliament voted in a new constitution, and Prince Sihanouk returned from France and took his rightful place on the throne. This began "Cambodia's Second Kingdom." This new liberty was fragile and limited, but it opened a door to hope.

Our family was going to walk through that door of hope only a decade since its resurgence. We were going to live among these traumatized survivors and their children. I glanced up at the map in the late-night shadows. Bats cried, hushed and soft, out my darkened picture window, and somewhere far away, perhaps under a metal tin roof, a child cried, shushed by his grandmother as she wrapped in him in a soiled *krama*.

I needed to introduce Cambodia to my children. The following weeks, I read them Cambodian stories of playful monkeys, Khmer princesses, and rare Mekong dolphins.

But I left out the darker stories: stories of children forced to watch the execution of their family members, of families broken up and sent away to camps to starve, of fathers hacked to death with "elephant" hoes if they did not work hard enough in the fields. Those stories haunted me, but I kept reading. I knew this history, this cultural understanding, was critical to our success, to our survival. Cambodia's eerie past and traumatized present was going to become our reality.

The church mission team had a plan for us. They needed missionaries to start and run an orphanage. We knew nothing about this work, how it looked in Cambodia, what the long-range implications would be, but that did not matter. In my heart, a confusing mixture of excitement and dread churned. I'd never admit the dread aloud— what kind of Christian feels dread about serving others? Yet there it was, a persistent shadow lurking behind my prayers.

Images online showed young, dark faces, masked with sad eyes and down-turned smiles, urging us to help. I found myself studying these children's expressions at night, wondering about their stories, imagining myself coming to comfort them as I would my own children. The thought filled me with a warmth that I recognized as pride, though I quickly reframed it as divine purpose.

John and I discussed it in whispered conversations after the children were asleep. "Are we really qualified?" I'd ask, voicing the doubt that gnawed at me. He would speak quietly and remind me that Moses wasn't qualified either. Neither was David. Or Peter. The Bible was full of unqualified people doing God's work. Who were we to question our calling?

We had a harmonious family, a firm faith, and a determined zeal. I repeated these qualities like a mantra, trying to drown out the occasional voice of reason that asked uncomfortable questions: What about the language barrier? The cultural differences? The complex psychological needs of traumatized children? I pushed those thoughts away, labeling them as fear, as weakness, as lack of faith.

Placing my hand over my growing belly, my thoughts turned to pregnant Cambodian women—women who, during the reign of the Khmer Rouge, were being strung up on poles, wombs ripped apart with machetes, and their unborn babies bashed against trees. Swallowing, I glanced back at the faces of orphans gazing back at me from my computer screen. Their pleading eyes blurred, and waves of nausea washed over me. Even if, on paper, we were perfect for the job, I knew I was protected, coddled, and not ready for this adventure, but it was too late. The move had already been set in motion. I knew at that moment we were no longer living in "cheap grace," as Dietrich Bonhoeffer, the great Lutheran martyr, had taught.

The way forward would be costly. Our new life was going to be infused with "costly grace." Bonhoeffer wrote, "Such grace is costly because it calls us to follow, and it is grace because it calls us to follow Jesus Christ. It is costly because it costs a man his life, and it is grace because it gives a man the only true life."[1]

We must follow; the way forward was too clear. But guaranteed, it would entail suffering. I knew I was not ready, but I also knew Who would hold me and never let me go. That was what I clung to. That was my hope.

---

1. Dietrich Bonhoeffer, *The Cost of Discipleship* (1937).

BIRTH STORM

Six months after John returned from Cambodia, I took my nine-months-pregnant, overdue body and lumbered out to the mailbox at the end of our sloping driveway during a sweltering 102-degree July day. Birth was an adventure I was ready for. Too ready.

For weeks, I had watched the heat waves dance off the barn roof and disappear into the cloudless Colorado sky. As the bone-dry grass crackled under my swollen bare feet, I wondered if today would be the day that this baby, number seven, would decide to be born.

My slow-moving legs and hardened feet carried me over the rocks to the mailbox. I peered over my children, who, despite the heat, were playing under the tall cottonwoods. I smiled at them all so full of life and strength. Grabbing the mail and heading back to the house, I considered my options for inducing labor: black and blue cohosh, castor oil, long walks.

Days of pre-labor had tricked me into hope. Enough hope that I had called my mother-in-law, our midwife, the day before. She came both to help with the birth and to see her six other grandchildren. I calmed when she arrived, and together we set up the birth room. She moved like a quiet brook, unhurried, reminding me that "the apple will fall when it is ready" as she tucked in the last corner of the bedsheet. I wasn't so sure.

Later that afternoon, I lay reading before my afternoon catnap when I noticed out of my southern window a gathering of ominous clouds moving on the horizon. They crept like tin soldiers in my direction, swallowing up the blue sky and casting gray shadows over the dry, wheat-colored land. I smiled, knowing that we would soon have much-needed rain. The wind picked up, the barometer dropped, the clouds coalesced overhead, and, to my surprise, my labor pains began.

After breathing gently through one contraction, I folded the corner of the page in my book, then stood up and stretched, waiting for the next. Then, after a quiet moment with my body, I knew it was time.

John came first, his body smelling of the barnyard and his eyes worried. My mother had arrived that morning to take care of the children. She popped her head in to say hello and ask if I needed anything. I finished breathing through my contraction and smiled and shook my head. "No." John asked for a glass of ice water, and she scuttled off to the kitchen, wrangling some children away from the door as she went.

John's mother, Judy, came up from downstairs where she was resting. A busy midwife, she knew that if the baby did not come today, then most likely it would be tonight. Either way, she must be ready and rested. Judy had already birthed ten of her grandchildren at home. She was no stranger to being a mother, mother-in-law, grandmother, and midwife, all in one breath.

Judy's midwife assistant, Diane, came in last. She dropped cases of supplies onto our cluttered dresser. Judy grabbed a Doppler from her tattered bag and sat next to me, waiting for my contraction to end so she could find the baby's heartbeat. *Whoosh, whoosh.* The heartbeat was strong and steady. Baby was fine.

Labor continued to increase as the day wore on. As if we were all a part of a magnificent, celestial orchestra, the storm outside and I whirled together and apart in increasing intensity. Outside, driving rain pounded the stone-hard ground, thirsty from weeks of relentless drought. My driving contractions pounded at my surrendering body.

"Count and breathe through them," I reminded myself. In a moment of rest between contractions, I glanced out my window in time to view a tree bending in submission to the storm's forces bearing down. It did not resist the fury of the wind. I responded in kind to the pounding pressure of my laboring body. John and the midwives disappeared, and I turned inward for the final act.

Then, as quickly as it came, it left. The force of my body had done its work, and peace was restored. Outside, the downpour became a drizzle, the mighty winds lessened to a cool breeze, and the sky reflected a golden light magnified by the glistening grasses in the field beyond. The world was refreshed, renewed, and reborn with the life-giving rains.

As the pure white curtains billowed in the breeze, and after six hard hours, my contractions settled, and I knew it was time for the last act. I held my breath and pushed. One, two, three, four . . . The midwives counted until I needed to breathe again.

Leaning back onto the bed, I gasped for breath. "We see the head. Not long now." Judy peered down while Diane started unwrapping packages of gauze to ease the head out. Again, I took a deep breath and pushed, moaning and feeling the baby move lower. I stopped when Judy said, "Push slow and easy. Here it comes . . ."

Swish. The calm of the storm washed in Olivia, "peaceful one." Contentment came after the fighting rain, and my submissive body welcomed her. John placed her on my breast to nurse while the midwives continued to check me and wait for the placenta. Swish it came. It was over. Whole and healthy. My baby girl was born. Within the hour, both of us, clean and happy, drifted into a deep sleep.

The dawn broke with optimism that the heat had broken, and fresh air filled with smells of damp earth drew me from sleep. I looked at John's sloping back as he breathed rhythmically in dreams. Beside me, my wee daughter, still pink and fresh from the womb with tender wrinkled hands and feet, the smallest of fingernails showing off their beds of pink, nestled into my bosom with complete and absolute serenity. She started to rouse and root for the breast, and I repositioned myself to feed her. Half-asleep, she fed.

I looked out the window as the pink, lollipop sky licked the cottonwood trees in our backyard, at the dew-heavy fields where only a few months earlier, our two Scottish Highlanders grazed. We had butchered and packaged the cows for the coming months, leaving the fields silent.

I shifted towards the door as my youngest, Clara, shuffled in the room with her large, doe-like eyes laser-focused on the new baby. No longer the baby, she now had to find her place among her five other siblings as "older sister." After a pause of curiosity, she quietly, as not to rouse her father, climbed into bed and snuggled down behind me with her back pressed against mine. Soon I recognized her slow breathing as she catnapped in the peaceful morning.

Time passed like this until the entire house rose. John got up to tend to the breakfast routine and morning chores. I heard the older children chat and mutter outside my door.

I beckoned them, and the children entered with curious and bright morning eyes to meet their new sister. Joseph, the oldest, entered first, the leader with his commanding presence. Tim, the second, followed close behind with his goofy smile and gentle ways. Next came Seth, the third son, and Stephen, the fourth. Seth, quiet and thoughtful, and Stephen, talkative and impulsive, stood off to the side, tugging at each other's shirts to urge the other to go in first. Finally, four-year-old Emma strolled in.

These six leaned in to look at their newest baby in the morning light. Their voices were soft, then sometimes shrill, and other times irritated as one of them received an elbow in the ribs or a conk on the chin in their efforts to get closer to baby Olivia. The warmth of my children's bodies, their familiar smells and distinctive voices, made my heart swell with love and pride. My seven children were the highlight of my life, my reason to live, my elixir of life.

I raised my eyes as John entered the room. I saw him scanning the bundle of children strewn across my bed, talking and chattering about baby Olivia. His eyes were full of love for his children, coupled with a pained and distant look that took him somewhere thousands of miles from us to the sun-parched land nestled in the jungle of Southeast Asia. Cambodia.

Thinking of Cambodia's killing fields, I could not meet his eyes. I knew his eyes were so full of hope and excitement. Mine were full of questions.

DISMANTLING

Olivia, as peaceful as her name, cooed contentedly by my side throughout the day. At night, she tucked in at my breast with her soft fingers wrapped in mine against the comfort of my beating heart and rhythmic breathing. She was warm, dry, and full as a tick. I packed the days with cooking, cleaning, homeschooling, gathering eggs, baking bread, and harvesting vegetables, all while my sleeping newborn nestled peacefully.

The routine was familiar, but the stakes were different. With all the other children, after birth, I had burrowed down into my cozy existence and marinated in its warmth and peace. Creating the perfect nest with the right feather laid here and the well-positioned twig placed there, I had repeated this dance with each baby for the past fourteen years. My goal was the creation of a home and hearth where I could raise my children in comfort and security, with their every hurt assuaged by my undivided and devoted attention.

This time, instead of assembling another layer of my tender and delicate nest, I dismantled the home I had painstakingly built.

"Everything must go," John said, "except what can fill the twenty-three pieces of luggage. We can store the rest at Mom's farm or sell it."

I sold off my children's toys and winter clothes, household goods, quilts, and blankets. I sent my beloved chickens, whose motherhood wove a bond with mine, to John's family farm in Boulder, along with our orange cat, Sammy.

"We can get something like that in Cambodia," I said, trying to cheer Emma, whose eyes were wet with tears when we dropped Sammy off at the farm. "They do have kittens in Cambodia. Maybe we can get one someday. Or even a baby chick . . ." By the dark, searching look in her eyes, I knew she did not believe me. She was still trying to imagine the place with palm trees, coconuts, kittens, Khmer princesses, and baby chicks.

We passed our heirloom furniture and some precious goods among family members or sent them to the farm's storage shed for safekeeping. John said one night, "We will be like the missionaries of old. They used to take their caskets with them on the mission field. They planned to never return. Our time in Cambodia will be . . . indefinite."

Indefinite, I would tell people when they asked. One-way tickets and no plans for return, except for the occasional furlough to visit family and stock up on coffee beans in bulk. In some ways, it felt brave and adventuresome to answer in that way.

But as I dismantled each piece of my soul, I felt like *indefinite* was a dark void of nothingness, with no hope of returning to the safety of my family, or America, my homeland. How would I ever be able to build my nest again? It had taken so long and required so much tender care the first time around.

That night, after tucking the children in, I stood in their half-empty bedroom and felt the panic rising. What if they got sick? What if they couldn't adjust to the culture? What if this move shattered something in our family beyond repair? Moving to our room, I sank onto the edge of our king-sized bed, overwhelmed by what we were about to do. John found me there an hour later, still staring at the wall.

"Hey," he said, sitting beside me.

"I don't know if I can do this," I whispered. "Take our children halfway across the world to a place where we don't speak the language, don't have any family . . ."

"The kids will be okay. They have us. Your love has been their safety net," John said.

I wanted to believe him. As we lay in bed that night, I pulled our children's passports from the nightstand, running my fingers over their hopeful faces in the photographs. I would make a home for them anywhere, even if right now I couldn't imagine how.

Weeks later, the undertaker's hammer pounded the last nail in the coffin when three things converged in one short week. First, the realtor took down the "For Sale" sign from the front of our home. We had a buyer for our five-acre paradise on the South Platte River. The house on Dos Rios Street was no longer ours but the next family's home with an exchange of money, a signed document, and a handshake.

The second pound of the nail resounded when John returned home one afternoon waving nine one-way plane tickets to Phnom Penh, Cambodia, with a departure date of May 1, 2003. Seeing the darkened numbers floating above the triplicate ticket, with their dancing feet singing of adventures and mission, made me swoon with apprehension.

The tickets looked so final, with each name spelled out meticulously. My hands trembled as I arranged and rearranged the tickets after John placed them on the kitchen counter, as if changing their order might somehow delay our departure.

The sound of the final nail in the coffin drove away in the back of my parent's Toyota Highlander. Moments before, a bundle of wiggling fur had bounded into the back seat of the Toyota, not knowing that she, our two-year-old Rottweiler Annabelle, was leaving the only family she had ever known to live with Grandma and Grandpa and their German shepherd, Heidi, on their lake property in Longmont.

I turned and saw my children's tears. Their mouths formed cries as they watched a beloved sibling disappear in the dust down our empty dirt road.

"Oh no . . ." The words escaped my lips as a whisper, hardly audible above my children's soft weeping.

"She's gone?" Clara clung to Stephen's arm, looking up into his dark, frozen eyes. "Is she coming back?"

Emma stumbled out to the road. "Wait, Grandma . . . Grandpa!" Her voice broke as the dust continued to settle behind the disappearing car.

I stood there, staring at the spot where our bounding, joyful Annabelle had stood, feeling a crushing weight of guilt unlike anything I'd ever experienced before. My arms, usually so quick to gather my children close in moments of pain, hung uselessly at my sides. My throat closed.

"Momma?" Clara tugged at my dress; her face streaked with tears. "Momma, why won't you say anything?"

I turned so numb that, for the first time, I could not comfort them. Not a single word of reassurance would come. Not a single gesture of comfort. I simply stood there, as empty as the dirt road stretching before us. I moved back into my bare house, which was no longer mine.

I dropped into one of the few chairs left and tucked Olivia into my breast to nurse, to comfort her, but more to comfort myself. I mused to myself that I must "do the next thing" as Elisabeth Elliot would counsel from her many books on motherhood and mission, which lay threadbare at the bottom of one of the twenty-three pieces of luggage stacked in the garage.

Do the next thing. I did. I finished nursing the baby, cooked dinner, ate on paper plates, cleaned the sparse kitchen, snuggled the toddlers, read to the children, and put them to bed. Repeat, repeat again, until May 1, 2003, the day the airplane came for us.

THE FARM TABLE

The new year, 2003, crept in. We moved to John's childhood farm in Boulder to wait out the last days. To keep track of all we had to get done before we left, we hung a large calendar above the fireplace in the family room.

The day of departure, May 1, was circled with red Sharpie, like a giant kiss from a muse. Each night, a child X'd off that day, moving us one day closer.

The kids were more excited as each day passed. They anticipated the adventure, and John awaited the mission, but I scanned the faces of those we were leaving behind, sensing their hearts were as heavy as mine. I saw the blank stares of my mother, my faithful companion, masked behind her feigned smile, attempting to be reassuring.

My younger sister, Barbara, spoke of the good work of caring for the Cambodian orphans as she hugged me repeatedly. On wintery afternoons, we sat watching our children play with each other as they had since birth. They were as close as siblings, and we knew that their loss would be as great as our own. We chatted as if nothing was impending, talking of new recipes, another homeschooling curriculum to try, or a new diet we were determined to undertake this year. Grasping at each moment, we knew, deep down, that our time was short.

Spring at the farm had arrived. Clara and Emma spent many waking hours in the barnyard with the new baby goats. Two little girls and two baby female goats romped through the churned soil of the vegetable garden. I stepped among the tilled rows in my bare feet, feeling the rich loamy soil between my toes, soil ready to receive the seeds for the new year of planting.

This was not my garden, but my mother-in-law's. I had left my garden back at my Dos Rios house and my Bluebell Avenue house before that. My gardens had boasted of large, bountiful harvests year in and year out without fail, from the early crop of spring lettuce, spinach, radishes, and carrots to the summer abundance of summer squash, eggplant, bush beans, tomatoes, and an extensive variety of peppers ranging from mild to fiery.

When the long-past evenings waned colder, crisper, and darker, we loaded up on winter squashes: acorn, spaghetti, decorative gourds for our Thanksgiving table decorations, pumpkins for winter soups and pies, along with the last vestiges of peppers popping with reds, yellows, and oranges.

My gardens were my happiest places, where I could watch life sprout, grow, and ripen, and then die after the first frost, all within a five-month period.

I spent the winter months poring over mountains of seed catalogs, dissecting every description for that perfect grouping of seeds for our climate and palate. The catalogs arrived every January, spilling with beautiful pictures of old varieties, new varieties, heirloom seeds, and hybrids, each with their own unique genetic code. I tried as many as I could, working to get the perfect combination of beauty, resourcefulness, and hardiness. The very combination of traits I nurtured in my children.

John and I would spend hours preparing and seeding the soil after the springtime sun warmed the earth. Then daily I pulled the weeds and watched the growth of both my garden and my children, each with their own genetic code.

The children loved the garden as much as me. I often had a sleeping baby nestled in my homemade baby carrier as I hoed, sowed, and harvested. The older children planted seeds in the spring, watered and pulled weeds in the summer, harvested in the fall. The youngest collected stones tossed up from the earth during the winter freeze, pulled roots from last year's crop, and collected squirming tomato worms to feed to the chickens, who fought for the delicacy.

All summer long, our clan of children foraged and nibbled on the produce as it ripened; bush beans, tomatoes, carrots, and cucumbers were fan favorites. Each fall, we spent long hours harvesting, canning, and freezing vegetables. The older boys built cornhusk huts decorated with pumpkins, gourds, and pinecones, with chairs and tables crafted from varying sizes of tree stumps.

They created elaborate villages and then tasked the younger children with manning the trading posts, where they sold green tomatoes and chicken eggs stolen from the coop. The older boys went off to battle with tree branches as weapons of war flickering in the distance. They played until the winter frosts and snowstorms forced them inside, where they watched from the windows as their village succumbed to the elements and returned to the earth.

Today, walking through the churned soil of my mother-in-law's garden patch felt like walking through a cemetery, getting ready to accept a new grave. Buried in that hole were my dreams of this year's garden. I kept one small doorway of hope open. Deep in my luggage, I had packed a dozen seed packets. Earlier that winter, I had scoured the seed catalogs for the most heat-resistant varieties of our favorite vegetables, and when they arrived in the mail, I stashed them away with hope and a bit of daring.

The back door opened; Tim called us in for supper. My girls ran ahead of me with the baby goats jumping at their heels. I followed along, savoring those last moments as the sun set behind the Rocky Mountains. To my surprise, some of John's siblings had arrived with their spouses and children. The house bustled with laughter, smells of soup and buttery baked bread, and shrieks of cousins chasing each other through the kitchen.

More siblings and cousins came through the door stomping their feet from the cold, which descended when the Colorado sun went down below the mountains. Bearing more food and farewell gifts, they hugged and kissed and lingered over each of my children. The dinner lasted for hours as we laughed, reminisced, spoke about the orphanage we were planning to open in Cambodia, and dreamed of future visits.

During dessert, Michele, John's oldest sister, sat down next to me on the creaking oak chair. She had been a missionary in Nepal and the UAE. She knew things. She had survived. I averted my eyes to avoid breaking down. But her radiant confidence shrouded my sullen unease. I caught her eye.

"I'll be there. I'll come to visit. You don't have to do this alone." She squeezed my hand.

I nodded, looking at the floor, picking at a piece of yarn hanging from the cuff of my dark red sweater.

After dinner was finished and the last dish dried, we sang. A Roberts tradition dating back to a time when Rich Roberts, their long-deceased father, would ring in the evening with folk songs dashed from his banjo. Today we sang with two guitars, John's and his older brother Mark's, which romped in harmony with all the old favorites.

The cousins laid on the floor like puppies, soaking in one of their last evenings together. Joy and boisterous singing lasted late into the night, when babies were fast asleep on beds in the guest rooms and small children collapsed where they sat on the lap of an older sibling or aunt.

They sank into sleep dreaming of "lemon trees, oh so pretty" and girls "five foot two with eyes of blue." Mark paused, strumming. John placed his guitar in his lap and waited for Mark's lead. Mark sang, his deep voice ringing in the lamplight, an old family classic. Only this time, he changed the words to commemorate this moment, when his only brother and his family were about to leave the family home.

The Lord let His face shine down upon you
 The Sun rise up to meet you on your way
 The Spirit of His love invades the circle of your friends
 His visions keep you changing day by day.

. . .

Good times be the jingle in your pocket
Life's hearthstone there to warm you when you rise
Forgiving and foregoing be the way you know your soul
Your heart be always open to surprise.

Your life and all its seasons
In the hollow of God's hand
His heart will be the ocean
Storing all your footprints in the sand.

Falling down be only London Bridges
'Down and out' be only words for rhyme
A suitcase full of dreams be all
That weighs your body down
Your life poured out like sweet and good red wine.

And time will tell your story
We will listen once again,
Your song will have its moment.
Share the gospel and make each man a friend.

John and Sheryl, you're off to new horizons
We'll miss you
It's so hard to sing this song
We've shared so much,
the memories will sustain us for a while,
Praise God, He promises it won't be long.

Our Lord see you in safety
To the place He calls you now.
May love be how you're known there

Trusting God awaits to show the where and how
Your rest be peaceful, sleep, a fond companion.

Jesus mark the road you choose to roam
If death should carve a canyon in
between us for a while,
Then sing this song for me 'til I come home . . .

The song's melancholic tone matched the family's mood.

"*Til I get home . . .*" The last traces of voices—high, low, sweet, choked, whispered—died off. Silence ensued. A sadness hovered. My heart ached to rewind all the way back to the day I said yes to my husband's call. The day my life shifted, and we ended up here, staring at the red circle on the calendar.

Happy plans, visits with friends, parties, and dinner gatherings filled all the days before the circle. The days that followed were blank, white, and alarming in their unknowingness. My deepest prayer was about to be answered, and I was terrified—yet somewhere deep inside, I felt the quiet stirring of possibility.

I let my gaze come back to the room, noticing silent tears, hugs, and tenderness.

In me, I found stiff resignation and something deeper—a fragile but persistent belief that this void might hold our purpose.

I stood and smoothed down my wrinkled skirt. Turning to see cousins embrace and tears flowing, I knew. This is the reality of the choice I made. We could not turn back; we could only go forward into the white void beyond the red circle.

THE HOUSE ON STREET 576

We landed with a thud on the tarmac. After over twenty-five hours of travel, we had arrived. We jumped to gather our belongings, which the kids had scattered about the empty cabin. It was mostly chaos—crying, jet-lagged children and orders from John as he struggled to handle all the passports and customs and immigration papers. He grabbed the back of Stephen's shirt before he disappeared down the gangway and out onto the hot asphalt.

I gathered Olivia's diaper bag and my backpack and placed her sleepy body on my hip. I grabbed Clara, who was resisting Joe's attempts to help her, and made my way out of the plane. The rest of the children followed. Tim, tasked with checking the seats for forgotten belongings, was the last to exit.

Waves of heat and humidity that took my breath away blasted me, suffocated me, enveloped me in a steamy haze. Moving through that oppressive curtain of air, I instinctively waved my arm, trying to part it before each step. It weighed me down and tried to press me under a vise, only to have me bursting out dripping in sweat from every pore.

We sloughed on across the sizzling tarmac, through immigration, with its staunch Cambodian officials grunting as they scrutinized our documents and then hammered down their date stamp while waving us out of line and into the chaos of baggage claim. Counting heads and gathering papers and passports, we moved as one through the crowd to the carousels and gathered our luggage. We shuffled past more customs officers, who, after seeing all our belongings and disheveled children, let us through, and continued their animated discussion.

The airport doors opened. People packed in a tight, undulating mass searched for loved ones and colleagues, and tourists thronged, moving as one. The stench of body odor, fish sauce, and exhaust from the street, coupled with the scorching heat, caused me to stumble. John pulled us along, scanning for Panha in the rabble. We saw him standing off to the side. His crumpled, button-down shirt gaped on his slight frame. His animated, slender arms waved when he spotted John.

Smiling broadly, bowing, and shuffling, he grabbed a couple of our bags, ushered our tired crew into two vans, and directed his hired local men to stack and drive our luggage in a third truck. My stomach, hard as a rock, churned as my head swiveled to scan the chaotic jumble as we careened out of the parking lot. In my mind's eye, I tried to keep our caravan of three together in the busy, churning madness that was Phnom Penh traffic.

Before I knew it, we turned down a residential side street and bumped down a dusty, rutted dirt road with an occasional chicken fluttering hastily out of the way. We stopped in front of a tall yellow wall with a green gate. The gate loomed in front of me, both imposing and protective. I glanced at its ironwork grates, decorative along the bottom, morphing into straight rows of pickets topped with gold-painted fleur-de-lis, reminiscent of Cambodia's French colonial era.

A small hole a third of the way up allowed me to reach in and unlatch the gate from the inside. It swung open into a spacious and beautiful courtyard. Up ahead was a two-story house, brick facade, with a welcoming, ornately carved twin wooden door on the ground floor and an inviting veranda above, beckoning everyone to come and rest from their journey.

Matt and Jean waved their arms, greeting us from the driveway.

My heart felt light to see familiar faces from home. It had been almost two years since John had seen them in Colorado on that fateful Sunday that led our family here. Today, they were a welcome link from the life we left in America.

"Matt, thank goodness." John stumbled out of the van. "That was quite a flight." He wiped his brow with his shirt. His large hands grabbed the first piece of luggage and dropped it onto the tile courtyard.

"Never gets easier either," Matt said as he pushed his dark wavy hair from his eyes and snatched the second bag. "But you can't beat the service on Asian flights. Come and see your new house. I've got a few hours before our kids return from their classes." Matt and Jean had given up their time and energy running an orphanage and an international school to set up our home.

The kids tumbled out of the vans, shoving and laughing as they scattered to explore. The house, much larger and more beautiful than any of us had imagined, pleasantly surprised me. Three young men from Matt and Jean's orphanage, Ponlou Home, meaning "little sprout," came around the corner and whisked our luggage off to all the different rooms Jean waved them into.

John and I wandered inside. With awe, we moved about the house, admiring its tall ceilings, bright tile floors, and spacious areas. This was a palace. *Suffering missionaries don't live in palaces*, I thought, biting my lip.

Heat rose to my face as I imagined explaining this arrangement to my support group back home, the ones who had donated their hard-earned money, expecting me to live simply among those I came to serve. "We can't live here. It's too . . . comfortable."

Matt threw his head back. "Never mind, you will have plenty of hardship here. At least you have a nice place to return to." *Hardship. Suffering.* My fingers curled into my palms, nails digging half-moons into the flesh.

I moved into the adjoining kitchen and gasped with pleasure. In the middle of the room was a large, twelve-foot-long table that could seat twenty people. I thought of all the dinner parties back in Colorado. Behind my eyes, pressure built. Around the table, I saw my burgeoning family and the many guests we could welcome around this gathering place. At that table, I glimpsed our life here. A thread of hospitality which could knit both our worlds together.

I kept wandering, following Jean as her tall, lanky figure glided through the rooms. She waved her thin hands like a maestro directing the moving pieces of luggage. We moved to the bedrooms with their cavernous closets and enormous adjoining bathrooms. I turned the shower on and off, spraying lukewarm water directly onto the sparkling tile uniform and level across the floor.

"Kids," I hollered, "you can bathe and clean at the same time."

Seth wiggled between my arms, sliding on the now-wet floor. "Slip and slide!" I grabbed his collar before he tumbled into the back wall.

"Let's save that for later. Get your bags unpacked. What room did you guys pick?"

"Stephen and I want the biggest one." He pointed to the next room, which was twice the size of all the others.

"That works. Great place for building block creations." I followed him in to admire the space.

The rest of the children ran from room to room, claiming or changing their claims on rooms depending on what new things they discovered. John and Matt walked downstairs to the kitchen, discussing the errands they would run that afternoon.

Phone lines needed setting up, electrical service needed to be turned on, and a driver's license for John applied for. Jean and I set about making the beds quickly before the younger kids dozed off in need of naps.

I glanced at myself in the mirror as I rounded the corner to the next bedroom. My face was haggard. Sweaty brown bangs looped around my widow's peak and behind my ears. My green eyes looked tired. But I noticed the strength of my walk, the hands holding sheets and pillows with their long, tan fingers, and the curves of my body which had held, birthed and nursed seven children. "She can do anything," I heard myself say to the reflection, moving a wisp of hair from my neck. "She's done so much already."

THE STREETS OF PHNOM PENH

I t took little time before we realized that the sheets I had carefully culled from my collection in America did not fit the extra-long and wide twin beds common in Asia. Jean tugged my arm and whisked me to her van waiting in front of the house. I lugged Olivia downstairs, not wanting to leave her behind, and yelled at John over my shoulder that we needed to run out and please make sure the kids unpacked.

I climbed in the passenger seat with a squirmy baby in my lap. Jean, noticing my discomfort, apologized for not having a car restraint. "Not a thing here. The kids get used to it." She twisted to look out the window; her bright red hair stood out from the dark heads of the Cambodians on the streets.

Jean and Matt had two of their own children, and all of them lived in Ponlou Home with the orphans. It was an orphanage model we had considered, moving in with the orphans, living as one family. But the implications, John and I discussed late into the hot Colorado evenings, did not feel right.

We had decided that we needed to keep our family and the future orphanage separate. That it was important for both the development and protection of our own children as well as the retention of the cultural identity of the orphans. We passed Ponlou Home on our way out of the neighborhood, and I noticed several Khmer teenagers gathered on the second-story balcony playing ping-pong or reading on the wide cement railing.

My gaze shifted from Ponlou Home to the scene in front of me. As we left the suburbs and entered the city center, the streets pulsed with an energy that defied conventional traffic logic. Motorbikes swarmed like insects, weaving impossibly tight spaces between lumbering Land Cruisers and compact Camrys. Horns blared. Motos carrying entire families, sometimes four or five people balanced precariously, darted between larger vehicles with an almost supernatural sense of spatial awareness.

Pedestrians navigated the chaos, stepping out into the streets, trusting in unspoken rules. Traffic would part and fold back to surround the pedestrian, who kept walking eyes straight ahead. If there was a system to this madness, I could not see it. The trash, poverty, beggars on the road strewn with garbage, and swirling smells of rubber, exhaust, and durian assaulted my jet-lagged brain.

Jean continued to point out landmarks for me to remember and chatted about the fastest way to the common Western markets. I blanked out all her words as I struggled against Olivia's squirms and my internal struggle to run. Jean watched me flinch when we barely missed getting sideswiped by a left-turning car at a busy intersection.

The new traffic light above blinked red, yellow, and green, but nobody paid any attention. Jean turned to me and said, "Yeah, we recently got our first traffic light." She swerved to miss a moto that turned in front of her without looking. "Cambodians still are getting used to them. You need to double- and triple-check every time you drive through." I won't ever be able to figure this out, I thought, and what if triple-checking was not good enough?

Moments later, we arrived at Bayon Market on a major Phnom Penh thoroughfare. In a dazed silence, I let Jean drag me along to the entrance to the market. Inside, a blast of cool air met us and gave me a moment of reprieve.

We walked through the home goods aisle where all the linens, with their patterns and colors, swam before my eyes. I searched for a floral pattern with a nice color palette and, finding a close match, I grabbed eight identical sets. I fled to the checkout with Olivia in one arm and a tower of sheets in the other. Jean followed.

I handed over a $100 bill that I had brought from America. The cashier eyed me suspiciously and brought the bill up to her nose, scrutinizing every inch. She returned it, pointing with her long fingernails to a small tear in the upper left corner. "No good."

Jean swiftly plopped her own $100 bill onto the counter. "You can pay me back later." She grabbed her change and paraded me with my stack of sheets of roses and thorns back to the gray van.

Half an hour later, I lumbered into our noisy house with the sheets and baby, wondering where to set both. The linens I handed off to each child to run up to their beds. Glancing around, I noticed that the tile floors were sparkling clean, so I gently let Olivia down. She wiggled out of my arms and looked up at me before heading off to explore the expansive space, a room we eventually referred to as the Great Room.

While keeping my eye on her, I meandered through the Great Room, inspecting all its features in a sleepy daze. I heard the others babbling about rent payments, more fans, and wondering when the bottles of water that were ordered an hour ago would arrive. We couldn't drink from the sink, and we hadn't yet set up our American water filter.

I was in a dream. The surrounding conversations floated in and out and around, melting into the stifling wall of heat, and stayed glued there, waiting for me to retrieve them.

I glanced at John buried in conversation about logistics that now shifted to rent tax. Giving his head a quick shake, he took out his wallet and doled out four twenty-dollar bills to give to Panha to pay the never-ending setup costs. I sat in a straight-backed teak chair pushed up against the heavy curtains along the side of the room near an open window.

Hoping to catch a breeze, I looked at the broad trees dripping with green mangoes. Something caught my eye, and my gaze shifted down. I saw many black, oblong specks scattered about the windowsill. On every windowsill, I found out, as I got up and wandered about the room. I motioned to John, who came and peered down, scrunching his dark eyebrows. He shrugged and went back to counting bills, but not before I saw Matt and Panha exchange knowing, concerned glances. Well, if those were creatures, they would have to wait until rent had been paid and dinner found. I was starving.

"Isn't it time to eat?" I stood up, brushing my sweaty hair out of my face. "Is there somewhere we can pick up some fast food or something?"

Matt and John, realizing that business would have to be postponed until tomorrow, smiled. Matt looked at his watch. "Yeah, I'll take you to our McDonald's equivalent." His brown eyes smirked when he said this. "Grab the kids."

I looked about. The children were folding like flies. One by one, they had curled up in fetal positions on the tile floor or flopped down semi-comatose in a papasan chair. Jean came down the stairs after making up the beds. "Keep them awake. They will get over jet lag faster if they stay upright for a couple more hours." Her green eyes flashed. *Impossible.* I thought. *I envy them.*

Matt and John ushered us all back into the van for a short drive to Lucky Burger, down near the Independence Monument six kilometers away. Once in the car, five children fell asleep. We had to drag them into the restaurant when we arrived, while the others reluctantly walked in and collapsed into the nearest booth. I watched but, in my haze, I was not sure how much sustenance they took in as some stayed dozing, some stared into space, and a couple drooled in their French fries. I stomached down a burger and fries while cradling a sleeping, sweaty baby. I could not take another moment. John and Matt continued to talk.

I stood up. "I need a shower and a bed. Can we get going?"

I woke those asleep in the booth and carried Olivia while holding Clara's hand. She slumped against me, whining into my skirt. John and Matt shooed the rest out the door and into the hot, sticky air. The house on 576 was calling. I was all too eager to oblige.

~

The next morning, the sun shone on my face as it peeked over the horizon and streamed into my room. Birds and dogs shared the stage for the first noises to hit my ears on our inaugural daybreak in Cambodia. I rolled over to look out my window at the beauty of the crimson sky and the waving mango leaves dripping with fruit and dancing to the tune of the birds.

We made it. We are here. This is our new life. How many more mornings were we going to wake to dogs, birds, and mango trees? *Indefinite*, I sighed.

In the distance, I heard car horns, clanging gates, and music—a strange, somber tune billowing in with gracious, rhythmic strains. The traditional Khmer music floated across the sky and landed on my bed, dancing in tune and beckoning me to come.

I eased my legs over the side of the bed, tiptoeing so as not to wake the baby or John, then slipped on some clothes folded in a black tote, yet to be unpacked from its flight across the ocean. A red short-sleeved shirt and jean shorts.

I wandered to our front veranda. At home in Colorado, it would be a porch, a place for sitting and reflecting with a cool beer or iced lemonade. But here, in a past colony of French Indochina, it's a veranda with its high roof, classical colonnades, and shiny tile floors. A large, low, wide wooden dais, a *krea*, carved from prized rosewood from the northern forests, was used for eating, sleeping, entertaining, and even giving birth.

The krea was the only piece of furniture on the east-facing veranda, so I sat down to soak up the breaking dawn with its brilliant colors and sweet rays, hoping this land wouldn't swallow us up.

Khmer music lulled me back as I searched for the direction from which it came. It floated down from the northeast with fine sounds of xylophones, buffalo horns, bamboo pipes, flutes, a dulcimer, and a traditional spike fiddle. The offbeat, cheerful tune sang with joy. Only later would I learn that this is the traditional wedding music played for days in front of the bride's home on loudspeakers pointed out to the world to pronounce a new Khmer family being born to the homeland.

Today it could have been a wedding, funeral, or a Buddhist prayer as far as I knew. But it was exotic and captivating in its off-beat style and drew me into this new land where we had been planted. I closed my eyes to feel the early morning rays of the rising heat, felt the hard wood beneath me and the cool tile under my feet. I smelled roasted pork and steamed rice mixed with jasmine flowers.

Then the wind shifted; sewage and rotten food with a tinge of smoke and ash from the neighbors' early morning cooking fires wafted in and out. My new home was going to delight and terrify as quickly as the shifting scents.

I heard a shout and movement in the house. I turned to go inside; the family called. I went. Forward, always forward. Today was the first day of indefinite, and maybe I was ready.

A couple of hours later, a new van sat in our driveway with its doors wide open and the children scrambling in and out.

John walked over and handed me the keys. "It's yours. Big enough to take the kids wherever. You can even put the seats down if you find some more furniture you want for the house. I heard there is a street on the other end of town that is lined with wicker shops. You might check it out in a few weeks."

I placed the keys in my bag, looking at the blue van with Grand Saloon written on the side of it. It was neither grand nor a saloon, but it was mine. It was my ticket to freedom or disaster. I would choose the former. I would learn to drive in that crazy, confusing chaos. It was my only chance to thrive. And, thriving was my only option.

OH, RATS!

That evening, we all piled into the new van for a drive to dinner. The children's afternoon naps under the blowing fans had left them well-rested. And after a couple of hours unpacking our totes in the kitchen, I felt accomplished. Deciding to try something different from Lucky Burger, Matt suggested Steve's Steak House, a small but delicious restaurant in the middle of the city. We were game to try it.

First, we stopped by Ponlou Home to pick up Srey Ning, so she could be our translator for our evening out.

She chatted in perfect English, directing us up and down streets to find the side road which hid Steve's Steak House. We were pulling away from a stop sign when a police officer in a light blue uniform stepped out in front of our car. Another one rapped on our hood and came up to John's window.

Srey Ning quietly said to John, "Stop the car. Don't say a word. I'll talk to them." John rolled down his window, and in a flurry of Khmer and sweet smiles, Srey Ning rattled off a litany of apologies.

The officer gave her no heed as he spoke in Khmer. "You were driving with your lights on." Srey Ning translated to John, who shook his head, "So . . .?"

While the police officer rested his arm on the window and placed his hand on the steering wheel, she explained to John, "It's illegal. Only government officials can drive during the day with their lights on."

Srey Ning and the police officer had a heated exchange for a few seconds before she looked back at John. "Do you have 2500 riel? He wants twenty dollars, but the law only requires 2500 riel, about fifty-five cents. He said he would accept that."

John fumbled in his pocket as I grabbed some riel from the center console of the van and handed it to the police officer. He let go of the steering wheel, stuffed the riel in his pocket, and waved us on.

Srey Ning motioned with her hand. "Go, go now past the next group of police officers at the next corner. And turn your lights off." John guided us back into the fast-moving traffic, weaving and bobbing among the motos and cars. We stayed in the center of the road to avoid the next set of blue-clad police officers.

Passing them, I breathed a sigh of relief, and I realized two things: First, we didn't know the traffic laws in Phnom Penh. John had gotten a Khmer driver's license by simply paying a bribe, not because he knew the law. Second, as foreigners, we had targets on our backs. The only saving grace? Negotiations were on the table. However, I had lost my first shred of dignity. We were not above bribing police officers. Here, no one was.

Dinner was another scene of meltdown with a glassy-eyed, jet-lagged bundle of children at a sit-down restaurant. The servers, however, swooped in and gushed over Olivia. They took her squirming form out of my arms to walk her around the restaurant so I could be free.

I watched as each member of the family was served, some within minutes, others later. My plate came last. I looked at my thinly sliced steak. I push the plate away, longing for a proper American steak—thick-cut, generously marbled, and tender. But the hot fries, unlimited Cokes, and a refreshing cold, mango salad provided by the mango trees dripping with fruit in the open-air restaurant gardens redeemed my meal.

I leaned in to nibble on the cool mango salad when Seth called out, "Look, a rat."

I dropped my fork and turned as a rodent as large as a small cat lumbered across the brick wall, deftly stepping over the shards of glass embedded in the cement. My meal suddenly looked less appealing. I turned, searching for Olivia with a strong need to protect her from becoming a rotund rat's appetizer.

Olivia was smiling with the Khmer girls as they banged tin plates together in rhythm to the song on the speakers in the background, and in the distance, the rat scurried into the darkness.

Soon enough, I left my half-eaten plate of steak and fries to help John gather the crew and pile them back into the stuffy van. Only a few seconds after driving off, all the children lay sleeping on each other like a pile of puppies. I used that quiet moment, holding Olivia, while Srey Ning quietly navigated us back home, to gaze out the window.

Outside the air was heavy with exhaust and smoke. The dark streets were devoid of police officers, who had all gone home for dinner and a restful night of sleep. The police slept. The city still hummed along, and we were on our own for protection. As the traffic thinned, the night's buzz dimmed as lights sprang on in homes across the city. Some *pteaya-l'vangs* (longhouses) boasted open cooking fires in ceramic pots placed near front doors, and the smells of charred fish and steamed rice wafted in as we drove past.

The night was quiet and peaceful when I spotted a beautiful Khmer girl, looking a few years younger than Srey Ning, strolling down the sidewalk with her high heels and short dress. I looked twice, assuming that parents would keep their beautiful, young daughters safely inside their homes, as traditional Khmer propriety demanded.

She strolled with her arm placed hesitantly on the arm of a man gimping along, burdened by age and a rotund body nursed for years on a standard Western diet. They were so incongruent, her youth, beauty, and delicacy and his age, decaying body, and hardened stature.

I realized I was witnessing, on my second night in Cambodia, the number one tourist attraction: the prostitution of minors.

"Almost home," I murmured, settling back against the seat, trying to keep my mind from racing down the dark road of Cambodia's underworld. My eyes drifted closed as I thought of our green gate's familiar clang and the promise of safety behind it.

Minutes later, we herded seven groggy children up the stairs. "Straight to bed, everyone," I called out, my evening routine forgotten as I collapsed onto our mattress, still half-dressed, Olivia soundly sleeping beside me.

It felt like minutes later when Joe's urgent whisper cut through my dreams. "Mom!" He stood in the darkness, clutching Emma's trembling hand. "There are rats downstairs . . . dozens of them."

"Come here, love." I reached for Emma while Joe darted back downstairs, John's footsteps echoing behind him. Through the hallway, moonlight revealed Tim already below with Seth silhouetted behind him.

"Let's get you back to bed," I whispered to Emma, padding across the cool tiles toward her room. As I reached her doorway, something small and quick skittered across my bare foot.

I stumbled, tumbling Emma onto her bed. "That was a rat." The words escaped my mouth in a horrified whisper. Emma's wide, blue eyes found mine in the darkness, reflecting the dim light from the hallway.

"Scoot over, sweetie," I murmured, easing onto the bed between her and a sleeping Clara. We listened to the chaos below as the boys killed the rats with brooms and mops

Emma pressed closer as each new shout filtered up. I stroked her hair, my heart pounding. There we were at 3 a.m. in a rat-infested house. *How can I create a home here?*

Emma drifted back to sleep, and John came up to get me. "Come to bed. There shouldn't be any more."

The rats lost the battle that night. The death count ran up to twenty-five. They piled their iron-gray bodies in black plastic bags in front of our house, leaving them for the morning trash collectors to bury in their rolling tombs.

That night, while drifting in and out of sleep, I envisioned rats dropping on me from the light fixture, running over my feet in the dark, or hiding under my children's beds. There was no safety in Cambodia, not even in my house behind the yellow wall and green gate.

OHM

The next week was a fuzzy dream of heat, smells, new tastes, and an endless list of to-do's to survive. Each day brought new curiosities, such as the mansion next door, a monstrosity that grew higher every day.

Local artisans labored in their shorts and flip-flops, swinging from bamboo scaffolds dozens of feet in the air. Once the evenings quieted down, the artisans' wives and children gathered, and each family found a quiet corner to pitch their hammocks, build a cooking fire, and have their evening meal.

Joe and Tim stood with me one evening on our veranda, looking over the forest of fires cooking and warming the little families. Children vaulted over rebar and bricks, playing tag. I shuttered, noticing more rats run along the walls silhouetted by the cooking fires.

Joe mentioned the sparsity of their existence. A few stitches of shirts and shorts stretched on lines crisscrossed across the yard like electrical wires. They laid reed mats for sleeping wherever they found a flat place.

My boys watched with disbelief and turned to their own home, palatial, and to their own belongings brought across the sea in twenty-three pieces of luggage. This was more than those laborers' children would ever see, yet by comparison, it was meager compared to the lavish living of children in the West. Joe, Tim, and I paused in the humility of this realization.

The days moved on with the heat rising in intensity as the sun moved overhead. The children astounded me with their adaptation. One afternoon, I found Stephen, seven years old, sitting with two half-naked children in front of the neighbor's house on a pile of construction sand playing with his Batman and Superman figures.

They could only communicate through the language of play and youth. When the sun started to set, Stephen gave each of the boys his cherished toys to keep and then wandered back inside the gate, unfazed that his belongings were irreplaceable in Cambodia.

I watched him from the corner of my eye as I squatted in front of our home practicing my few Khmer phrases with my neighbors while graceful Khmer music floated in and among the flowering bougainvillea and wafted down our street, bathing the scene of play and relaxation with the perfect tune.

The neighborhood children grabbed an old soccer ball to play on the rutted, dirt road, not caring when the ball stuck in the deep pits. With the sun setting, Seth, Joe, and Tim braved the cultural and language barriers and jumped into play. The Khmer boys rumbled and competed while the Khmer girls giggled and blushed under the Rambutan trees as they watched the new foreigners.

John arrived in the van. I opened the gate and waved goodbye to the grandmas. He jumped out with arms full of Styrofoam containers. I smelled freshly steamed rice and roasted beef surrounded by lettuce and tomatoes. We called in the boys from their play for dinner. Rice was the staple of every meal in Cambodia. In fact, the Khmer phrase for "eating a meal" is *num bye*, or "eat rice." One Khmer greeting is "*Num Bye Howie?*" or "Have you eaten rice yet?"

Tonight would be the last night we would have to search for food outside our gates. A week earlier, I decided that Ohm would come to work for us. I had met her in the cramped office at Matt's school.

Ohm sat on the edge of her chair, her foot tapping, and, in her hand, she held a fake leather pocketbook. She opened and closed the clasp, clicking it nervously. As both a friend of hers and a prominent member of the expatriate community, Matt knew where to find her next placement.

When I walked into Matt's small office, she stood abruptly and placed her hands together, dropping her pocketbook on the floor, and bowed in a low, respectful *sompeay* greeting. Rising with a smile, masking the fear in her weary eyes, she scooped up her pocketbook, fiddling with the clasp once again.

Matt looked at me. "She needs this job. She's been bouncing from expatriate family to missionary family and back again." Ohm, only guessing at his words, nodded her head and watched his mouth. "Families never stay here long enough for her to have stable employment."

I felt a sinking feeling in my stomach and bit my lower lip. I would let her down. We would not stay long either, I had decided after the rat infestation. But I needed her. House helpers in Cambodia did all the difficult and labor-intensive work of a home: daily shopping at the crowded, local markets, cooking from scratch, washing dishes by hand, washing clothes and hanging them to dry on the line, and endless cleaning of dust, which perpetually crept in through every open window, coating surfaces in a fine gray film. If I tried to do those things, I would struggle with the language barrier, the increased prices at the market for foreigners, and the time-consuming household chores that would take all day. Yes, I needed her.

I placed my hands together and bowed awkwardly.

I turned to Matt. "I imagine we can give her years of employment." My head tilted to the side, and I looked out the window, surprised at my blatant lie.

He smiled and translated to Ohm, who again bowed profusely. "*Ackoon, Lok Srey, Ackoon.*" (Thank you, ma'am, Thank you.) *Lok Srey*, Ma'am, Mistress of the Household, that was going to be me if I hired her. I pictured ringing bells to summon servants and a tray of tea coming every afternoon. I was unsure what it meant to be Mistress of the Household, but I knew I needed someone to help me.

Her smile comforted me, and her earnestness affirmed that she really needed this job. I put out my hand. "You are hired. Can you come over tomorrow to cook dinner?" I bit my lip again. Maybe that was too bold, but, goodness, I needed a cook. After Matt translated, she turned, *"Jah, jah."* (Yes, yes.) We spent a few minutes negotiating her salary, which seemed meager.

Matt explained we could not give her more than her skill's market value. We agreed on eighty dollars a month for shopping, cooking, laundry, and cleaning Monday through Friday. I watched her face for signs of anger. *What a measly salary this was.* Instead, she smiled broadly and bowed, thanking me. I fished in my purse for a twenty-dollar bill for food, which she could use in the local markets.

We parted out in front of the gate as she puttered off on her small moto with my bill placed gently in her pocketbook and then stowed in her waistband to keep it away from pickpockets.

Later the next week, Ohm buzzed into our courtyard with her moto basket overflowing with produce, colorful fruit, and slabs of raw meat wrapped in plastic. She parked the moped and gawked with pleasure, her eyes darting at our palatial home and ample kitchen.

Marching in with her arms loaded, enlisting Emma to carry a large pineapple and a hand of tiny bananas, she got to work shifting around my supply of pots and pans, clicking her tongue in either pleasure or judgment. I could not be certain.

Panha had arrived earlier that day for Khmer lessons and to help translate for Ohm. She jabbered to Panha, who calmly replied, *"Baat, baat."* and scribbled on our lesson book. He turned to me, "She needs a wok, rice cooker, mortar and pestle, clay cooking pot, and meat cleaver . . ."

He glanced at me out of the side of his eye while trying to still listen to Ohm mutter under her breath about my inadequate American cooking pans. Panha looked down at the long list. "She will need another fifty dollars to buy all these things."

Moments later, Ohm jumped on her moto and headed back to the market with fifty more of my dollars. I turned to look at Panha, helping John with the Khmer alphabet. The strange sounds of the letters confused me as I thought about Ohm and Panha's conversation about simple household items. Not a word of it was familiar. Not knowing the Khmer language was going to prove limiting. I must start my language classes soon; I knew that, but creating a home was taking precedence.

A yell and a cry from upstairs jarred me. "Mom, Olivia slipped again and hit her head!"

Footsteps thudded on the cement staircase as Emma came down to find me. I passed Stephen and raced upstairs to grab the crying Olivia just learning to walk and scuttled into the bedroom, checking the back of her head for a goose egg or blunt cut. She showed no signs of injury, and I breathed a sigh of relief. She quieted as I put her to my breast for comfort.

She looked at me with her green eyes and twisted my long hair in her chubby fingers. Sweat soaked the two of us, so I leaned over to switch on the standing fan and placed a cloth diaper between her sweat-soaked hair and my arm. I settled back in the bamboo rocking chair that clicked and clopped as it rocked on the tile floor.

She soon fell asleep, and I gazed at her sweet face. My baby and youngest girl. Girl number three, she was sweet spirited and silly with her wrinkled nose and little snuffles when she laughed. But my heart sank when I glanced down at her little mouth and chubby legs. She had developed thrush, and her body had reacted to the relentless heat with an outburst of heat rash that inflamed her whole lower body.

I unpinned her cloth diaper to let her body have some air that was circulating from the fan. The breeze soothed her oozing sores. Normally, I would have bathed her before her afternoon nap to bring down her body temperature.

Today, we both fell asleep in the rocking chair with the clip and clop of runners soothing us to sleep. The undertow of my children's needs in this sea of tiresome newness dragged me down and sapped all my strength. I was exhausted.

KHMER MEAL

A n hour later, Clara startled me awake by bouncing into the room yelling, *"Num bye,* Mommy, *num bye!"* Her quick little mind had already picked up the Khmer language, at least for the important things like eating. I dressed Olivia and wandered downstairs, following the din of excited voices wafting from the kitchen. I walked in and pressed my fingers to my smiling lips at the spread of food filling our large dining room table.

Rice in a beautiful blue ceramic bowl was at the center of the table. Next to it, a platter of sautéed beef with onions and green beans swam in a sauce punctuated by fish sauce, oyster sauce, freshly grated ginger, ample cloves of garlic, and a dash of soy sauce.

Olivia sat on my lap quite ready to nibble on the strange smelling food, banging her little spoon on the table to get my attention. She ate bits of rice from my plate and then asked to nurse again by rubbing her chest with her hand, the American Sign Language sign for "please." I shook my head no and tried to distract her with a piece of pineapple to suck on until I found more suitable baby food later.

The children chattered about their day. Their discoveries included three species of geckos, cockroaches crawling out from behind the toilets, and an assortment of license plates that were found behind the house, one of which was from Colorado.

The children talked over each other, and the excitement escalated to a loud din that overwhelmed my sleep-deprived system. I was about to ask for some quiet when John spoke up. "We should take a trip to the beach this coming weekend. What do you all think?"

A loud cheer erupted as Joe and Tim high-fived. The beach! For our previously landlocked family, this was luxurious—an enjoyable break from the heat and noise of the city. John continued, "Maybe we'll leave Friday morning. I heard the coastal town of Kampong Som is nice. We will take Route 4." He looked at me and smiled.

I looked down. "What about that story that Jean told us the other night? Wasn't it only a few years ago that the embassies warned travelers to avoid Route 4? That it was one of the last strongholds of the Khmer Rouge?"

I stopped talking. The kids were listening. But I remembered the rest of the story. Three young men, an Australian, a Brit, and a Frenchman, had defied this warning and hitched a ride on top of the train running between Phnom Penh and Kampot. The Khmer Rouge attacked the train and took the three men as hostages. The Khmer Rouge forced them to work in the blistering sun, and they soon fell ill. Later, the Khmer Rouge executed them.

"Yeah, in that instance"—he glanced at the children, their eyes glued on him— "a car would have been safer."

I knew full well he remembered the second story. That one week before the train abduction, three young Western professionals were driving in a taxi back to Phnom Penh to get food for their newly opened cafe in Kampong Som when they got stuck in a Khmer Rouge convoy holdup on Route 4. The Khmer Rouge abducted them on the spot and then shot them. Later, villagers found their bodies, deep in the jungle. These stories echoed through my mind so loudly that I barely noticed John getting up from his seat.

John took his plate to the sink. "Oh, and I ran into another missionary at basketball this afternoon." The plate clanked. The sound reverberated along the tile floors and concrete walls. "He asked if we needed a guard for our house. He has a student who has come from the province of Kampot living in his driveway. He could sleep in the garage on the spare bed. He only needs to bring his own mat."

Sitting back down, John glanced in my direction. "What do you think? He can watch the house while we are at the beach." A cook and now a guard. I felt the control over my household start slipping away.

John noticed my distress. "Mark says he is very gentle. He is also a new Christian. His name is Ly." He waited for my reply.

I nodded. "That sounds okay. For now." The conversation shifted back to the beach and how long the drive was. I heard John mention a restaurant there that we must visit called the Snake House. "It has tables with clear centers that harbor all kinds of tropical snakes. You can watch them while you eat."

"Eat what?" I shivered.

"Lots of things. I hear they have some exotic meats. Some of them are illegal." The boys roared in excitement and the girls grimaced and looked at me for support. I got up to find Olivia some food while trying to find a reasonable argument for skipping the Snake House.

Ohm leapt to attention from her perch in the kitchen corner. Speaking in rapid-fire Khmer, she grabbed Olivia from me, then commandeered a plate of freshly cut mango in the other. She placed the plate in front of John, who engaged the kids in conversation about Cambodian snakes and exotic, illegal meat while passing around the sweet mango.

Smiling and bowing, Ohm backed away with Olivia from the table to her perch in the corner. Continuing to fawn over Olivia with coos and cheek pinches, she spooned rice from the pot and smashed it with a fork, then poured a dollop of beef broth and meat scrapings from the bottom of the large pot over it. She fed Olivia with the tiny, pink baby spoon that I had brought over from America. Rubber-tipped, soft for baby hands, and tiny, the spoon rhythmically went from the rice baby food concoction into Olivia's gaping mouth. Looking like a baby bird, she gulped and swallowed, all the while not taking her eyes from Ohm. Pleased that Olivia loved her Khmer baby food, Ohm snuffled Olivia's cheek repeatedly.

Snuffling, a strange word for a Khmer kiss, but the only one we could come up with in our limited English language. Blow out through your nose while waggling your head back and forth. Olivia giggled as Ohm's snuffles tickled her cheek.

We had, over the past days, pieced together Ohm's story. As she loved on my youngest child, I reflected on her frightening and courageous life.

Ohm's life had unfolded against the backdrop of Cambodia's tumultuous history. Born in the rural province of Takéo, she grew up surrounded by rice paddies and the gentle rhythms of village life. What set her apart was her education, rare for a girl from the countryside, which included proficiency in French, a leftover from the colonial influence that would later both endanger and save her.

At eighteen, she married and soon moved to Phnom Penh to work as a schoolteacher with her husband, a civil servant in Lon Nol's government. By twenty-two, they had settled into city life and were busy raising their four-year-old son. In April 1975, black-clad Khmer Rouge soldiers shattered their modest comfort when they emptied Phnom Penh. Ohm and her family were forced back to Takéo province at gunpoint.

Upon arrival, the Khmer Rouge separated the little family. The communists, suspicious of education and urban connections, sent Ohm to a women's labor camp, her husband to a men's camp, and her small son to a children's barracks.

Her French literacy became both danger and salvation when the commune leader's wife faced complications in childbirth. Medicines scavenged from abandoned clinics, French labels indecipherable to the Khmer Rouge cadres, sat useless. In desperation, the commune leader summoned Ohm.

Standing before the boxes of medicine, she understood the deadly gamble: Reveal her education to save a life or deny it and watch a woman die. With trembling hands, she sorted through the vials, translating the labels, knowing each word could condemn her as an intellectual. The woman and baby lived.

The commune leader never forgot her courage. Though he wore the checkered krama of the regime, he quietly ensured that Ohm and her husband received protection. He overlooked their former government connections in the endless purges that devoured hundreds of others.

Once every two weeks during that time, Ohm could see her son.

His hollowed cheeks broke her heart anew. The children's camp provided even less food than the adults camp. Each night, Ohm would carefully scrape the burnt rice from communal cooking pots, hiding the precious grains in a scrap of cloth tied around her waist. During their brief visits, she would press these morsels into her son's small hands, watching him devour them while she pretended not to be hungry.

When Vietnamese troops drove out the Khmer Rouge in 1979, Ohm's family fled to a Thai refugee camp. For years, they lived in the limbo of displacement, sleeping under UN-issued tarps and standing in endless lines for water and rice. When they returned to Takéo, Ohm joined the village security detail, taking night shifts with others to watch for Khmer Rouge guerrillas who still terrorized the countryside.

Remarkably, the former commune leader remained in their village. Unlike many Khmer Rouge officials who had ruled through terror, he had shown small mercies when he could. The villagers protected him in return, a complicated grace in a country where victim and perpetrator often had to rebuild side by side.

Loss continued to shadow Ohm, even after the fighting ended. Years later, her husband, weakened by years of forced labor, died of illness. Then came another cruel blow—her adult son, the child she had saved one handful of rice at a time, died during what should have been routine surgery. At age fifty, Ohm found herself utterly alone.

With nowhere to turn, she returned to Phnom Penh, now transformed by an influx of foreign aid workers and missionaries. She took her village cooking skills and adapted them for Western palates, learning to prepare meals that satisfied foreign tongues while remaining true to Khmer traditions. By fifty-three, her reputation led her to our gate.

I watched Ohm across the room, her small frame swaying as she cradled Olivia in her arms. My ten-month-old daughter, usually so particular about who held her, nestled against Ohm's chest. I thought about Ohm's history—the labor camps, her child stolen away to collective housing, those desperate scraps of rice hidden at the risk of her life—and now here she was, holding my daughter, her weathered hands supporting the weight of a child not her own, after losing everyone she had loved.

My exhaustion suddenly was shameful; my complaints were petty. I had chosen this disruption, this uprooting. Ohm had had no choice when the Khmer Rouge forced her family from Phnom Penh at gunpoint. She had survived genocide, watched her husband and only son die, and still found the capacity to care for my child.

A complicated emotion rose in my chest—part gratitude, part guilt. Ohm began humming a melody I didn't recognize, a Khmer lullaby perhaps centuries old. I wondered if I could be so resilient, so gracious in my suffering.

She caught me watching and nodded toward Olivia, now sound asleep in her arms. *"Kon-sreay s'aat,"* she whispered. Beautiful child.

"Thank you," I said.

Her weathered face creased into a smile, and she gestured toward my half-eaten plate with a questioning look.

"Chnang Nah," I said in halting Khmer, patting my stomach. Very good. Her eyes crinkled with pleasure as she nodded.

I rose from the table, carrying my plate to the sink. The clinking of forks, the talk of beaches and long drives, a reptile restaurant, a strange man coming to live with us, the confusion and horror of Ohm's story. It was a strange dream. I slipped away and disappeared up the darkened cement stairway to my bedroom.

At 6:20 p.m. night after night, the sun dropped out of the sky. Night did not descend gently, like in Colorado, with a rich drawn-out sunset. No, here, the day exited like an Irish goodbye. In its place came the hoard of mosquitoes. They feasted on our fresh blood, sweet and new. Our arms and legs were evidence of their starvation.

Fans, mosquito coils with their slow-burning wicks of repellent wafting out from under tables and beds, mosquito nets draped like wedding dresses over our beds, and fast-moving battery-operated swatting wands like tennis racquets were heavy in our arsenal of weapons against the dengue fever and malaria potentially lurking in every mosquito bite.

The fan only kept them off temporarily while I kicked off my flip-flops and crawled under the mosquito net to escape. The heat under the white, billowy netting was almost unbearable, so I snuck up to the switch next to the door and flipped on the air-conditioning unit mounted high above the north-facing window.

A blast of cold air drenched me and, for the first time in days, I felt some relief and my nausea dissipated for a moment. This act of rebellion felt glorious until I heard John's voice in my head. *We can't afford air-conditioning. Electricity is too expensive. We must acclimate.*

I flipped off the switch, and almost instantly, the soothing coolness dissipated like the sun on the Cambodian horizon. I crawled back under the net and tilted the fan so that the billows of netting were blowing and filling like Marilyn Monroe's skirt. I laid back and sobs leapt up, choking me.

LOOPS AND ARCS

I sat straight up in bed, sweat pouring down my back. Then I heard it again—the cacophonic clanking of sticks echoing under my window. The sun pierced the sky at 6:20 a.m. sharp.

The noodle man was passing by. His clattering announced breakfast for two thousand riel—fifty cents—if you hurried to flag him down. I wanted neither noodles nor to be awoken so early, yet there I was.

My door opened and Clara bounded in on her tippy toes, both excited to come in but mindful of John and Olivia still sleeping.

"Mommy," she whispered, "my pants are dry. Can I have a chocolate?" I am not above bribery with Cambodian police or my three-year-old daughter who does not wet the bed.

I ushered her out and down to the kitchen to rifle through the freezer to find the bag of chocolates stowed away from America in one of our twenty-three pieces of luggage. She sucked on it happily while I turned to unlock the bolted kitchen door.

Emma was now up, and the two girls wandered out into the courtyard to play, and I set water to boil on the small propane stove, the same stove that housed the clan of rats we exterminated our second night here. I peeked hesitantly into the oven to make sure a new rat family had not taken up residence.

The water boiled. I added American coffee to the French press and took a cup up to John, who was checking his email on the clunky computer positioned in the sunny open space outside our bedroom. Behind the desk, two large wooden acacia doors carved with flowers and scrolls opened onto the front veranda. I set the coffee down on the bamboo desk while John typed a letter to our mission organization asking for more money for a washing machine.

I took my cup, journal, and Bible and claimed my throne on the veranda and surveyed my small domain. From my perch, I watched the courtyard where my girls played, glimpsed the street beyond, and when curiosity struck, peeked into the neighbor's yard.

"Momma, look at my cartwheel!" Clara called from below.

"Beautiful, sweetheart," I answered, steam rising from my mug as I sipped. Emma waved from her spot under the mango tree, deep in a book. Only after confirming all was well in my realm, I settled into my morning ritual of reading, prayer, and contemplation.

The boys' sleepy shuffling and cabinet-opening eventually drew me from my sanctuary. "Mom, is there anything to eat?" Joe's voice carried up the stairs.

"Coming," I called back. In the kitchen, I sliced crusty French bread, arranged fresh fruit on plates, and set out a bowl of jam on our oversized table.

"Can we have rice pudding?" Tim asked, appearing in the doorway.

"Already warming it up." I stirred last night's leftover rice with milk and palm sugar. Then I grabbed the muffins from the oven.

"What are those supposed to be?" John peered at the sunken tops.

"I made muffins," I sighed, dumping the failed batch into the trash. My mind drifted to my kitchen in Colorado, where perfect blueberry muffins once rose golden and light in my dependable oven, their aroma filling our home.

As I finished the kitchen dishes, Ohm and Panha arrived at the same time. "Chumreap-Sua!" Panha greeted us with a sompea, a slight bow with hands folded in respect. We responded awkwardly and practiced our few Khmer greetings.

Ohm placed bags of raw slabs of pork, fresh vegetables, and tropical fruit on the counter. Clara and Emma raced in from the court-yard to rummage through the bags to try to guess the evening meal. John and Panha talked briefly about ministry with Panha's church, the plan for the orphanage once our language skills increased, and a bit about the latest political news since the national elections were coming up soon.

Ohm clucked her tongue and looked at Panha out of the corner of her eyes, as if to say, "Don't say too much." Panha lowered his voice and looked around but continued to talk about the elections—the Cambodian People's Party and their political opponents, Funcinpec. As if it were illegal to talk about such matters, we all kept looking over our shoulders. I had enough of political talk and left to gather the kids for our morning of homeschooling.

The kids whined and complained that their cousins in America were on summer break. Why did they have to do school? I reminded them we took months off from school while we were getting ready to move to Cambodia. The Cambodians, I explained, have year-round school, so we will too. They moaned but settled down to take up their math, handwriting, journaling, science, and spelling.

Later that afternoon while the little ones napped and the older boys read books, and the middles played in a tote filled to the brim with building blocks brought over from home, I had the arduous task of language learning.

Srey Nut, my Khmer teacher, with her floppy sun hat and sachet full of Khmer language books, beeped her moto horn in front of our gate at two o'clock that afternoon. She smiled and sampeahed me then drove her moped into our courtyard.

Making our way into the empty schoolroom, I brushed aside the half-finished math papers from the morning to clear space to work while also trying to clear my mind of all my fears about language learning.

I sat down on the hard teak chair while Srey Nut chattered in Khmer. Her fast-moving hands told me she said something about books, pens, and tracing the letters of the Khmer alphabet.

I smiled at her, hoping to mask the voices in my head beating me down. Srey Nut slowed down her speech and gently walked me through my first lesson. Khmer has a Sanskrit alphabet with thirty-three consonants and twenty-three vowels that, combined with the consonants, create over sixty vowel sound combinations, more letters than any other language in the world.

The letters are placed in, around, above, under, and next to each other, creating fresh sounds—vowels embracing consonants and both running together into words and words into sentences, neither stopping for a breath. There are no spaces between Khmer words. It becomes one long sentence. Loops and arcs flowed across the page, reminiscent of the flowing Mekong. Its curves and waves tumbled down to the South China Sea. *I must conquer this language river to survive*, I thought. I pulled my weary brain along.

"The only way to get better is to practice," Srey Nut said in halting English as she gathered up her books at the end of the lesson. I smiled and agreed as I glanced at Ohm working in the kitchen. But language was only the beginning of the chasm that was before me in this land.

The vast contrasting traditions of Eastern thought (particularly Cambodian) and Western (particularly American) thought resulted in a cultural standoff. I didn't understand the Cambodians, and they did not understand me. For a moment, the weight of centuries of divergent histories hung between us like a heavy curtain, making even the simplest exchange feel like navigating through fog. I needed a guide. When Ly arrived, I knew we had found that person.

ROUTE 4

L y arrived late in the afternoon the day before we were to leave for the beach. He quietly rapped on the front gate, and Tim, dribbling his new basketball, opened it. Ly peered around the corner as his eyes darted around the courtyard. Tim invited him in, and Ly walked his moto in and parked it in the courtyard while more of my curious children peeked through the doors and windows to see who this student was that was coming to live with us.

Nervously, Ly smiled and sampeahed and, to my surprise, greeted us with grammatically perfect English, though still heavily accented. My relief must have shown on my face, as Ly responded in kind with a large, toothy grin, which caused his eyes to squint and disappear. Conscious of his large, crooked teeth, he closed his mouth so only his eyes sparkled and laughed.

"Come in," I welcomed him, beckoning the children from their hiding places to come and meet him. John joined us in the Great Room. Ly sat down on the edge of the chair and spoke softly and now with a pronounced stutter, which caused his face to turn red.

John encouraged him. "We need a guard, someone to pay our bills, monitor the gate, and sweep the courtyard. Can you do that between your classes?"

Ly relaxed back in his chair with a sense of relief. "I can do that."

John stood and put out his hand. "Then this weekend will be a trial run. If all goes well while we are at the beach, you have a job. Forty dollars a month and room and board." More comfortable with a sompeah than a handshake, Ly timidly took John's hand. They sealed the deal.

Ly moved in that afternoon and didn't leave for twelve years. He was reliable, intelligent, personable. Everyone benefited. It did not take more than a few days for my boys to warm to his gentle, older brother ways. The girls enjoyed his protective posture and funny jokes. To John and me, Ly became like a son. And Ly was there on that early Friday morning when we left for our beach trip to Kampong Som.

"Everyone in the van . . . don't forget your overnight bags." I searched for my flip-flops in the pile accumulated at the front door. "Clara, here are your shoes." I threw a small pink pair into the court-yard. "Joe, grab the box of cinnamon rolls on the counter . . . Get your water bottles. Let's go, everyone." Like scurrying ants from a shaken ant hill, the children ran back and forth: making one more last-minute bathroom stop, grabbing a book to read in the car, filling a water bottle from the kitchen water filter. One by one, they trickled into the van.

John checked the water in the radiator and washed the front windshield. Once in the van, I counted heads; as I got to six, I turned to see Emma with her head in a book saunter out and grab the last seat in the van.

A tussle for the window seat ensued, but as one of the youngest, Emma squeezed into the middle with Stephen's overnight bag beneath her feet. Kicking off her flip-flops, she settled in to finish the page before putting the book away to keep her eyes straight ahead to stave off car sickness.

We backed out of the driveway with Ly standing and waving in the driveway. He closed and latched the gate behind us, and we were off on our first adventure since arriving in Cambodia two weeks earlier.

～

Kampong Som was a horrendous four-hour drive down a busy two-lane highway. The ride was an endless dodging of schoolgirls on wobbly bikes, roaring tourist buses, slow-moving for-hire moto drivers (called *motodups*), sprinting teenage boys racing to school, stick-thin Brahman cows, chickens, and mangy dogs. Not to mention that in the recent past, Route 4 had gobbled up six Westerners assassinated by the Khmer Rouge. The road was too bumpy and the dodging too chaotic to read the book I clasped in my hand. I turned to the side window and watched the distant green rice fields and thatched stilted houses with hammocks strung underneath to escape the relentless heat.

Within a few hours, we arrived at an open-air restaurant at the top of a hill. A small Khmer woman showed us to a large table right in the middle of the restaurant, far from the hot kitchen in the back and the exhaust-filled street in the front.

Trash, dirty white paper napkins, and an assortment of dropped silverware littered the ground while mangy dogs wandered between the tables to lick up dropped rice and chew dirty napkins. Other dogs lounged in shady corners to escape the heat, and a bitch with a litter of pups sprawled out under a banana tree in the dirt parking lot. The pups rooted and nursed on her dried out, tired teats.

Our table was sticky. I rummaged through my bag for a pack of wet wipes and scrubbed.

I handed out one for each child. "Don't touch anything and wipe your hands thoroughly. Seth, don't let Olivia put that in her mouth. Wipe her hands!"

The waitstaff dropped dozens of lukewarm cans of cola on our table and a few tall tumblers of boiling water with silverware stuck face down to sterilize the utensils. They gave us grimy menus in Khmer with blurry pictures of the meals.

John pointed to three or four local dishes we could recognize had pork, chicken, or beef. He added a few plates of *bye cha* (fried rice), a family favorite. Soon, a young boy around eleven years old brought platters of food and steaming pots of rice and placed white plates before each of us. We served food and rice all around and ate family style. The kids downed cans of cola while John had an Angkor beer, and I drank a glass of iced green tea. It turned out to be delicious, and I was pleasantly full at the end of the meal.

"Run to the bathroom, kids, before we pack back up." I grabbed Olivia to wash the sticky rice off her face, hands, and toes with a wet wipe. John and the boy of eleven counted soda cans and totaled up the bill while I followed the kids around the corner of the restaurant to a rectangular cement building snug between three banana trees.

A covered porch in front anchored a counter with sinks for washing up, minus soap or towels. Opposite the counter were two doors with the universal signs for male and female. The boys took turns in and out, washed their hands minus soap or towels, and headed back to the car. Meanwhile, I found the girls staring at the door to the bathroom. Neither of them dared to go in.

Emma looked up at me. "What are we supposed to do?" I laughed as if she had never used a bathroom before. I peered into the dark cement room and saw why she was so confused. One hole in the ground, one cistern of murky water, and one blue plastic pail with a long handle. I looked at the girls and said, "I guess we squat . . . like camping." I tried to make my voice cheery. Clara squirmed and looked at me with her green eyes. "Me first. I can't hold it."

I gave Olivia to Emma and took Clara into the bathroom. I assumed the pail and cistern of water were for cleaning. After holding her while she peed, I took the pail and dipped it into the cistern and tried to splash her privates. It only resulted in wet pants and water all over the already wet floor. Disheartened, I took Olivia from Emma while she went in next, looking like she would rather pee in the forest. Emma emerged, looking a bit horrified but with dry pants. Somehow, she had already perfected the use of the squatty potty. I still had much to learn.

Back in the car, we were soon careening down the chaotic highway and continuing south to the beach. We passed Pich Nil, the highest point on our drive. Several phallic-shaped shrines to Yeay Khmao (Dark Grandmother), the spirit guardian of the Southern Cambodia region, stretched skyward through the mountain mist, while incense smoke and the sweet, ripening scent of fruit offerings filled the air—tributes left by devoted travelers to appease her spirit and ensure safe passage.

Reaching the beach a couple of hours after passing Pich Nil gave us all a rush of joy. The ocean, with its brilliant blue, greeted us at the top of the last hill on the journey. Here it was, the Gulf of Thailand. It looked inviting, and we already felt the salty water on our skin and the gentle movement of the waves. Even the early evening breezes with their salty, fishy smells and cooling touch whisked away the stress of Phnom Penh.

Sihanoukville was a serene coastal town, dotted with nightclubs and lined with palm trees along the road leading from Route 4. The peaceful beaches were home to open-air eateries serving up specialties like pepper crab, fried squid in tangy pepper lime sauce, papaya salad, and juicy mango and pineapple. This quiet paradise for backpackers and locals alike was far removed from the hustle and bustle of Phnom Penh.

Within minutes, we found our hotel, a four-story cement building, which, for Cambodia, was stunning—clean, delightfully landscaped, and with a gleaming pool of clear water. We found our two rooms and placed our luggage onto enormous beds with stiff sheets and flat pillows. We quickly changed and asked the small teenager tending the front desk which beach we should try. He motioned across the street, and we headed that way.

As we crossed the courtyard, I glanced at the crystal-clear swimming pool. My body tingled as I recalled years of swimming on our local neighborhood swim team in Southern California, starting from the age of ten. I pictured my tall, lanky self trembling on the starting blocks waiting for the gun.

Ten years of swim team, from the neighborhood pool to the varsity swim team at Dana Hills High School, flashed before my eyes. Chlorine, water, stroke after stroke, lap after lap, had been an integral part of my young life. I yearned for that kind of movement, stretch, and rhythm in my body again. And, even more, I missed that sense of the complete obliviousness to life above the water. For an introvert, it was heaven below the water with only the sound of my arms slicing and my legs kicking. It was a world unto itself, that swimming pool and my body moving like air within it.

"Mom, we are crossing the street. Catch up?" I looked up to see Joe waving at me from the curb. With towels draped over skinny shoulders, the children, in varying sizes, were already dashing across the quiet road.

"Coming!" I left my silent, aquatic reveries and jogged up to meet him. He smiled and we stepped off the curb together, chasing the dashing crowd of towels and laughs.

We spent the day sunning on the beach, playing in the gentle, gulf surf and eating various foods that were hawked to us by women in large sun hats with flat baskets of food placed precariously on their heads: grilled squid, bags of cut mango with a spicy salt dip, fried sesame balls, and boiled peanuts. We ate, laughed, played, and swam. We even made it to the Snake House, which was not as scary as I had imagined. This trip was charming. It was what I needed to believe that Cambodia could be delightful.

Driving home on Sunday, John and I talked about how much we had enjoyed the trip. His brother Mark, with our niece Melissa and nephew Andrew, was coming for a visit next summer. We decided we would take them here and re-create this trip. We settled the matter. We would escape the heat of Phnom Penh for another charming beach holiday the next time we had visitors. It was the perfect vacation spot.

BANG, BANG

fter the serene vacation to the coast, we returned to the hustle of the city feeling spiritually adrift, starting to miss the familiar warmth of our home church in Colorado. We searched and hoped to find a place that echoed the worship style and close-knit community we left behind. Jean and Matt took their orphans and their own children to a Southern Baptist church, which rented a lecture hall at the Russian Center of Science and Culture on Norodom Street. The service across town started at 5 p.m. on Sunday evening. This Sunday, we decided to join them.

We left Ponlou Home in three vans packed to the gills with children. In our van, the Khmer girls sang show tunes from America's musicals. It was odd to hear Cambodian orphans in the middle of Southeast Asia singing "The Lonely Goatherd" and "Do-Re-Mi" from *The Sound of Music*. But it reminded me of home, so I settled back, listening to my little girls happily singing along.

We arrived at a lovely white villa with a circle drive surrounded by a luscious garden. Pastor George greeted us inside after we walked through a long white hall decked with Russian portraits of stern-looking men with thick, Coke-bottle glasses and starched suits. Pastor George led us to a stately hall with plush stadium seats and a large wooden stage. On the stage was one microphone, a podium emblazoned by a spotlight angled so that the speaker was awash in shadows, and a long, red velvet curtain hung from the ceiling, adding to the feeling of overbearing opulence.

Pastor George, with his thick Southern accent, began the service with prayer, but only after we corralled the orphans and our own children, some of whom were playing cards backstage on stage boxes. The chairs squeaked and moaned as everyone found a place.

We sang old Baptist hymns pounded out on the piano by Pastor George's vivacious wife. Then Pastor George preached long and hard on the Lord's Prayer. The shadows played out like umbrages on his face, his mouth moving with intelligence.

The sermon lasted almost an hour, and my thoughts drifted. Having grown up Episcopalian, I was accustomed to both male and female priests and pastors. But I found myself, in adulthood, more comfortable in traditional Christian services with male clergy. Women were not less capable or spiritual, but male clergy was what I understood to be proper biblical interpretation and historical church practice. There was something significant about that consistency across different traditions.

I was curious about whether changing these long-held practices, like more progressive mainline churches have done, might be moving away from something important, even if I couldn't fully articulate what that was or why it mattered so much to me then.

I glanced at Pastor George as he was wrapping up his sermon and wondered what role women, me included, would play in the nascent church in Cambodia.

Pastor George and his wife had not been in Cambodia long either and chose to live in Ta Khmau, a small market town on the south side of Phnom Penh. Matt had told us that a few Sundays earlier, Pastor George was driving home from church when his passenger window was shot out. Although shaken, he had arrived home safely. Someone had wanted his car. He vowed to get home before dark after that, but his long-winded preaching often got the best of him.

The story reminded me of what Panha had told us when we first arrived. "If you go out of your gate after dark, *bang, bang,* you're dead." We made sure to be behind the gate after dark, as did most of the citizens of Phnom Penh. After dark, it became a ghost town.

I looked around and checked my watch. We were going to be out after dark. Dark descended quickly at 6:30 p.m. The church service, with its lengthy singing of hymns and its fifty-five-minute sermon, dragged on as I watched my watch tick and felt my anxiety increase by the minute.

The last note of the final hymn rang out, and it was over. Breathing a sigh, I quickly gathered our belongings—coloring books and crayons, water bottles and a diaper bag—and scuttled for the door.

We set out from the meeting hall, down the hall of Russian notables and out into the darkness. After finding our shoes among the dozens at the door, we left with a passel of hungry kids. I looked for my children, scanning faces while the older Khmer girls linked arms and sang the showtunes again, their shiny black hair contrasting to my blonder girls.

The three vans were parked in the darkened circle nestled among the Areca palms, mango trees, and velvet tamarinds. I saw my boys jump into a van with their friends. I chose a van closest to the front door and peered in, hoping to count heads. I carried Olivia on my right hip as usual, and Emma shuffled on my left side. But where was Clara? She was not in this van. I scanned the parking lot for her near the other two vans, but it was so dark I could not see her anywhere.

"John, where is Clara?" I cried out as I saw him crawl into the van with the boys. He waved his hand as if to say she was somewhere in one of the other vans with the other children, and they drove off.

Our engine roared to life, and we jerked out of the parking lot. I was desperate to find Clara, but by now all three of the vans were dashing into the dark Phnom Penh streets. With my face pressed up against the window, I searched the pitch-dark parking lot and now-empty building. No movement. Was she inside there somewhere playing among the stage boxes or on the road in one of the other vans?

I clung to Olivia when we stopped at a red light. I glanced around to see if I could catch a glimpse of Clara in one of the other vans.

A bright white ambulance, running lights and sirens, squealed up next to us and obscured my view. The traffic remained stubbornly still. A handful of motorbikes attempted to make way, but they were pinned in by the crush of vehicles and the collective indifference to the emergency.

The light inside the ambulance flickered and lit up a grisly scene: Blood was everywhere. Dirty, mangled limbs and helpless paramedics with bloody gauze draped over their dirty hands. Emma gawked, and I tried to turn her gaze away from the gruesome scene. Too late, her face drained of color and fear filled her eyes. My brain swirled—a mangled body, a lost child, a traumatized five-year-old, and we were still out after dark. *Bang, bang.*

I held my breath until we got back to Ponlou Home, where the vans emptied, and the children ran inside to wash up for dinner. My heart stopped when I spotted one of the girls holding Clara and taking her inside the orphanage. I gasped and gave an inaudible shriek of joy. She was not lost among stage boxes, darkened pianos, and austere Russians. She had been fine all along. It was me who was not. I had catastrophized, panicked, tortured myself with all the worst things that could happen to a child in that twenty-minute drive.

I leaned into John when I saw him. I told him my fear, and he chuckled and kissed my forehead. "I knew she was fine. The Ponlou girls take care of our girls like they are their younger sisters."

I was glad he was so confident. I hoped his confidence could carry both of us.

MONEE

The slow summer days after our beach trip continued to delight me. The things that were foreign and strange at first were becoming charming and interesting, though I still lacked John's confidence and vigor.

I was still afraid of long, rambling sermons, lost children, and nighttime. But mornings were delightful, and I spent every one of them on the veranda listening to the waking of the city.

I noticed her while sipping my coffee on the veranda one morning. Monee would squat on a pile of construction sand near her mother's cooking fire, tending the morning pot of rice. She looked about twelve or thirteen with long, sleek black hair tied back in a ponytail. She would often look up at our house with her round and gentle eyes and watch our girls run in a game of hide and seek or sit quietly and play dolls on our veranda.

On a construction site, she had nowhere to run, and if she was not helping her mother cook over the open fire, she drew pictures with her finger in the piles of sand left over from cement making. Her younger brother, Di, would sit beside her and dig holes in the sand, bury broken pieces of brick, and then find them again. He could not run amongst the scrap wood, rusty rebar, and sharp metal shards hidden indiscriminately among the construction debris. So, he sat and played in the sand with scraps.

Occasionally, their mother would let them play outside the gate when she could watch them while her baby slept in the hammock strung between two poles inside the compound. It was one of those mornings when I saw Monee and Di and their mother outside the gate. I cocked my head and looked back at my palatial home. Feelings of guilt washed over me. I needed to be a good missionary. Here was my chance.

I put down my coffee and scurried downstairs and out the gate. Barefoot, I ambled over to Monee's mother and asked her if Monee and Di would like to come play with my children at our house. I pointed next door. She looked up with her black eyes shaded by the *krama* wrapped around her head. She glanced at my house, tipped her chin, and nodded. Monee and Di, shy yet eager, followed me into our gate and into our home.

My kids peered out from behind the couch where they were playing with building blocks. Monee and Di hid behind me as Stephen, outgoing and bold, came forward dragging a large sheet full of thousands of pieces. He dropped it at my feet and motioned for Monee and Di to come play.

Emma and Clara approached each with a half-built creation in their hands. I stepped aside so Monee and Di could join them. Stephen, with his happy chattering in English, must have made them feel welcome. Before long they were all engaged in building a world that only children can enter despite language barriers.

Over the next week, they came over daily. Then one day a few weeks later, I heard from Monee that she, her mother, Di, and the baby would be returning to their home village in the Svay Rieng province to start school. Their father would remain in Phnom Penh and work at our neighbor's house until the home was finished. I knew that time with them was short, and I hadn't told them about Jesus yet. This was the last chance I could be the missionary that I was expected to be for Monee. I invited Sombat, one of the girls that lived at Ponlou Home, to come over and translate for me. I wanted to show Di and Monee the *Jesus film* in Khmer.

One late afternoon, a few days later, we all watched the movie together in our upstairs living room. They were mesmerized by the story of Jesus's life and were sad at his death by crucifixion. Monee jumped for joy when he rose from the death and "found his friends again." When the movie was over, Sombat asked if they had ever heard that story before. Both shook their heads no. With wide eyes, they listened to Sombat elaborate on Jesus's gift of life and his death and resurrection as our path to eternal life. She gave them a Khmer Bible that I had on hand and taught them a couple of short prayers to take home with them to pray in their village. She asked them before they left if they would like visitors to their village, if we could come and see them again. Monee looked around at all of us and nodded yes. She would love a visit from Sombat and her new American friends.

I snapped a few pictures of Monee and Sombat for my missionary newsletter, waved goodbye to Monee and Di, and went back in the house to start writing a letter home. Here I was, doing what missionaries do. Though we were tasked to open an orphanage once our Khmer language was proficient, we could not wait. Here was an opportunity to share the gospel in a remote village. I jumped at the chance to prove my mettle as a missionary, to have something to write home about, to feel worthy to be here. But I had to push past a gnawing fear of things outside my gate.

A couple of months later, I sat in the backseat of our van looking out at the bright green, newly sown rice paddies. I took one deliberate breath, filled my lungs with air, and realized that today I was calm and ready for an adventure. Tall, elegant palms dotted the long stretch of green. Small, crouched women stooped and planted each tiny rice seedling.

I turned to look at Olivia sleeping in the seat next to me with her bangs matted down with sweat and dirt smudged on her left cheek. The rest of the kids chatted happily in the back seat while Michael, another missionary, sat in front with John discussing the plan once we found Monee in her village in Svay Rieng.

Sombat and Srey Ning were in the van behind us, with Tim, Joe, and Seth driven by one of the older Khmer boys from Ponlou Home.

We invited Matt and Jean's Ponlou orphans to join us after we realized that they were losing their Khmer language in their home. Matt and Jean had decided that the kids would be at a disadvantage if they did not know English and Western culture fluently. So the children were forbidden and even punished corporally for speaking their native language. We thought this strange and not in keeping with modern mission practices. Things were starting to feel off about their engagement with Cambodia. We filed that away and decided to help the orphans by taking them deep into the provinces in hopes that this would help them maintain their Khmer language skills and cultural understandings.

I was hot, tired, and bruised from bouncing around in the back seat on the rutted dirt roads. John swerved to avoid a gaping pothole, which bounced us to one side of the van. Then he turned to miss another one, only to hit a third. We flew into the roof. With no seatbelts, we had to hold door handles or ashtrays to stay in our seats.

With one hand I held on, and with the other I clutched Olivia in my lap. The road had been rough since we left Phnom Penh many hours earlier. I doubted Sombat's promise. I didn't need this torture to reach Monee. I could be a good missionary another way, couldn't I?

There was another reason I was anxious about this visit. This remote province was hostile to Christianity. Three weeks earlier—on a Sunday morning in July 2003—two hundred villagers had descended on a local Anglican church in a neighboring village. A three-year drought plagued the farmers, putting their livelihood and their lives at risk. They were desperate for relief. Armed with hammers, they broke windows and shutters and destroyed tables, lights, and ceiling fans. They took dozens of Bibles and dumped them into a nearby pond and rice field. The villagers believed that Christians were to blame for their long drought. The Khmer Christians were not giving sacrifices to the Spirit of the Land, the Neak Ta, so he had punished the whole village with a drought.

The van stopped and, looking up, I noticed we were approaching a river. A rickety ferry on the other side of the river slowly moved across while a long line of cars, motos, and trucks waited. We waited with them. Within seconds, twenty krama-wrapped women peddling their food, drinks, and wares swarmed and circled our van. The van's windows, designed to slide horizontally rather than roll down, were pushed along their weathered metal channel by grimy, dark hands. The hawkers stuck their hands inside, grasping for my children's faces.

I grabbed Olivia, who had a dark, dirty hand caressing her arm. One woman leaned in to kiss Clara on the cheek while Stephen tried to shut the back window where a man stuck a lit cigarette into his face, enticing him to take a drag.

I pushed hands out of the van's windows and slammed them shut, oblivious to any fingers lingering behind. I turned to the children and saw their eyes wide with fear and the smell of cigarette smoke swirling in the air.

I brushed ashes off Stephen's pants and gathered Clara, her lips quivering, in my arms. Glancing out the windows, I saw Khmer faces pressed against the glass, staring at my scared, light-skinned children. Some knocked lightly, smiling with teeth either blackened from betel nut juice or missing altogether. Some had kramas wrapped tightly round their faces and tattered straw hats pulled low over their piercing, dark eyes.

A few women held wide, flat baskets on their heads with little, naked sparrow heads deep-fried and tipping over the edge. Others held buckets of roasted black beetles and crickets, or congealed rice balls wrapped in banana leaves.

The van became claustrophobic and smelled of cigarettes and fish sauce. I climbed over the seat and opened the door and crawled out. Standing sentry to keep the hawkers out of the car while letting the faint breezes sift in, I noticed John had already left the van and had gathered a crowd.

Though he was not tall by American standards, in Cambodia, he was a head above everyone. He engaged with the sellers with a friendly demeanor and, with his halting Khmer and eagerness to try crickets and beetles, he wormed his way into their hearts. They smiled and joked with him, pressing up close to hear him tease affectionately. I cringed when I watched him pop a handful of crickets into his mouth and then laughed as he searched for riel in his pocket to buy a Coke to wash them down.

His ease and comfort with the Khmer people and his ability to make them feel his warmth triggered something deep inside of me. He loves it here. He loved our life in Cambodia and embraced it fully and deeply. He was drinking in all the flavors that this tiny country had to offer.

I had followed him here with my own dreams of adventure. I watched him move so naturally among the people, while I was still so terrified and clumsy in my embrace. I needed him to carry me, all of us, through our own fears and misgivings. He looked at me and smiled, and I knew at that moment I would follow him anywhere.

The crowd began to shift and peel back as the line of vehicles inched towards the returning ferry. John and I jumped back into the van in time to take our place in line.

Carefully driving onto the crowded ferry, we found ourselves parked next to a large cattle truck carting hogs to the distant provinces. Their snouts poked out of the slates to sniff and snort. The kids laughed and made faces at the pigs as we all moved noiselessly through the muddy, brown water.

Looking across the water, the bright sun silhouetted a shirtless fisher in his thin boat with curved prow. He rhythmically threw his net into the murky water and used his muscular forearms to pull it up slowly. A small boy in the stern of the boat would wrestle the fish into a bucket perched on the slated seat in front of him.

Wooden stilted huts hugged the shoreline. Each hut held a Khmer family—mother, father, children, probably a grandparent or two. The huts look painfully inadequate to hold any life, but the collection of rubbish and sewage that collected beneath each hut and washed back and forth with the river's wake was a reminder that life did exist there.

Two small children, naked and brown, gleefully splashed and played in the murky water while their mothers washed clothes downstream. My American sensibilities were assaulted. The river water must have been teeming with creatures—parasites, amoebas, typhoid, cholera, dysentery, and any number of bacteria. As careful as we had been at home in Phnom Penh, with a state-of-the-art water filter from America and an excessive amount of bleach and handwashing, our family still struggled with constant digestive issues and bacterial skin problems.

Back on the rutted, red clay road, we soon turned right and passed underneath an elaborate red and yellow stone archway showing the entrance to a village with its nearby *wat*. The arches were carved in traditional Khmer style, stylized with seven-headed Naga snakes, dancing Apsara women, and Dvarapala, the door guardians holding their clubs and spears with fierce grimaces.

Along the roadside, villagers appeased the Neak Ta—ancestral spirits who protected their land—by leaving fresh fruit, burning incense, and small cups of rice wine at wooden spirit houses, ensuring these territorial guardians remained benevolent. We scuttled under the lofty arches, inched down the road, and wondered how we would ever find Monee amid the Nagas and natives.

THE VILLAGE

few more turns, many stops to question local villagers, and a faded mile marker brought us to Monee's village. We stopped at a coconut stand flanking a small home with bare-chested men playing cards and drinking beer. With friendly smiles and wide eyes, they wondered at our question, "Do you know a young girl named Monee?"

Each of them shrugged, conversed together, and pointed down the road. At each stop we got out and, looking behind us, saw a small crowd gathering, obscured by the dust from our vans.

John slowed and, putting Olivia on my lap, I looked out the window. We had driven right down the center of a *toul*, a mounded path between two rice paddies. Our van barely had room to drive, and the steep sides of the toul dipped sharply into the rice fields below.

A shout went up ahead, and a small thin boy tumbled down the toul shouting at us to follow him. Someone had alerted the village that we had come. John drove slowly, following the boy as he gestured with his waving hands, excited to be the important messenger.

Across the toul and around the next bend on the dusty, rutted road, we saw her. Monee was helping her grandmother with the noonday meal. Her small, stilted home had a sleeping pallet resting in the shade underneath and a cooking hearth made of stones and bricks at the edge.

Monee, hearing the commotion, looked up. She saw Sombat, and her face beamed as her hand went to her mouth in joy and amazement. She looked around at the entourage of people who had driven three and a half hours from Phnom Penh to visit her. Her eyes widened.

This little village girl, whose name no one even knew except a small, thin boy, had become a person of great importance. The curious crowd that had followed us gathered around to see the visitors from the city and the foreigners from America. Monee's eyes swelled with tears. *"Khnom mun ha chue te. Mut robah khnom nou ti ni."* (I did not dare to believe it. My friends are here.)

Monee's aunt heard the commotion and, coming out from their home, raised her hand to her mouth. She straightened her skirt and drew her hand across her gray hair. In Khmer she said, "Foreigners have not come to our village in ten years. We are so honored."

She went back inside to wake Di and his cousin from their midday naps. The two boys stumbled out and ran down the wooden stairs. Di stopped in front of Stephen with wide eyes. Stephen smiled and put up his hand for a high-five. Slapping his hand, Di dragged Stephen under his house to show him a small building block set that he had bought in Phnom Penh.

More village children gathered to see Monee's visitors. Older girls would gently take my girls' hands and walk down the quiet road flanked with dusty mango trees waiting for the rain. The boys from the second van, along with Sombat and Srey Ning, grabbed large black totes off the top of the luggage rack.

Tim opened the totes as the children gathered around. They gawked as if it was Christmas in America when they surveyed the bounty. Each tote contained dozens of brand-new backpacks; each backpack held notebooks, pencils, erasers, and a picture Bible storybook in Khmer on top. Joe handed them out while Tim and the Ponlou boys corralled the crowd.

I watched with pride as my boys circulated among the children with tenderness and ease. It was hard to tell the ages of the children, as they were much smaller than their American peers. Even they didn't know their ages. They might tell you they were born in the rainy season, or around Khmer New Year, or in the year of the flood, but most had no official birthday.

The older girls, their hair wet from a fresh wash at the village well, held the hands of the smaller children. With their dingy clothing hanging loosely on their small frames, the children looked at us from the corners of their eyes. Their little bare feet with the characteristic splayed toes of the Khmer—feet growing without fetters—scuffed the dirt, making little lines and patterns.

Looking around, I noticed the children had few to no possessions. Some had a ball, a plastic bucket to play with by the river, but most amused themselves with rocks and sticks and the unlucky stray dog or scrawny chicken that crossed their path. I saw no books, crayons, or dolls. The only toy set I saw was Di's cherished small building set hidden in his mother's clay cooking pot.

Joe, Tim, Sombat, and Srey Ning gathered the children around to share a story. They spoke in a serialized storytelling mode built upon the children's existing knowledge of their Khmer storytellers. How did the world begin? The children jumped to answer this age-old question with their own Khmer story of creation. Sombat agreed, but what came before that? Who created the creator? The questions stumped them, and one by one, they lowered their hands to listen to the story of the "Great Mover," the "First Cause," God.

While the children, holding or wearing their backpacks, were engrossed in the story, I watched John mingling in the back, talking with the group of adults who had gathered to watch and listen.

The men would point to their oxen in the field or to a small child here or a teenager there to show their wealth or influence in the village. John would cross his arms, observing all they pointed out, his head nodding in admiration.

My lungs expanded with deep satisfying breaths watching John and the children move effortlessly in and among the villagers. Their language ability was adequate, even good, their openness to the culture admirable.

My eyes settled on an old woman sitting under a tamarind tree on a worn wooden bench. We made eye contact, and she patted the seat beside her. I moved closer and sat. We both watched the children listen to the stories while the afternoon heat pressed down.

"*Koun nuh sralahn nah*," I ventured, pointing to all the children. (Very cute, lovable.)

The old woman's face brightened instantly at my attempt at Khmer. "*Jah! Koun sralanh*," she agreed with a nod, her smile revealing betel-stained teeth. She added something in rapid Khmer that I couldn't follow.

"*Som toh* (I'm sorry)," I apologized, tapping my ear. "*Knyom mun yul te.*" (I understand little.)

"Ah!" She slowed her speech dramatically. "*Kon chhau knyom*," she said, pointing to a boy of about seven who was sitting up front. "My grandson."

Her weathered face creased with pride. She turned back to me. "*Neak Srey mawk pi Amerik?*"

"*Baat*," I confirmed. "*Knyom mawk pi Amerik.*" (I'm from America.)

She looked confused, then laughed, gently correcting me. "*Baat* for man. *Jah* for woman." She nodded as I blushed. She patted my hand. "America good."

"*Amerik l'or*," I agreed, using the Khmer word for good. "But Cambodia *s'aat nah*." (Very beautiful.)

A small girl ran up to us, staring at me with curiosity. The old woman spoke to her, and I caught the word *barang*—foreigner.

"*Chumreap sua*," I greeted the child with the formal Khmer greeting, bringing my palms together.

The girl giggled and hid behind the old woman, who laughed and stroked her hair. "*Kon chhau sreay*," she explained. (Granddaughter.)

"*S'aat nah*," I said, smiling at the child. She was indeed beautiful. We sat in comfortable silence, my limited Khmer exhausted. I felt tired of the struggle. I nodded to the woman as I stood and stretched and sidled away to explore. She patted my arm and turned back to snuggle her granddaughter.

Down the toul, I found a small path leading deeper into the rice paddy buzzing with cicadas. I ventured off and under a white-flowering jasmine tree; I kicked off my sandals and squatted down. Easing my way down to the edge of the rice paddy, I let my toes curl down into the mud.

A swirl of chocolate-colored water hid my feet as the cool, silky silt hugged them. I reached out to brush the tops of the newly planted rice shoots, planted by the villagers weeks before. In the distance, one lone woman crouched in her field, placing the last of her delicate rice shoots in ruler-straight rows.

The sarong around her waist clung to her stout dark legs as field water licked up the cotton. Her large reed sunhat cloaked her face. She grabbed each shoot from a sack hanging from her side, transplanting and never standing for a rest. Down into the life-giving, nutrient-rich mud she planted. The clutch of tender shoots in her left hand grew thinner as she made her way to the end of the row.

As John, Sombat, and the team planted seeds to nourish souls, this woman planted seeds to nourish the body. *What do I plant?* I wiggled my toes in the mud, my feet brown and slim. I plant both. As a mother, I nourished the body, within my womb, through my breasts, and in my kitchen. I also nourished the soul with that first kiss on a newborn's head, to the lullabies sung, to the rhythmic rocking, to the late-night conversations with teenagers sprawled across my bed in the dim light of the lamp. I am a nourisher, even in this corner of the world. A mother takes her job with her.

As my hands brushed the shoots in front of me, I gently tugged on a slender rice shoot. Its roots had taken hold, and it did not budge under my prompting. Rice was the lifeblood of Asia. All human existence depended on it. The Cambodians named the seasons of the year after the different rice-growing cycles. This was the end of the hot season and the beginning of the rainy season. Enough rains had flooded the fields, so each little, short shoot stood erect, as if in a sea. The lifeblood of my little field was maternal devotion, love, and a lot of sacrifice.

I flinched and jerked my feet out of the water. A long, brown snake slithered past, uninterested in me or my muddy feet. I laughed at myself and admired the serpentine wake the snake left on its way to find lunch.

The smell of the jasmine tree landed with the breeze and, mixed with the scent of petrichor rising from the murky water, I closed my eyes to take in the delicious and new experience. Enfolded in the moment, my heartbeat steady, I delighted in my immersion in Cambodia's natural beauty.

I had found my place of wonder and contentment in this rice paddy buried deep in Cambodia's interior, far from the hustle and bustle of city life. My fingers laced around my knees with my feet once again firmly planted in the silky mud, and I looked up once more to the hectares of rice standing at attention reflecting a brilliant yellow-green color so unique in the agricultural world. Blowing softly, the carpet of green and brown welcomed me to a Cambodia I could find peace in.

John called my name, jolting me from my trance. Looking up, I saw the cars already full of my family and friends ready to head back to Phnom Penh.

I jumped up and waved. "Here, coming!" I slipped on my sandals and made my way back to the toul.

The kids waved from the windows. "Where were you, Mom? We looked everywhere."

I laughed at their feigned concern and kissed their outstretched hands. "Just saying hi to a water snake and some rice seedlings." They laughed and moved over to let me in. Olivia crawled into my lap, and before we drove under the red and yellow Neak Ta archway, she was sound asleep.

ROBBED

A few months after I found peace in a rice paddy, Stephen, Emma, and I were working on math problems in the Great Room when someone banged on our front gate. I trudged out to see who it might be. Opening the gate, I found our new American neighbors, Amy and Jake, shaking and wide-eyed.

"We had our motorcycle stolen at gunpoint. While we were sitting on it." They looked a distance down the street. "I don't know who it was. Some young man. Stranger. But the gun . . . I can still see it." Jake moved from one foot to the other.

"Come in . . ." I shuffled away to let them in the gate, then peering down the empty street, I slammed the gate shut and locked it from the inside. "Come in. I'll get you some water." I ushered them into the Great Room and told the kids to go upstairs and to get Daddy and then to stay in their rooms to play. They ran up the stairs. John came down and, noticing the situation, questioned Amy and Jake, who stood shell-shocked. With Amy's staccato answers and John's experience in police investigations, they soon re-created the scene.

"We think it started yesterday," Amy started. "We had no problems with crime until something weird happened." She wrung her hands. "We heard an unexpected knock on our gate, and when we went to answer it, two policemen came into our courtyard. They were friendly at first, smiling as Khmer do. We thought maybe something happened in the neighborhood and they wanted us to know. But as time went on, and they did not get to the point, we were wondering what this was about. Finally, one of them said, 'You need to pay for our protection.'" She paused and looked at Jake. "Then the other guy said, 'Yeah, a couple of hundred dollars should do.'"

Jake looked out the window. His jaw clenched. "I will not do that. I won't have anything to do with bribery. We are missionaries. That would be so wrong. I said no and let them know we were busy and said, 'Thank you for coming.'"

Amy continued, "The police officer in charge said something to the other in Khmer. He had an angry tone which concerned me. I didn't understand his Khmer. They left quickly."

John put it together. "Let's go down to the local police station and report the robbery." John stood up and grabbed his motorcycle helmet. "They need to know."

Jake followed and grabbed an extra helmet from our rack. He and John left on the back of John's motorcycle, headed three blocks away to a small storefront-turned-neighborhood police station that crouched between a nail shop and a karaoke bar.

Amy and I went into the kitchen for lunch, our conversation turning to schooling for the kids and their latest trip to the beach. I avoided the subject of robberies at gunpoint and corrupt police. Amy's eyes softened as we talked. The tension in her shoulders eased.

Soon John and Jake returned looking pensive and replaying the scene as they came into the house.

"It was so weird when you walked into the station"—John unlatched the clasp on his helmet and set it on the rack—"that the first thing the captain said to you was, 'We had nothing to do with it.' Do with what? Did they know what you were going to say? They had something to do with it." Jake nodded.

Worry etched the men's faces. Amy wrapped her arms around herself, unable to stop the slight trembling in her hands as the men talked.

"I can't believe it," Jake whispered, breaking the heavy silence. "We went down there for help, and now . . ." His voice trailed off.

"I know what I saw," John said firmly. "Those officers weren't there to protect us . . ."

"They are out for themselves. They are corrupt," I finished, voicing what everyone was thinking.

Jake paced by the window, periodically peering over the gate. "Being a foreigner is like having targets on our backs."

"So, what do we do now?" I asked, looking around the circle of anxious faces. "Where do we go when the people who are supposed to protect us are the ones we need protection from?"

No one had an answer as we stood together, feeling powerless. My throat tightened as I stared at the floor. I'd believed in systems, in order. I had taught my children that police were there to help. Those years John worked at the Greeley Police Department had cemented in my mind that the police were the good guys. Now those certainties crumbled inside, leaving only hollow questions and the persistent thrum of fear beneath my ribs.

A few days later, as I taught the younger kids, we heard a loud rap at our gate. My stomach dropped and my hand froze in midair as I stared at Emma's spelling words on the paper in front of me. *Ignore it, they will go away.* But Ly opened the gate.

Two police officers in their tan uniforms stood stiffly. John noticed them from the upstairs veranda and slipped down, giving me a look of concern and nodding his head to let me know he would take care of it.

They sauntered into our courtyard, eyes searching our home. As one of them talked, the other scanned the outside of our house. I offered them water and a place to sit outside in our courtyard.

They jabbered to John in Khmer. I watched John's body language, lost in the situation.

Then they handed John a clipboard with some forms. It was all in Khmer, and I could not make it out.

John saw my concern. "They want us to register. All foreigners need to register when they move into a new *sangkeat*—a neighborhood."

I nodded. But I did not want them to know where I lived, let alone the names and ages of all my children. I watched John carefully writing down all our names. I wanted to stay invisible. But a Western family with seven children was hard to hide.

They left with smiles and kind words to the children, who wandered down to see what was happening. Their demeanor was disarming. Maybe we would be okay. They did not ask for money for protection. I wondered why. The question did not bring relief, only more confusion.

I woke the next morning and felt like something was off. The unease was strong. Maybe it was left over from the police visit, I told myself. But the moment I walked out of the bedroom, I gasped. The large wooden veranda doors were standing wide open. I was the one to open them first thing in the morning and lock them in the evening. Lock them. I must not have locked them during the busy evening managing everyone during yet another power outage. *I forgot to lock them.*

Turning quickly to the desk standing across from the veranda, I noticed my camera bag was missing. I started moving through the house, scanning the rooms for other missing belongings. John's wallet on his nightstand, Tim's CD player next to his bed, another digital camera last placed on a side table, all were gone.

My heart sank, and fear paralyzed me. The evidence was undeniable—the missing items, the subtle displacement of books on the shelf, a lingering scent that didn't belong to our home.

My eyes darted frantically around, cataloging the things that were disturbed or out of place. The thought of strange hands touching our possessions, invading our private spaces, made my skin crawl. But what turned my blood to ice was the realization that whoever it was had been mere feet from where Olivia had been sleeping, her tiny body curled up beneath her favorite blanket, completely vulnerable.

I stood frozen in the doorway of our bedroom, my fingers white-knuckled around the doorframe. I could not step further. It was no longer a sanctuary.

I forced myself to breathe, to push through the crushing weight of panic. The violation went beyond the physical disturbance of our home. They had stolen something precious: my sense of safety, the belief that these walls could protect what I loved most in the world.

MOVING IN

Two weeks later, a truck rumbled down our street. I could see it from the veranda. It paused and stalled at each crater-like pothole in the road, disappearing and reappearing. At the front gate, it stopped, and three men sauntered out and opened the back hatch. Carefully, with hands covered in thick gloves, they unloaded several coiled meters of razor wire and dropped them on our driveway.

The rest of the afternoon, they unraveled the coils like a concertina, laced them over the top of our wall, and tethered them off with heavy wire until it covered our entire front and gate.

Joe wandered up next to me on the veranda as we watched them finish with the last ties. The half-inch teeth, shaped like tiny guillotine blades spaced every few inches along the coils of wire, were sharp and menacing.

The landlord arrived soon after in his black Lexus with tinted windows and, with his hands laced behind himself, he wandered back and forth inspecting their work. He glanced up at me now and then, nodding and smiling. Embarrassed by the robbery, he did his duty to protect us and, more importantly, his investment.

Joe turned to leave. "We really live in a prison now. Looks like Guantánamo Bay." I took a sip of my coffee and sighed.

A few months prior, from my Dos Rios house in Northern Colorado, I had seen vast vistas of the Rocky Mountains from my back porch: brilliant sunsets over the mountains, low-moving clouds on the green corn fields behind us, the tops of golden cottonwood trees down by the river glimmering in the crisp spring evenings.

Now I stared at razor wire coiled like a snake on my dull yellow wall. It looked menacing, but at least it would be a deterrent. Or so I hoped. After triple-checking every lock on every door of the house for the previous two weeks, I might sleep easier that night and only check once.

Later in the afternoon, I heard Olivia's cry to get out of her crib and then a happy coo. Ohm hustled upstairs, and chattering in Khmer, grabbed Olivia and brought her to me on the veranda, both smiling broadly while Olivia reached for me from Ohm's arms.

"Neak Srey . . ." Ohm asked in Khmer. "Tau khmon auj sua neak avay muey?" (Can I ask you something?) Her rapid-fire Khmer challenged me even after months of study.

Putting up my finger to stop her, afraid of missing her request, I leaned over the railing and yelled for Ly, napping in his room outside. I turned back and plucked Olivia from Ohm's arms. I had recognized a couple of her words and felt proud of myself, but it did not take long for my inner critic to berate me with hopelessness. I was failing. Ly bounded up the stairs two at a time. "Yes, Neak Srey?"

"Can you translate for me? I don't understand." I waved my hand in Ohm's direction. I turned to smile at her, trying to reassure her that the misunderstanding was mine. She returned my smile with her eyes downcast, shamed that I could not understand her. Mutual discouragement and self-blame.

Ohm and Ly spoke. Ohm fluttered her hand, pointing up and down the street. I put Olivia down to play with half an ear still trying to reassure myself that my hours of language study were worth even a few words of comprehension. I returned to stare at the ominous razor wire, and it both comforted and horrified me in the same breath.

"Ohm wanted to let you know . . ." Ly paused as Ohm looked down at her feet and tears fell on the shiny tile below. "She wants you

101

to know that her moto was stolen by her second husband, who left her and went to live in the province with his other wife. She will be late for work, she says. It will take her over an hour to get here from the south side of town on her bike." Ly stopped and looked at Ohm, nodding his head in sympathy. Ohm still had a smile frozen on her face, even though her eyes were wet with tears.

"How sad . . ." I was trying to imagine a life with other wives. I knew that Ohm's first husband died after the Khmer Rouge. This was her second marriage to a much younger man. "Of course she can arrive late." Then, in a moment of impulsiveness, I added, "Why doesn't she come here and live with us in our spare room next to the kitchen?" I caught myself as Ly excitedly translated. *What did I just do!*

Ohm's head snapped up, and her eyes shone. She sampeahed me repeatedly, going lower each time showing deference and gratitude. "*Ackoon. Ackoon charain, Neak Srey!*" (Thank you, thank you very much, ma'am!) She swooned and stooped. She left, telling Ly that she would bring her things tomorrow. Bouncing and bowing, she backed out the door.

My offer horrified me, and at that moment, I heard John's motor-bike horn outside. Ly took off like a rabbit to open the gate for him. *I offered Ohm our spare room.*

"John!" I yelled over the veranda. "Ohm is coming to live with us." I bit my lip and watched his reaction. He furrowed his brow, then nodded.

The next day Ohm arrived one hour late on her dull red bike. A flatbed trailer pulled by a moto followed. On the flatbed were various pieces of furniture and several large plastic bags and a few tattered suitcases.

She cradled under her arm a carved rosewood box which held the only possessions from her deceased husband and her only son.

She gestured with her free hand to the flatbed moto driver to drive the monstrosity into our courtyard, scolding him for being too slow and careless.

Ly and Hok, Ly's twin brother, scurried her belongings to the spare bedroom off the kitchen. Clara, Emma, and Stephen—eager to have a diversion from schoolwork—jumped in to help with arms full of boxes and bulging plastic bags.

Ohm whipped out a handful of Khmer riel to hand to the driver and shooed him out the gate. She jumped back on her bike and wobbled down the rutted road to the market. On my way upstairs to chat with John, I peeked into the spare room piled high with bric-a-brac and smelling like mold, fish sauce, and Tiger Balm ointment.

The girls wrinkled their noses and retreated to the Great Room to finish their school assignments. I slowly closed the door to keep the foreign smells and sights from leaking out. Ohm was here for indefinite.

A HOUSE OF FOURTEEN

few months later, I had to find Ly again for translation. "What is she saying?" I waved my hand in Ohm's direction. Ly listened and then turned to me. "Ohm has a niece from her home village in Takéo who is looking for work. She is wondering if you know of any work for her with other foreigners?"

"I can ask around," I said. But I knew nothing about her niece. How could I vouch for her? John and I talked about it later that evening. Ohm suggested her niece could live with her in the spare room. We vacillated, then agreed. It was the right thing to do, but I was feeling claustrophobic and closed in. It felt as if the walls of our home were shrinking around me. The thought of another presence—another set of footsteps, another personality to navigate—sat heavy in my stomach.

Later that morning, Ohm returned with her bicycle basket over-flowing with fresh fruits and vegetables with cuts of pork for the day's meals. Behind her rode a thin young girl with a floppy hat, pink frilly shirt, and dark green striped pants. She hopped off the bike and stood with her head so low I could not see her face as she fussed with a small bag attached to the bike rack.

Ohm thrust the overflowing parcels from the market along with a pineapple and bag of mangosteens in the young girl's free hand and marched her into the house. I stood in the doorway of the Great Room.

"*Neak Srey, Jim Reap Sua.*" (Hello, ma'am.) Ohm smiled and her eyes disappeared into her lined face. Motioning with her hand, she continued, "*Ni cu chia, Maiy. Neak mok be Takeo.*" (This is Maiy. She comes from the province of Takéo.)

Proud of myself for understanding her Khmer, I glanced at Maiy with a smile. She looked up at me, and my smile froze. Scars marred the right side of her beautiful brown face, and she was missing her right eye. In its place was an empty socket. A caved-in eyelid dripped over the void. Her other dark brown eye met mine with confidence and intelligence. As she made eye contact, she bowed low, her back bent straight and proud.

Clara and Emma snuck into the room and hid behind my skirt, while Stephen peeked over his book from the corner of the room.

There was a moment of silence, then Maiy squatted down, fished in a bag that Ohm had handed her, and gently offered Clara a mangosteen. Clara looked at her for a moment, her head tilted to one side, and then with a smile, she grabbed the mangosteen Maiy had popped open and sucked out the sweet, juicy innards, without taking her eyes off Maiy. Emma emerged, and Maiy handed her another mangosteen with an open smile and her one kind eye inviting the girls into friendship.

By the time John got back from language class, Maiy had created her home in the spare bedroom with Ohm—Ohm with her many bags of clothes, fabric, and books, and Maiy with her one small backpack from her village home.

Ohm made up her bed with flowery sheets and a Mickey Mouse pillowcase, which seemed out of place for a middle-aged woman who had survived the Khmer Rouge. Maiy would sleep on a reed mat on the floor next to Ohm with a thin Hello Kitty blanket and a small pillow. Every morning, Maiy would roll up her mat and tuck it away under Ohm's bed. The room was now theirs.

The two women spent the rest of the afternoon in the kitchen.

Ohm taught Maiy to cook the evening meal, and Maiy wrote Ohm's instructions in a new lined notebook. Savory eggplant cooked with crumbled pork and Khmer spices; Banh Keo, a crepe made with rice flour stuffed with crumbled pork, bean sprouts, and green onions; Lok Lak beef with lettuce, onions, and tomatoes; deep fried whole fish laced with lemon grass; Key Teau soup with noodles, spices, hard-boiled egg and cilantro—these recipes filled Maiy's notebooks as the weeks passed.

Ohm knew that Maiy's success as a house-helper for expatriates depended on her knowledge of cooking, cleaning, laundry, and child-care with an eye towards detail and impeccable sanitation. Some of the Khmer ways would have to be adapted for her to be marketable to foreigners who paid better and treated their house help with more respect than rich Cambodians who were also looking to hire.

We later learned that Maiy's scars stemmed from a childhood accident. She and her schoolmates had been playing in an empty field. Several boys discovered an unexploded ordnance, a lethal remnant of the civil war. In their innocence, they began striking it, hoping to break it down for scrap metal to sell at the markets. In moments, an explosion shattered the morning—killing one boy instantly and forever changing the lives of the others. The blast took Maiy's eye and mutilated her face, yet she survived.

Despite her hardship, Maiy's natural brilliance shone—she grasped reading and writing Khmer with extraordinary speed and showed a particular gift for numbers. But by seventeen, the strain of reading and calculating with one eye had produced such crippling headaches that she had to abandon her formal schooling in the prov-ince. Unable to continue her studies, she left school to help her mother tend their modest sugarcane stand, which stood in front of their village home in Takéo.

Maiy was smart as a whip, a hard worker, and honest. Sassy, fun, and eager to please, she became a joy to our entire household. She balanced Ohm's more sober and commandeering presence. Since Maiy was a quick learner, we soon found her a job with another American family. She rode on moto taxis daily to their house five blocks away.

Our home was soon bustling with the Khmer language spoken from all corners. Ly brought his twin brother Hok and his sister Sothea to live with us. Sothea created a proper home out of the long, open attached garage we gave them free to live in. The nine of us spread out through the rest of the house. Now we were fourteen in the house on Street 576.

KHMER CHURCH

J ohn found me in the Great Room typing away at my computer. I was in the middle of writing a newsletter for our supporters. John sat down. "I think it's time for us to go to Khmer church instead of an English church. We need to immerse ourselves in the language and culture more."

I looked up and shifted in my seat. We had already left the Baptist church and had settled into another American church closer to home. I felt comfortable in this one that hosted the kids from Ponlou Home and other missionaries of the same Reformed theological bent as Matt and Jean and the new American pastor. John Calvin and his TULIP theology was interesting and intellectually stimulating. I hated to leave that community, but also, I knew John was right. We needed to branch out. It's what was best for our language and cultural understanding.

One Sunday morning in March, we pulled up next to a nondescript cement building. We sidled into a large room with colorful banners filled with Khmer Bible verses.

Some young boys were fiddling with the microphones. "Hello, hello." They tapped on the mic with their fingers. We found some seats in the back, and the pastor and his wife greeted us.

The church started on time with an animated trio of worship

leaders singing translated versions of 1980s American worship songs. Their off-tune lilt, reminiscent of Khmer traditional music, was hard on my Western ears. But their rousing energy lifted the mood of our kids, who clapped when they recognized the familiar tunes.

Singing ended when the pastor came forward, and for the next forty minutes, he read from the Bible and preached. John followed along in his Khmer Bible, mouthing the words as he read and following the sermon with amazing accuracy.

At the end of the sermon, the pastor looked at the congregation and mentioned something about the beach. John looked at me and smiled, nodding his head. "Yes?"

I shrugged my shoulders, not knowing what I was agreeing to. The pastor saw my confusion and said in English, "Baptism at the beach next Sunday. We will bring lunch. Leaving the church here"— he pointed down—"at 7:30 a.m. Please come." I looked at John, his eyes sparkling. A beach day with the church could be a lovely family outing, especially since our last time there had been so delightful.

"Sure," I mouthed to John as the service wrapped up.

The following Sunday, we left for the church at seven o'clock. The kids were excited as they held their backpacks with beach toys and fresh clothes. They insisted on wearing their bathing suits and had their towels draped around their shoulders. The back of the van held a Styrofoam cooler where I packed peanut butter and jelly sandwiches, sliced mangoes, a giant bag of chips I'd found at the Western market, and dozens of small bottles of water all buried under two pounds of ice.

John tried to discourage me from making lunch for everyone. "They're going to feed us," he kept reminding me.

"The kids might not like the food, and I don't know who prepared it. I feel better about having options." So earlier that morning, I had the boys carry the cooler packed with ice to the back of the van.

Once we arrived at the church promptly at 7:30, the pastor came over to greet us, smiling and poking his head in my window to look around. Glancing at the nine of us spaced out in the nine-passenger van, he exclaimed, "Oh good. You have plenty of room." He opened the sliding door of the van and motioned to a group of youth huddled near the church entrance. He ushered them into our van for the four-hour trip to the beach.

John looked at me with a bemused smirk. Annoyed, I turned to shoo two girls out the door who were going to sit on the laps of their friends. I shook my head. No more room!

My kids moved to the back seat and pressed close together. Stephen crawled in the back with the cooler and the extra beach towels. It grew even hotter with four more people crammed inside. We left to get the air flowing through the windows.

We arrived four hours later. The beach was overcast and windy. The salty air assaulted my eyes when I got out of the van and stretched my legs. We parked near a group of open-air thatched huts where people from church gathered, each claiming a wooden plat-form to unroll their *kantails* (reed mats) and laid out their rice buckets and plastic baskets full of food and soda.

The Khmer church gathered with their boisterous chatter while I kept my eyes on my children at the seashore. The pastor grabbed a bullhorn, and over the noisy din of the excited crowd, he gathered them for prayer. With hands raised, the Khmer youth prayed and sang and readied their hearts for baptism. I watched Joe mingle among them.

At only fourteen years old, taller than most, he bantered with the boys and teased the girls, blending in effortlessly. Tim, now twelve years old, had the best command of the Khmer language of all my children. Cambodians often asked me if he was *"Kon Khmer"* (half Khmer). I would chuckle and shake my head no, admiring my artistic and linguistic second child. After prayers and singing, the youth lined up along the shore. I followed with Olivia toddling at my side, and Clara chasing the gentle waves of the Gulf of Thailand.

One tall Khmer youth gently strummed his guitar facing the parishioners ready to be baptized in the warm, tropical water. The gentle plucking of nylon strings carried across the shoreline, blending with the rhythmic lapping of seawater. People joined in singing, their voices rising and falling in melodic Khmer hymns. The songs carried notes of hope and renewal, a stark contrast to the coun-try's troubled past.

The pastor stood waist-deep in the dark blue water, his white shirt clinging to his shoulders as he beckoned the first candidate forward. Twenty-two new Christians waded in one by one, the women clutching their traditional krama scarves that fluttered in the breeze, the men with hands clasped reverently before them. Each face reflected a mixture of nervousness and profound joy.

People joined in singing until the pastor baptized all the new Christians. The overcast, breezy day dried their thin clothing quickly, though some cocooned themselves in *samputs*, wrap-around skirts in vibrant patterns of burgundy, azure, and emerald. The fabric rustled softly in the humid air.

My heart soared to see so many new Christians join the nascent Khmer church. Cambodia had a growing and vibrant church before 1970. The Catholic Church first came to Cambodia and brought Christianity in the 1500s. Protestants arrived on the scene in the 1920s. The Khmer Rouge's horrific autogenocide in the 1970s killed about 80% of all Christians, including nearly every Catholic priest and Protestant pastor. Today, the church is just beginning to grow in a land so corrupt and disorganized that they have few restrictions on evangelization and church-planting.

While my heart lifted at the sight of young people stepping forward for baptism, my mind wrestled with the church's approach to their spiritual formation. The path to membership asked little beyond an expressed desire to be Christian. This minimal foundation proved fragile; I had learned that within three years, many new converts would drift back to their Buddhist roots. Glancing at the newly baptized, I was curious how many of them would finish the race. What were we doing here if most of the converts would not stay Christians? Why did Christianity struggle to take root here?

My eyes traced the coastline to the south where a mountain range emerged from the jungle. Unbeknownst to me in that moment, beneath its dark green canopy, at the very peak, stood a forsaken, abandoned church, once home to the area's small Catholic congregation. Now it kept a lonely vigil, accompanied only by ocean breezes. War-torn walls bore bullet holes, while graffiti spilled from its doorways. Inside, an altar remained, with the ghostly outline of a crucifix still visible behind it. Like this abandoned sanctuary, Catholicism had become a quiet presence among the people, its traditions flowing into the cultural waters of Cambodia—integrated, subtle, uniquely Khmer, but also damaged by war and neglect.

I picked up Olivia and walked back up towards the thatched huts. The women heated pots of rice and soup, prepared in Phnom Penh and stored in Styrofoam coolers, over small propane stoves on the wooden platforms. Everyone gathered and prayed before grabbing a bowl and a spoon from the plastic baskets brought from the church. They waited to have the lukewarm soup and rice slopped into their bowls, then squatted under the shade shelters, and spoon to mouth, they gobbled down their lunch.

My kids gathered around me, and I motioned for Joe to grab the cooler from the back of our car. With all the platforms taken, I spread out a picnic blanket on the sand and handed out wet wipes. I passed out sandwiches, mango slices, bottled water, and the bag of chips.

John wandered over, taking another bite of Khmer soup. "It's delicious. Do you want some?" He held the spoon out to me.

Normally, I loved Khmer soup. I looked at my dull sandwich. "Smells great, but I'll play it safe." I took another bite.

The pastor ambled over to thank us for coming. He and John talked for a bit. I heard him ask John if he'd like to help with the music for the Sunday services. John nodded and looked at me, raising his eyebrows. I shrugged, fiddling with my water bottle. I glanced back at the crowded shelters swarming with excited youth, chatting and laughing. The kids blended; John had found a place within the Khmer church. But who was I sitting here alone on the beach with my peanut butter sandwich?

I didn't fit in with the Khmer women. Our lives were so different, with too many cultural barriers. I didn't fit in with other missionaries who were busy with their full-time mission work.

I missed my family, our friends with their large families, and mothers who stayed home to tend their gardens, chickens, and their many children whom they homeschooled.

The drive home was quiet. Everyone slept in the dense, humid car. The salt from earlier still clung to my skin, tiny crystals catching the afternoon light. Grains of sand had worked their way into the creases of my clothes, my bag, even the pages of my book. Fields of rice stretched beyond my window, but my attention kept snapping back to the buses hurtling past, their turbulent wake threatening to push us off the narrow road.

John was unfazed by the narrow misses, his hands steady on the wheel as if we weren't constantly a breath away from disaster.

"I found cheap flights to Bangkok," John said, his voice breaking through the hum of tires on asphalt. "We should get away for our anniversary."

The idea of Bangkok alone with John conjured images of golden temples rising into hazy skies and romantic dinners where we could remember who we were before we became the people who worried about huge buses on narrow roads.

"I'd love that. But what about the kids?" I turned to look at the children's sunburned faces peaceful in sleep. I envied their ability to surrender to rest while my own nerves remained raw and alert.

"I figured Ohm, Maiy, and Ly will be around. Michele will stay with the kids overnight." Michele, John's sister, was a nurse, and she had moved in with us a month earlier to work at an international medical clinic. She kept her promise to me that night around the farm table. Michele came to help.

My heart started to warm. "We can see a movie. They have theaters there." There were no movie theaters in Cambodia.

Now distracted from the turbulent drive, my mind raced with plans for the trip coming up in a month. Fancy hotels, movies, shopping malls, decadent restaurants. They had a famous outdoor market where I could get the kids new clothes and shoes that weren't knock-offs from China.

The rest of the road trip flew by. We dropped the Khmer youth off at church and drove our sleepy crew home. Ohm had dinner waiting for us, and after we ate, the kids cleaned the kitchen. We went upstairs to shower and read before bed. Soon everyone sank into a deep sleep, and I dreamed of Bangkok and our perfect romantic getaway.

BANGKOK

One humid morning two weeks later, John and I were packing in our bedroom to leave for Bangkok. I grabbed a pair of nice black slacks and a short-sleeved cream-colored blouse. Holding it up, I turned to John. "When we go somewhere nice, I can wear this."

His face looked pale. He held a pair of socks and stared out the window. Teetering a little, he sank onto the bed.

I went over to him. "Are you okay?" I sat down.

"I feel a little off. Like I'm getting a fever."

"Darn. Do we need to cancel our trip?" I felt his forehead.

"No, it'll be fine. I should be able to kick this. Maybe I'll lay down for a few minutes." Pushing his suitcase to the other side, he curled up on the bed.

He was warm. "I'll go grab you some Tylenol and some cold water." Down in the kitchen, I rummaged through a box of drugs and came back with water, painkillers, and a pile of clean clothes that Ohm had finished folding.

John was fast asleep. I gently placed the water and painkiller next to the bed and finished packing. I closed the door and let him sleep for a few hours. Early afternoon, John woke up. He said he felt better, though I was not so sure looking into his bloodshot eyes, but he finished packing. We left for the airport that evening.

The Phnom Penh airport, only twenty minutes from our house, had only four gates. We arrived with plenty of time to spare for our evening fight. The flight was brief, and the Thai hostesses brought us a meal of Pad Thai. I devoured mine in three bites. John did not touch his. Dozing on and off the entire flight, he spoke little.

From the airport to the hotel, he was quiet. But Bangkok was bustling with noise, life, and smells. Our driver only knew a few English words. When we asked if he knew the Khmer language, he sniffed in disgust. "Oh no. Why would I?" The sudden change in his demeanor was startling. His previously carefree expression had transformed into unmistakable contempt, his shoulders stiffening as if the very mention of Cambodia had offended him personally.

I soon realized that mentioning Cambodia was the quickest way to shut down a conversation in Bangkok. Centuries of mistrust, prejudice, and even hatred between the Cambodians and the Thai, some of it as recently as January of that year, had bred suspicion and avoidance. I had heard only months before, about Khmer demonstrators who burned the Royal Thai Embassy in Phnom Penh and vandalized Thai businesses after a Thai actress allegedly said that Angkor Wat belonged to Thailand. She, in fact, never said this, which later became public knowledge, but it was too late. Long-latent hatred fueled destructive fire in Phnom Penh against Thai properties.

As I looked out the window, I thought about what I had read while still in America. In the 1980s and 1990s, Thailand became one of the strongest economies in Southeast Asia. Coupled with its larger population and its openness to Western ideas, it became the envy of the Cambodian nation. Cambodia, by contrast, struggled to dig out from under the devastation left by the Khmer Rouge and the subsequent communist government, which failed to secure its recognition by the United Nations.

Cambodia remained economically weak, which made them rely on Thai businesses to keep their economy afloat. This fueled Cambodian resentment towards Thailand coupled with a perception that Thais were arrogant and racist.

Both countries were angry about a century-long dispute involving the area surrounding the eleventh-century Preah Vihear Temple on the border between northern Cambodia and northeastern Thailand. The dispute had led to periodic military clashes and diplomatic tensions since the 1950s. While the International Court of Justice awarded the temple to Cambodia in 1962, disagreements over the surrounding land and access routes have continued to cause friction between the two countries. I now understood the extreme reaction of our cab driver.

Bangkok slipped past while we drove down the wide roadway from the airport. Glittery and shiny, tall and new, Bangkok was all splendors. We arrived at our hotel and shuffled into the large reception hall with windows full of glass climbing two stories. A massive chandelier hung over the center of the room, and below it were luxurious couches and tables with massive vases of exotic flowers dripping over the bowls.

After being shown to our room, John collapsed on the bed. I opened every drawer and peered in every cupboard. I kicked off my shoes and laughed as my toes curled around the soft gray piles of carpet. I had forgotten what carpet felt like.

"The towels are so white and fluffy," I yelled from the bathroom as I buried my face in a massive bath towel hanging on a golden rod. Wandering to the window of our fifteenth-floor room, I gawked at the city full of skyscrapers and twinkling with lights. Phnom Penh had no skyscrapers or any buildings above eight floors. In Phnom Penh, the streets went dark at night, with everyone inside their locked gates afraid of roaming bands of muggers or packs of stray dogs scavenging for trash both territorial and dangerous.

I turned from the window. "Let's find a Thai place for dinner. Maybe the one that the receptionist mentioned."

John did not move. I went over and felt his forehead. He was burning with fever and sound asleep. Sitting beside him, I adjusted his pillow, took off his shoes, and called room service to order two plates of Pad Thai, a couple of waters, and some Tylenol. Turning on the TV, I curled up and resigned my first night of our anniversary weekend to watching Thai TV and eating room service next to my sick husband.

The next morning, his bloodshot eyes and sweat-soaked pillow showed he was no better. I ordered breakfast via room service and more Tylenol as John stared at the soccer game flickering across the TV screen and barely touched his food.

When I mentioned leaving and going back to Phnom Penh, he shook his head no. "I'll be okay later. Why don't you go exploring?"

I looked outside, my eyes darting up and down the busy Bangkok streets. Part of me was sad to leave him, but I was so looking forward to an adventure.

"Sure, I guess so." Turning to him, I asked, "Are you gonna be okay?"

"Yeah, order me some Sprite and a couple eggs before you go." Looking at his untouched plate of cold scrambled eggs and nibbled toast, I gathered our dishes and placed them outside the door.

Twenty minutes later, I hailed a taxi on Sukhumvit Road. "Take me to the Chatuchak Market." I pointed at my tourist map while holding my purse snug against my chest. The driver nodded and peeled out of the hotel circle and onto the busy street.

The picture of John lying in bed watching soccer with cold eggs beside him caused me to wince. He'd never want to shop for a full day anyway, I reassured myself. We could spend the evening watching a movie. Maybe he'll feel up to eating out. I doubted it by the look of him when I left. At least he had air-conditioning.

Hours later and loaded down with packages, I quietly opened the hotel door and shuffled in. I dropped the goods in the open closet and peeked around the corner. John was sleeping with the shades pulled down.

The room was dark and smelled of warm Sprite and unwashed, sweaty bed linens. I felt his back as I sat gently on the bed. He was burning hot and sweaty. The covers were kicked off and wrapped around his legs. His breathing sounded rattled and shallow. Best to let him sleep it off, whatever it was.

I showered, changed, and went downstairs to eat alone in the dining room on our fourteenth wedding anniversary. It was normal at this point to have all my good intentions in Asia sabotaged by some unsuspecting event. Rats, heat, robbery, aloneness—so much aloneness. I was alone again. I picked at my cold Tom Kha soup, with lemongrass and chunks of chicken swimming in a pale-yellow, opaque broth. Delicious when hot, but I lost my appetite as my disappointment in my Asian life grew. I sipped the rest of my Thai tea and left a few baht at the table.

I didn't want to go back to the dank sickroom, so I wandered the Thai streets outside our hotel room on Sukhumvit Road, a busy thoroughfare in an exclusive area of Bangkok. It boasted fancy restaurants, swanky hotels, glittering banks, and raucous nightclubs. Well-dressed, affluent Thais and expats floated in and out of the loud, bright enclaves, laughing and pushing past me.

Cars honked and brushed past while smells of roasted pork, fish sauce, and fried noodles danced in the air. So much energy. A bursting city much more modern and affluent than Phnom Penh. It made me sad for Cambodia, the poor stepchild to its richer, more popular sister, Thailand.

I was, at that moment, happy we had chosen the more troubled nation in Southeast Asia. I didn't fit in Bangkok. I didn't fit in Cambodia either, but at least I didn't have to be pretentious in Cambodia, which I was terrible at doing.

Gazing up at our darkened hotel room, I marveled at how Cambodia had transformed John. It had awakened something in him those years on the Greeley police force had buried. He had found a new purpose in Southeast Asia, immersing himself in the language and culture with natural ease. The hardened edges of his former life had softened; he had become more gentle, more present with us than he ever was in America. If this journey offered me anything, it had given me a kinder husband—and for now, that was enough.

TWO PINK LINES

T wo days later, back in Cambodia, I was unpacking my black pants and the cream-colored top that I never wore. I checked my watch to confirm we had time to get through the traffic for John's doctor's appointment across town. He was still lying in bed where he had collapsed after our flight home.

We had returned home to Phnom Penh the night before to find three of our children sick with the stomach flu, Stephen suffering from a double ear infection, and the rest sleeping in our room under the air-conditioning. Our bedroom had become an infirmary. I had moved throughout the night dumping bowls of vomit, wiping down brows, and putting warm garlic oil and cotton balls into Stephen's oozing ears.

Now, my eyes burned with exhaustion. As I unpacked, I felt a tickle in my throat and a wave of nausea and panicked. I can't afford to be laid up with the stomach flu, I thought as I weaved through the sick kids in our room. Who would do all this? I waved my hand about me as if to wish all the sickness away.

Emma moved her leg so I could step over her to get to my bamboo armoire with the cracked mirror. She looked up at me with her peaked face. "I can help, Momma."

I leaned down to kiss the top of her head and picked up the warm washcloth off her forehead. "You rest. I've got this." I smiled.

~

"Typhoid," the Khmer doctor, with her round, steel-rimmed glasses perched on the end of her nose, blurted out after reading John's test results. Dr. Ly Srey Vena, our favorite physician in Phnom Penh, and the only one we trusted, managed the small clinic.

She looked up. "You must have picked it up eating out somewhere. Incubation period averages between seven and fourteen days. Any thoughts?" Her dark brown eyes peered over at us.

I looked at John, and we both said, "The beach baptism."

"I'll give you a prescription, but you're going to feel terrible for a while. Watch for relapse. It happens often. If you have a setback, you'll have to come in here and get an IV."

I glanced at John. "Michele?" I raised my eyebrows.

"Could a nurse who lives in our home administer the IVs?" I looked back at Doctor Ly.

"Sure. That's possible."

On the ride home, my belly twinged. Perhaps I should have gotten tested. Maybe I should have brought the kids as well. No, they had a stomach flu, not the same symptoms as typhoid. *We might have worms.* I was always worried about parasites after hearing other missionaries' horror stories. Jean's daughter threw up spaghetti one night after dinner, only to realize it was a wiggling, squirmy, slimy pile of roundworms. Anytime someone complained of stomach issues, I went right to deworming medicine as my first line of defense.

At home, I got John settled with icy rags and turned on the air-conditioning. His face was ashen and slick with a cold sweat. His shallow breath whistled through his parched lips, interrupted by bone-rattling coughs. I laid a hand on his shoulder and noticed his limbs trembling beneath the thin sheet, alternating between feverish heat and chilling shivers that made the bed frame creak softly.

I needed to get out. So later while John slept, I drove down to the pharmacy at the end of the local market and, with no prescription, bought eight boxes of worm medicine, John's antibiotics, and a pregnancy test, a precaution I took before taking the Albendazole, the worm medication, which was contraindicated with pregnancy.

Back at the house, I gave John his antibiotics and more painkillers and handed out the boxes of worm medication to the kids who grumbled and wrinkled their noses. Then I walked into my bathroom with my pregnancy strip. Behind me, I shut the solid wooden door. The musty smell of our bathroom was comforting. My place. Alone.

The evening tokay geckos were crying. I placed the pregnancy strip on the counter and brushed my teeth. When I looked again, I saw the first bright pink line. I washed my face and looked again. A faint second line. My eyes went blurry, and my stare drifted up to the eight-foot ceiling, noticing a dark, forgotten cobweb stirring in the corner. My pulse hummed with anticipation and a slight tremble rumbled beneath my breastbone. Number eight.

Tiptoeing back to the bedroom, I paused, heart hammering. The news felt both momentous and commonplace. My fingers traced the bed frame. The scent of Tiger Balm ointment hung in the air, mingling with the faint traces of our home.

I leaned close to the bed, studying John's face in the soft light filtering through the gauzy curtains. Even in illness, I could see reflections of the children in him—Emma's contoured jawline, Tim's chocolate-brown eyes, Stephen's ruddy skin.

"A baby's coming," I whispered.

John stirred, blinking as my announcement penetrated the fog of his fever. For a moment, confusion clouded his features before understanding dawned. He offered a weak grin. That smile—half joy, half wonder—broke something loose inside me.

I sat on the edge of the bed, feeling the mattress dip beneath my weight. Seven pairs of flip-flops already lined our entryway each morning. Seven bedtime routines, seven fastidious food preferences, seven unique rhythms of breathing I could identify in the darkness. And now, an eighth. The practical voice in my head—the one that managed spelling tests, skin rashes, seats in the van—was already rearranging mental furniture.

Yet beneath the logistical calculations lay a stubborn, quiet joy. Despite the fever that wouldn't break, the distance from grandparents and cousins, and the loneliness that came with raising our brood in a place where we still stumbled over words, we would find a way through this. The new life growing inside me, small but present, was a testament to our shared belief that there is room for one more.

I placed my palm against my still-flat stomach and watched John's breathing even out as he drifted back to sleep. Outside, tokay geckos called to each other in the gathering twilight, their songs both strange and beautiful. Like our life here. Like the promise of number eight.

MOTHERHOOD

That month, in May 2004, the temperature spiked, the dank air brooded with humidity, and the mood at the house on Street 576 was queasy. Black garbage bags bloated in the heat and split open, spilling their putrid contents onto the dusty street. Our bedroom, a blur of invalid drama, cocooned John as he lay sick with soaring fevers, cold sweats, and severe abdominal distention. The rest of us fluttered about, trying to keep him comfortable. I floated between nausea, heat-exhaustion, and sleep deprivation. Every night, I tumbled into the sweaty, sickly sheets, only to wake up as tired as before.

Each morning, it started over. I changed sweaty sheets, stumbled over to the toilet with morning sickness, fanned John for hours with palm fans during the electricity outages, homeschooled the children, studied Khmer, and nested in my hot, dusty, germ-filled house. Then every night I fell into bed again next to John, hoping the electricity would stay on for the next few hours.

But joy was underneath. Olivia's contented babble would wake me each morning, and her pert smile gave me hope for that day.

Olivia turned two. And now, with my new pregnancy, our little family of nine was going to be a family of ten. Double digits, a nice round number divisible by ten. Ever since I sat in my damp, musty bathroom with the two pink lines, I spent the days considering all my possibilities for a safe birth. I dwelled on my peaceful home births in Colorado with midwives, state-of-the-art medical care around the corner, and loads of family and friends to care for me. None of that was available to me now.

I watched Olivia sleeping in her dirty tattered portable crib we brought from America. I rested a hand gently on my belly, saying hello to the new life within me. The logistics of this pregnancy rumbled across the landscape, swallowing up the pleasant memories of pregnancies, births, and babies. Derelict Cambodian hospitals, a long trip to Bangkok, or an unsafe home birth, these were my only options.

Eventually, John came out of his delirium and fever. Even before fully healed, he rode his motorcycle down to language school to continue studying Khmer while I slept through most of the morning, and the children crept away to play when they should have been practicing spelling words and writing book reports.

A few weeks later, John ate heartily, putting back on some of the fifteen pounds he'd lost, and I edged out of the worst of morning sickness. It looked like we were going to make it. He was well. I could start homeschooling again, and Michele would take care of all of us.

The next week, John crashed and landed in bed with a horrendous fever and intense bed sweats. He was relapsing, and IV fluids with antibiotics twice a day were his only hope. In our bedroom, each morning and night, Michele poked his arm and strung up his IV on a makeshift bamboo pole. While he sweated and slept, I suddenly stopped feeling nauseous. Both happened overnight. Neither was a good sign.

One night, two short weeks later, on August 26, 2004, I clutched my cramping stomach late in the night. Blood gushed from my weeping uterus, and somewhere in the red mire was my baby. I cried, I panicked, I flushed. I weaved my way to bed and collapsed in a sweaty, disheveled heap.

Morning came with cruel brightness. I moved through the house a ghost, changing diapers, preparing breakfast, speaking words that felt disconnected from my mouth. My other children watched me with careful eyes, sensing something had shifted but unable to name it. How could I tell them? What words did I have to explain that their sibling had been flushed away?

Our neighbors continued their daily rhythms—the old woman across the street sweeping her patch of sidewalk, the fruit vendor calling out prices, children in pressed uniforms walking to school. I watched them from our balcony, these people for whom August 26th was just another day, not the day that cleaved my life into before and after. Cambodia continued turning while I stood still.

At night, insomnia became my companion. I would place my hand on my now-empty abdomen, trying to remember the slight firmness that had been there days before. Seven weeks wasn't long enough to show, wasn't long enough for others to acknowledge the pregnancy as real, but it had been real to me. Real enough to name, though I never spoke that name aloud. Real enough to dream about. Real enough to mourn.

"Maybe we shouldn't have come here," I said one night, staring at the ceiling as shadows traced their paths across it. My husband's labored breathing paused beside me.

"Do you think it would have been different at home?" He rolled over to face me.

I didn't answer. An internet search came up with results that explained miscarriage in clinical terms—chromosomal abnormalities, incompatible with life, nature's way. Nothing to do with Cambodia's heat or water or air. Nothing to do with stress or travel or adaptation. Just biology's cruel lottery. But rationality couldn't compete with my narrative. Cambodia was the villain; I was the accomplice.

Weeks passed. The hot season began its slow retreat. My body healed while my heart remained splintered. There was no grave to tend. My baby had become water, had joined Cambodia's rivers, its rice paddies, its ocean.

Seven remained seven. The baby I flushed away remained gone. Cambodia remained Cambodia—complex, challenging, indifferent to my pain, yet somehow cradling it within its chaos.

And I remained here, breathing, counting, living—despicable perhaps, but surviving, contemplating something I had taken for granted: fertility. For fourteen years, I never had to wait to get pregnant, had no anxiety that I might never get pregnant, had no lonely months ticking past as I desperately tried to conceive. And I had never lost a baby before. I had expected my fertility to be uncomplicated.

From the earliest days and months of our dating relationship, John and I realized we had something in common. We both valued the gift of children and were open to a large family. People looked at us incredulously, mumbled something about our ignorance about where babies came from, and moved away, leaving us both chuckling and lonely at the same time. Sometimes, after perusing our office walls littered with degrees and career awards, those same people would conclude that a lack of education was not the problem. Must be something more.

We knew it was love and faith. Faith informed our laissez-faire attitude toward fertility, reminding us that God was the one who opened and closed the womb. We had no reason to doubt it. Pregnancy and birth came easily, and we happily lived within our means to make a police officer's paycheck spread as far as possible. Each new baby added joy to the existing family.

A week after my miscarriage, I sat on our veranda reading. The dark clouds teased us with hope of rain and then relinquished a spit of moisture here and there. We waited for the rainy season to enter when the clouds would deluge the earth with its fury. Relief from my grief came in spits and spurts, but my bleeding body was a constant reminder of what I lost.

Sitting there, I got a call from Panha. "*Neak Srey?*"

"Yes, Panha. Hello . . ." I tried to sound cheerful.

"*Neak Srey*, there is a pregnant mother in the village of Neak Vieng who already has two children, and she is very poor." He paused, and I sat up. "She doesn't want her baby. Can you and Lok John take the baby?" A baby!

"Umm, let me talk to John and get back to you." I quickly hung up the phone and found John teaching English to Ly, Hok, and Maiy. John was teaching idioms today, and the Cambodians were straining to understand "being boiled like a frog." I laughed for the first time in days.

John, looking frustrated at their lack of understanding, glanced at me, saw me laughing, and relaxed. I put my hand to my ear and tried to mouth that Panha called me, then I pretended to rock a baby in my arms. He realized what I was trying to say, pursed his lips together, and shook his head, his eyes boring into me. My heart deflated, but I left, determined not to let this conversation die.

Later, John found me reading on the veranda while Olivia napped in our room. "Now what did Panha say?"

I relayed the conversation, exaggerating details about the despair this young mother must be going through.

John let me finish and sat down. "I know you are struggling. I get it. But this baby cannot replace the one we lost." I shifted in my seat. He continued, "We had decided a few months ago that the best place for these babies was with their families in their villages, with their relatives. It does these babies no good to live with a Western family and lose their Khmer culture. Plus, there is no avenue for adoption in Cambodia right now for Americans. And it will be many months before we are ready to open our orphanage."

I knew he was right. I knew that bringing a Cambodian baby into our house, a baby we could never adopt, a baby who had a mother would be complicated if not wrong. I looked down at my hands, rough and worn from mothering, yearning to rock another baby again.

Olivia stirred from her nap. When I grabbed her, I heard John on the phone with Panha, discussing the family in Neak Veing. John asked how we could help this mother keep her baby and care for her other children in a culturally appropriate way. In a way that would not take away from the family's and village's need to care for each other.

Panha mentioned we could help by buying the other children's school uniforms and paying for their school fees. We could help the mother by providing her with some extra rice and vitamins for herself and her children. John agreed and told Panha to make the arrangements. He was to swing by our house in the next few days to pick up some money to get started.

Olivia smiled and babbled, pointing to the swirling fan above our heads, telling me a story. My mind was far away as I changed her cloth diaper and rinsed it in the toilet with the bidet sprayer. I placed it in the plastic bucket filled with water and some bleach next to the toilet to be washed the next day.

Laundry was an all-day, every-weekday affair in Cambodia. With no hot water, our clothes came out of the washing machine dingy. We hung them from the four lines stretched across the cement wall of our compound. In the hot season, they could dry in fifteen minutes. In the rainy season, we strung them around the house on every railing, bedstead, and flimsy clothes rack, creating perfect forts for the little girls.

Today was Monday, and the diaper pail would be full. Ohm would gather and wash and hang the diapers after washing the fruits and vegetables from the market. They would soon wave in the dusty, musty breeze on the side of the house.

In Colorado, nothing had been more satisfying to me than seeing dozens of dazzling, freshly cleaned, satisfyingly soft diapers pinned to the clothesline and dancing in the summer breeze. Cloth diapers symbolized my down-home mothering style. I had received dozens of new, out-of-the-package diapers at Joe's baby shower a decade and a half earlier. Plastic covers and large diaper pins with yellow ducklings at the head completed my diapering set. Hanging these diapers on our wooden clothesline with balsa clothespins was meditative. Time to escape the house. I could remember breathing in earthy, wet leaves, laundry soap, and the tangy odor of the barnyard.

Even in the depths of winter, I trudged out in my snow boots and barn coat to hang diapers. They dried slow and crisp, partly frozen when brought inside hours later. I folded them one by one, breathing in the Rocky Mountain air still lingering in the cotton, and then placed them in a tidy pile next to the baby's crib.

The cloth diapers became Ohm's domain in Cambodia. She'd gather them each Monday. In the afternoons, when the house grew quiet, I'd find Ohm humming ancient Khmer lullabies as she hung them to dry. During these times, she often watched my children with an expression that mixed wonder with an old, familiar ache.

I thought about Ohm, the loss of her own son, and how she nurtured my children, especially in days that I could not. In the early weeks, I remembered how Ohm had navigated our household chaos with the instincts of someone who had learned to read children's needs without sharing their language. She moved through our mornings anticipating which child would need what before the tears even started.

Emma, our seven-year-old with the tangled hair and perpetual dirt smudges, became Ohm's first conquest. While I fumbled with breakfast preparations, overwhelmed by the humidity and my own inadequacies, Ohm would appear at Emma's side with a perfectly ripe mango, already peeled and cut into neat strips. She'd click her tongue disapprovingly at Emma's attempts to brush her own hair, then gently take the brush and work through each knot with patience.

Seth, once suspicious of this weathered woman who'd appeared in our kitchen, softened when Ohm began saving him the choicest pieces of meat from her cooking pot. She'd catch his eye across the dinner table and nod toward his plate, a conspirator's smile creasing her face. He didn't know yet that she had once saved burnt rice grains for her own son during the worst of times, that feeding children well was written into the very fiber of her being.

But it was with Olivia that Ohm's maternal instincts bloomed most fully. My ten-month-old would reach for Ohm with the certainty of a child who recognized something familiar. The rice Ohm prepared for her was purely Khmer—smashed and mixed with chicken broth and meat scrapings, rich with flavors my daughter devoured with more enthusiasm than she'd ever shown for my careful American preparations.

129

Ohm had the wisdom of someone who knew how quickly children could be taken away. In her careful attention to each child's needs, I glimpsed the mother she had been.

I was contemplating Ohm, cloth diapers, and Colorado air when I sat down to nurse Olivia in the bamboo rocker, clicking and clacking on the tile floor. My mind drifted back to babies: the one that I recently lost and the one in a faraway province. A baby that was born to another overwhelmed but poor mother. That family would not have cloth diapers, a washing machine to clean them, a fan to cool the baby in the heat of the day from their rashes, or a crib to place the baby in at night. These mothers had a murky river or a village well to clean their children and owned few clothes and bedding and, if they were lucky, a plastic pail and a small package of laundry soap purchased from a corner shop. These mothers had hammocks to rock their babies to sleep for their midday naps or kramas to wrap their babies close to their bodies so they could walk down to the rice paddies to catch late-afternoon breezes.

I couldn't picture myself raising my seven children in Cambodia's traditional manner, while my friends in America struggled to understand our daily reality here—two worlds of motherhood, separated by more than the ocean.

It was about mothers. Centuries of mothers, in climates hot and humid or cold and arid, doing the best that they could. Mothers loving their children, brooding over them, and keeping them close in heart and mind.

I tucked Olivia closer as she gazed at me with her large green eyes. A smile broke out on her little face, which caused her eyes to squint and her tiny nose to wrinkle. I laughed in return, and we stared at each other with utter love and joy.

I found that my other hand had crept and lay protectively over my womb, as if to comfort the grief that lay inside. We sat there together —mother, daughter, and grief—until the sun set.

NO SAFETY NETS

Time passed, even when I wanted it to stop. Days became weeks, weeks folded into months. The acute pain dulled. I learned to breathe around the wound in my womb and my heart.

One evening in June the following year, John suggested a trip back to the beach, his voice gentle but firm as he placed a glass of iced coffee beside me. "You need this. We all do."

I nodded, surprising both of us. "Okay," I said. "Let's go."

The planning gave me purpose—something I hadn't realized I'd been missing. I arranged accommodations at the beach; Mark, John's brother, and his two children, Andrew and Melissa, were arriving in a few days. To make room for them in our home, I moved kids to different beds and stripped all the linens, discovering forgotten toys and books under mattresses. I made hospital corners the way my mother taught me, with sheets smelling of plumeria. Now I had something to look forward to.

Weeks later, the beach breezes blew through the van windows. "That's not it," John mumbled as we tried to find parking near the overcrowded tourist beach in Kampong Som. "Lewis mentioned heading farther south where there are fewer people." We were interested in settling at a more deserted part of the beach, away from the hustle and bustle on the north side.

John turned the car around, and after passing thatched huts selling tropical fruits, Angkor Beer, and fried squid on a stick, we saw a deserted part of the beach looming ahead. This was perfect, a whole beach to ourselves. My chest tingled. *Why is no one here?* The blue of the water lured us in, and I didn't even consider the question until later, when I wished I had trusted my gut to ask.

The kids jumped out of the car. We laid down our towels and grabbed the inner tubes we'd rented from a local shop near our hotel. The older kids raced into the ocean and paddled out in the tranquil surf. I stretched out to enjoy some sun, Olivia played in the sand next to me, and Clara and Stephen built a sandcastle near the breaking waves.

A short time later, out of the corner of my eye, I saw them. Some dark storm clouds were rising on the southern horizon. I leaned up on one arm and shielded my eyes. They moved quickly, more quickly than I was comfortable with. I saw John and Mark talking up by the road.

I motioned to them. "John, I don't like the look of those clouds." The wind rose and stole my words.

A moment later I heard a shriek and looked out to the sea, spitting and foaming. The boys and Melissa were paddling hard as their inner tubes were being swept out to sea on a riptide. The yells were muted by the wind, but my mother's ears, accustomed to faint cries in the night, heard them as clear as day.

"John! Mark!" I screamed, jumping up and running to the water. "The kids . . ."

They looked up at the same moment, saw the danger their children were in, and ran into the growing surf. John grabbed Emma first and hoisted her ashore.

Another shriek and I saw Melissa lose her inner tube and go under a pounding wave. She popped up again, only to be lost in the surf. John and Mark were struggling in the waves. The other boys were fighting for their lives in their own flimsy inner tubes.

I turned towards the road. There was not another soul in either direction. *No wonder no one comes here; it's a death trap!* The storm moved menacingly closer, and I felt the spit of rain.

"Someone help, please . . ." I yelled into the wind, my voice cracking. The cry echoed back at me against the roar of the churning surf.

Seth, Joe, Andrew, Melissa, and Tim—and now John and Mark—were out somewhere in the roiling, deadly riptide. Their heads appeared and disappeared among the white-capped waves, sometimes visible for heart-stopping seconds before being swallowed again by the hungry sea. Every time a dark head vanished beneath the surface, I felt my heart constrict, wondering if they would resurface. The distance between each of them grew wider as the current pulled them apart, their frantic arms waving in diminishing strength.

Again, I searched up and down the beach for any sign of someone who could help, my eyes burning from the salt spray and my briny tears. The shoreline stretched desolate in both directions, the normally inviting sand now a vast wasteland.

No lifeguard stood at their post. The red flags that should have warned us of riptides were missing. No one even knew we were there, having made the impulsive decision to visit this secluded stretch of coast, telling ourselves how lucky we were to have found such a private paradise.

What a devastating mistake that was.

I threw up my hands in the air, a gesture of utter helplessness, and dropped to my knees in the coarse sand. The impact sent shockwaves of pain through my legs, but it was nothing compared to the agony tearing through my chest.

Rain spat on my face, the storm clouds overhead darkening further, as if nature itself was closing in to witness our tragedy. I turned my face to heaven, my eyes blurring with tears that mingled with the falling rain.

"Please," I cried out to God, the word barely intelligible through my sobs. "Save my family. Don't take them. Please don't take them from me."

I felt the sharp sand etch into my knees, grinding against my skin. Each grain cut deeper as I rocked back and forth, the physical pain a welcome distraction from the unbearable weight of watching my loved ones struggle.

Through tear-soaked lashes, I kept my gaze fixed on the water, counting heads when I could see them, losing count when the waves rose too high. The minutes stretched like hours.

I looked up in time to see Tim, his young arms somehow still fighting against the current, grab Melissa, who was going under for possibly the last time. Her limbs had stopped thrashing, her strength entirely spent. With a surge of desperate energy, Tim hoisted her onto his tube, his face contorted with the effort. Melissa looked lifeless, her head lolling to one side, her long hair plastered across her pale face like dark seaweed. I caught my breath as I watched, unable to tell if she was breathing.

It was at that moment that the surf calmed, as though some invisible hand had passed over the water. The waves that had been crashing with such violence moments before subsided, their roar diminishing to a gentle murmur.

Tim, with Melissa still draped across his tube, Joe, Andrew, John, and Mark made their way back to shore. Their movements were slow and exhausted but approaching safety. Seth, closest to the shore, bobbed in last, his boyish face strangely peaceful, somehow oblivious to the danger he had been in, protected by innocence from the full understanding of how close they had all come to being lost forever.

Emma, Clara, Stephen, and I stumbled to meet them. My legs were weak with relief, my face streaked with tears and rain. The sand shifted beneath my feet as I waded into the shallows, reaching out with trembling hands to pull them the final distance.

We all collapsed in a crying, gasping, terrified heap on the wet sand, a tangle of limbs and sodden clothing. I counted them all with frantic precision—one, two, three, four, five, six, seven, eight, nine little heads. Melissa coughed as color returned to her cheeks.

I looked to the sky with the clouds parting and the sun peeking through, golden rays breaking. In that moment, I felt something beyond relief—a profound gratitude that transcended words.

Emma, Clara, and Stephen snuggled in their large towel on the sand. Joe, Andrew, and Seth gathered up the inner tubes. Melissa and

Mark huddled together a way off. Tim stood apart; his eyes glazed over, staring out into the sea. I went to him, put my arms around him, and held him close.

He did not move. "I caught her just in time, Mom. She would not come up again. I knew it."

My voice was gravelly. "She would have drowned if you did not grab her at that last moment."

"I was so tired. I didn't think I could make it over to her." He continued to watch the soaring surf return to its placid calm.

I held him. He started shaking. We both stood gazing out into the sea, deceptive and dangerous, which was placid once again.

The next morning, I stared out the window on the long drive home. The van was quiet except for an occasional request from Clara for a snack or Olivia for her water bottle. Most of the kids slept, some read, and some stared out the window.

What was this place we had given our lives to? A place with no safety nets—no police protection, no lifeguards on the beaches, no signs to warn you about riptides and dangerous surf, no emergency numbers to call if you were in trouble, and no adequate medical clinics or hospitals. What if someone had drowned back there in that surf and needed immediate medical treatment? I was struck by the realization. We were on our own.

Back in Colorado, my mother, while she helped me pack, had gasped as she picked up a book I had bought called *Where There Is No Doctor* full of step-by-step instructions to fix broken bones and to suture wounds for the non-medical person.

"Why do you need this?" She looked at me with concern, her bottom lip quivering slightly.

"Not sure about the medical situation in Cambodia," I deflected as I shuffled a first aid kit under some clothes. "Can't take any chances."

But I lied. We knew what we were up against. We heard the stories, and they were horrendous. Cambodia was a dangerous place with limited medical care.

"But neither you nor John have any medical knowledge," my mother said as her well-manicured hand with her heirloom rings flipped through the pages of the book.

I shrugged and gently pulled the book from her shaking hands, placing it on top of a pile of third grade spelling and high school math books. It was so romantic and so daring to go, solely relying on ourselves. Self-sufficient lifestyle at its best. Looking back, I should have noticed what it was: foolish and terrifying.

As we sped along Route 4 back to Phnom Penh, I scanned for hospitals and medical clinics along the roadside. They were stark, single-story buildings, distinguished only by red crosses painted on their white walls. Motos and bicycles dotted the dirt lots out front, their shapes reflected in grimy windows. These forlorn structures looked more like sets from an apocalyptic film than places of healing.

Moto accidents, typhoid, stitches, broken bones, bloody rags in brightly lit ambulances. The medical book and our measly medic kit were useless. Medically, we could not take care of ourselves, but looking at the forlorn medical clinics on the side of the road, I knew I could not trust Cambodia to take care of us either.

I remembered reading that the Khmer Rouge had methodically destroyed Cambodia's medical system. They'd executed 90 percent of doctors, condemned them as "enemies of the revolution," while converting hospitals into centers of torture and imprisonment. Ineffective revolutionary practices replaced modern medicine. Some patients became unwilling subjects for medical experimentation. This reign of terror left more than physical scars—it created a generational void in medical expertise and instilled a bone-deep fear of medical facilities among Cambodians. The country remained decades away from rebuilding a trusted healthcare system. I wasn't willing to gamble with what remained.

I turned back to the rolling countryside and occasional peaceful village, fighting fear for the next four hours. It was a long time later that I looked at John with his hands grasping the steering wheel, his face stoic, eyes straight ahead.

ONLY HOME

Once behind the green gate, I didn't leave home. I had learned to drive in the chaotic traffic of the city months ago. I was proud of myself for getting out and was hopeful that this would give me more freedom. Driving to the local Western markets for a block of cheese from Malaysia or some boxed milk from Thailand, I was gaining back some agency.

But after the beach trip, I did not leave the house. John could do all the errands; I would stay home, the only place I felt safe.

I tried to make the children stay home as well. But we realized at the beginning of the previous school year that Joe's, Tim's, and Seth's education needed more structure, and they needed friends. The orphans at Ponlou Home were their companions, but they were in school all day. When we first arrived, I had let the older boys walk over to the local international school to check out books at their extensive library and to play on the nascent high school basketball team.

John and I decided to enroll the three oldest boys in school. The boys ended up loving it, coming home every night with electric excitement and interesting stories about learning in an international community of students. I conceded we could trust the school as a place of safety for our older children, but the younger ones would stay home with me, the only true safe place.

Soon it was rainy season. One late afternoon, I studied the Khmer alphabet at our bamboo desk. "*Ga, ka, go, koh, ngo . . . jah, chat, jo, cho, nyo . . .*" I wrote the words like a preschooler in my grid-lined notebook. Discouraged and bored, I looked up and off to the horizon over the rooftops of the houses and saw rain clouds roiling and rolling in our direction. It was a sweltering and blistering day, and the cooling rain was about to bring respite.

I slammed my book shut and shouted to the kids, "Rain's coming!"

We darted downstairs and out into the front courtyard, hearing the monsoon's primal roar blocks away as it moved in sheets down the dusty streets. In minutes, it reached our little courtyard.

Dramatic, drenching, cleansing. The tumultuous thunder and sheer sheets of rain poured down on me as I raised my hands to heaven and let myself get cleansed of grime, sweat, and fear. I loved that warm, tropical rain. For that one moment, when it rained, I was very happy we had come here.

I watched my children laugh and play in the rain—catching raindrops on their tongues, sliding along the tile courtyard in a game of slip and slide. Their joy was my joy. I smiled and laughed with them, spinning in circles, then catching them as they slid into me.

They were not suffering here. They were thriving. I felt a sense of guilt that I could not enter their daily, pure joy of being in Cambodia. At least for now, as I gazed outside the gate, we were safe. With Ohm, Ly, and John to take care of us—and the padlock on the green gate, locks on the doors, and razor wire on the wall—I could go on nurturing and building a home here. Rebuilding my nest was possible.

That night, we gathered around the dining room table to share our meal and talk about our day. Joe described the snacks he bought on his way home from school—fried sesame donuts, fried bananas, ice cream sandwiched inside a French baguette. I smiled and nodded while my stomach turned imagining the pathogens lurking in street food.

John shared what he learned in language school and about the political pressures that continued to mount in the city. "Today a newspaper reporter criticized Hun Sen and was found shot outside his house," he said, putting another bite of rice and fried fish in his mouth.

The Cambodians have little freedom to talk about their political opinions. No wonder Ohm and Panha spoke in whispers when discussing politics. I grabbed another slice of mango from the plate that Ohm placed before me and thought that political shootings were another reason to stay home.

"Mom, what did you do today?" Seth asked.

My head shot up. "I prayed, made breakfast, homeschooled, took a nap with Olivia, studied Khmer, and played in the rain a bit . . ."

"Sounds boring." He took another slice of mango and turned to tell John what he'd learned in Khmer class that day.

Not boring, safe. I stabbed another mango slice. Safety is not being a missionary. That was John's job, not mine. I kept everyone safe and cared for, so he could go outside the gate for the mission work. I stayed home.

After quizzing the boys on their Khmer lessons, John turned to me again. "Panha has a family he wants me to visit in Prey Takeo. I will leave with him after my language class tomorrow and return around dinnertime."

"Okay . . ." I muttered, my mind quickly flipping through all the things that could go wrong with this trip.

"There is a sick woman with tuberculosis. Her husband is a Christian, but the rest of the village wants to bring the witch doctor to their home for a healing ceremony. Panha wants us to pray instead."

"Okay. That's fine. Sounds necessary." John had to do these missionary things. That was why we were there, why the checks came to our bank account every month. We needed results. We needed to show our financial supporters that their sacrifices were worth it.

The boys were about done cleaning the kitchen, and Emma went upstairs to put away some clean, folded clothes. Outside the kitchen, I continued our evening routine, bathing Olivia and Clara in a large plastic tub outside the kitchen, water coming from a spigot on the cement wall.

Suddenly, without warning, the house went pitch black and silent. Another evening power outage.

"Mommy! I can't see anything!" Emma cried from somewhere in the bowels of the house. I couldn't leave the two littlest still soapy, wet, and naked. I called up to the open windows above, "Keep your hands in front of you and make your way to your bed. I will meet you there in a few minutes. Ask the boys for help if they are upstairs." I heard her carefully make her way across the room.

Downstairs, Joe and John found some candles, mosquito coils, and a dim flashlight in desperate need of something other than cheap Chinese batteries. Tim came outside to help me and gathered Olivia in a towel. Joe led the way with a candle, while Tim took her upstairs to the girls' bedroom. I wrapped Clara in her towel, and she followed close behind me, holding the back of my shirt in one hand and her towel in the other. I kept the lit candle steady and made our way upstairs.

We sat on the girls' bed and watched the candles move around the house while John and the boys wet towels to wrap around their necks to lower their body temperatures and to keep the mosquitoes away. I placed a sheet around all of us girls. This kept us from getting eaten, but without the fans blowing, we soaked the sheet in sweat.

Olivia and Clara whimpered with discomfort and their fear of the dark. Despite my frayed nerves, I sang to them. We sang hymns and silly songs. Our spirits lifted even in the heat and darkness. John found us and handed me a lit mosquito coil to place under the bed. Then, he went with the boys downstairs to finish washing the dishes by candlelight. Afterwards, they sat outside in the courtyard trying to catch some breeze.

I laid the girls down, placed the candle on the table, and sat in the chair. I waited until they were deeply asleep, fearing they might wake up afraid and call for me. Even if I tried, I couldn't sleep right then. I waited and watched them tossing and turning until they drifted away.

Once they were asleep, I found John and the four boys sitting in the courtyard with their candles extinguished. We lit more mosquito coils and sat on the swing in the darkness.

My shirt adhered to my back and a musky smell came off my

body. I needed another shower. Pulling my shirt from my back and fanning the hem to get some breeze, I didn't know how much longer I could bear it.

Two hours later, the lights blinked on, the fans blasted, and the music from the boys' CD player blared from the kitchen. We headed inside to get some sleep.

This ritual became routine, to the tune of two to three times a week during the hottest part of the year. It continued until the heavy rains came in September and filled the rivers so that the electrical dams could continue their work supplying electricity to the bustling city of Phnom Penh and its two million people. We were at the mercy of the rain for reprieve, respite, and replenishment.

THE SCHOOLYARD

S creams of laughter and scurrying feet filled the wet schoolyard as the students flooded out of classrooms at the end of the long day in the middle of September. The international school enrolled many multinational families in Phnom Penh for work or mission: Khmer, Vietnamese, Chinese, Sri Lankan, Korean, British, Kenyan, and American.

A year had passed since my miscarriage, and it had been months since our near miss in the Gulf of Thailand. Life had gotten back into a routine. As I sat in front of school, I watched parents on motos gather their children with their toppling helmets perched on small heads, backpacks full of books and papers sporting Hello Kitty or Ben 10, and three-tiered, circular tin lunch pails held precariously on parents' laps.

Some students left with their older siblings on sporty motos. Some left on wobbly bikes. Some walked. Today Seth needed to go to the dentist, so instead of walking home with his brothers, I planned to pick him up in the car and drive across town. It was rare for me to attend the end-of-day pickup, and I was usually grateful to be spared the mayhem.

I watched the missionary students closely. Their mothers worked in missions next to their husbands. Khmer nannies watched the younger kids while the missionary mothers studied the Khmer language, taught Khmer women's Bible classes, served as midwives for pregnant Khmer women in poor villages, or ran elaborate after-school programs for Vietnamese children living in isolation near the flooded parts of the Mekong River.

Then there was me. I stayed home, managed our household, homeschooled my young children, attended my sons' sporting events, and studied Khmer each afternoon. My routine had been plucked off the plains of Colorado and plunked into the center of Southeast Asia.

But I noticed large swatches of empty time. Ohm had taken over most of my homemaking duties: shopping, cleaning, cooking, laundry, and even sewing the children's clothes became her happy domain.

I often watched her sing while working and remembered my own American days filled with the joy of simple work done out of love for my family. In Cambodia, after the children settled to play, Ohm's dinner simmered on the stove, and laundry was cleaned, folded, and put away, I would sit on my veranda and stare out into the street. I had too much time.

The days crept by like that. I created new projects such as gardening, crocheting baby blankets, or baking bread. None of them materialized. The lack of resources, the brutal climate, or antiquated tools sabotaged my best intentions. The garden seeds, brought from America, sprouted, withered, and died. My Christmas baking floundered with flat, unappetizing cookies. My attempt at sewing had Ohm snickering and clucking her tongue.

My long afternoon walks on Colorado's country roads pushing a double stroller became short stints around the block dodging trash, human feces, biting dogs, and catcalls from the construction workers high on the buildings. I had too much time and no success in bringing my expressions of home to Cambodia.

I checked my watch for the fifth time, scanning the school entrance.

"Where is he?" I hoped Seth remembered I was coming for him today and did not stay to play basketball with his friends. I watched the gray sky darken overhead. He needed to come quickly before the next deluge of rain.

Staring at the gate, I noticed one frazzled missionary mother race to the front of the school, motioning wildly to her third grader. She scooped him up and placed him on the back of her moto. With him clinging to her waist, his backpack bouncing down the road, I wondered if I should be busier, frantic, rushing off to do important work.

Frowning, I saw Seth racing to the car with his left shoelace untied and dragging in the dirt. Before he reached the car, I decided I had nothing to offer as a missionary here in Cambodia. I wasn't a teacher, a nurse, a project manager, a Bible scholar, or a midwife.

He bounded into the car and slammed the door shut. "Can we get something to eat?" He smiled at me in his light-blue school uniform, which was already stained from the Khmer soup he'd had for lunch. He was hungry.

"Sure, do you want fried bananas or sesame donuts?"

"Fried bananas!" He put out his hand for two thousand riel.

I handed him the money from the center console of the van. He jumped out of the car and raced down the block to a small food cart. Standing in line, holding his money protectively, he waited for the middle-aged Khmer woman crouching over a hot sizzling wok to notice him. She smiled and place two small fried bananas in a plastic bag.

He handed her the riel in his hand and then fished around in his pocket. Finding more crumpled bills, he handed them to an older man sitting on an orange cooler next to her cart.

Seth blurted out one of his favorite Khmer words, "*Coke-ah.*"

The man smiled, his mouth full of black and crooked teeth, while he opened his cooler full of sodas, green tea bottles, and Angkor Beer.

Seth meandered back to the van, munching on his banana and holding the can of Coke under his arm. We drove in silence as he finished his snack and soda then catnapped with his head against the windowpane.

I glanced at him during the occasional traffic stop, admiring my ten-year-old boy. The third son, quiet and thoughtful, with boundless energy and athletic prowess. Seth was growing up. I noticed his head flopped over on his chest, his brown hair matted with dried sweat, and his olive skin needed a good wash after eating the greasy fried banana. All my kids were growing up. Maybe they didn't need me as much anymore.

With Ohm at home holding down the domestic front, maybe I should give more thought to this missionary thing after all. I figured there must be something I could do. If I was no longer a homemaker in the traditional sense of the word, then I could be a missionary, too.

That night around the dinner table, I told my family that I was going to be a missionary, too. The idea spurred a flurry of discussion. The little girls wondered if I would still be homeschooling them. Stephen asked if he could go to school with his older brothers now. The older boys looked at each other and shrugged. They did not care as long as I still made them breakfast.

Then John asked, "What would you do?"

My heart stopped, and I swallowed. "I don't know."

The table was quiet for a moment and then Joe spoke up. "We are studying AIDS this term. Maybe you could plan a field trip or something." I sat up straight. Maybe that was it.

My American neighbor, Amy, visited an AIDS hospital twice a week. Maybe we could take Joe's ninth grade class there for a field trip to really see the face of AIDS and not just read about it. Yes, that was a good start. It would get me out of the house, braving the Cambodian landscape again, to start my new life as a real missionary.

Joe's voice buzzed in the background. "AIDS . . . T-cells and transmission rates . . . social biases . . ." He paused, reaching over to spoon more rice. "Mr. King showed us these old pictures. From the eighties, I think . . ."

I glanced up at the humming LED light above the kitchen window. Like clockwork, Anthony and Cleopatra, two geckos named by the kids, came out from behind the lamp, lapping up gnats and mosquitoes. They knew instinctively who they were. Where their home was. What their purpose was in their little corner of the world. They were my unusual companions, showing me that finding purpose and rhythm was possible.

THE AIDS HOSPITAL

The plan to visit the AIDS hospital in Phnom Penh came to fruition after months of planning. Amy and her team at the hospital helped me put the field trip together for Joe's class. The day arrived. It was a sweltering afternoon when ten students, one teacher, four Khmer teacher aides, and one wannabe missionary piled into the school van.

The van arrived at the hospital and parked in front of three dilapidated cement buildings. Walking to the entrance, we passed a brood of scrawny chickens and a ragged collection of small children scratching and playing among a pile of discarded Styrofoam food containers, old used needles, and bloody wound wraps.

We tiptoed our way around the refuse and into the hospital's front doors. I felt the sickness hovering, slinking around the corridors like a miasma, filling the whole hospital. A hell. This hospital served the poor Khmer soldiers, not the ones who moved up the ranks of the Khmer Rouge and into the elite class. They took their sicknesses to Bangkok or Singapore. No, these men, covered in tattoos and scars, underpaid and malnourished, came from the poor villages in the north. They were a forgotten subculture in Cambodia.

With trepidation, our little group of five, breaking off from the larger group, meandered up a dark, dank staircase. Making our way down a dirty hallway smelling of urine and sweat, we headed toward a room at the far end of the hall. A new patient, a man in an advanced stage of AIDS, had just arrived from a northern province. The foul and stale room was dingy and empty except for a rusty iron bedstead and one metal chair. It was sparse and desolate.

He lay curled up in the bed's corner. This former soldier was now a skeleton with wrinkled flesh, drowning in a military uniform that once fit a muscular man. His reed mat was filthy. Flies buzzed around his gaunt face. I watched one land on his ear and crawl inside. He didn't flinch. I waved it away. It flew erratically, only to land on his skeletal hand.

The man, staring distantly, faced the crumbling plaster wall. Ming, our Khmer translator, moved closer and brushed his shoulder. He turned to look at us with empty eyes. This was someone's son, brother, friend, comrade. Now he was alone and dying.

I asked him in my halting and rudimentary Khmer language if I could pray with him. He nodded and turned back to stare blankly at the wall.

I sat on his bed and placed my hand on his bony leg, shifted my weight, and prayed in Khmer. I stumbled over words and butchered pronunciation. I kept restarting, stuttering, hesitating. But as I pushed through and plodded along, something came over me.

The words began tumbling out. They became effortless, fluid, clear. *Is this supernatural? A speaking in tongues?* It was new and exciting. My speech was confident, clear, concise. I prayed stories of Jesus that I had learned as a small child on my mother's knee. Stories I knew that brought me comfort and peace. I gave him, in the Holy Spirit, my gentle Jesus.

As I prayed, the sick soldier transitioned from resigned to agitated. My prayer was having the opposite effect on him. I felt peace, but he coughed, sputtered, gagged. He made strange, gurgling noises in his throat. His limbs went rigid.

Then, I felt it. A heavy darkness settled within the room, filling every corner. The hot room turned colder with an inexplicable chill, and my skin prickled with static electricity. Shadows deepened and ordinary sounds of the creaking bed frame and shuffling of feet became muffled and distorted. The oppressive shadows, the smell of decay coating the back of my throat, metallic and ancient, and an eerie sense of being watched overwhelmed me. My peace was gone.

I, desperate for relief, turned to the man and pleaded, "*Lok, tuk jut, tuk jut Prea Jesu.*" (Sir, trust, trust in Jesus.)

He turned and looked up at me with his bloodshot and pleading eyes and whispered, "*Tuk jut, K'nyom tuk jut.*" (Trust, I trust.)

With the same energy as it arrived, the oppression lifted.

The room was brighter and warmer with a sharp, ozonic freshness, like after a lightning storm. Shadows snapped back to where they should have been, and the temperature equalized. He stopped coughing and choking and fell into a deep, peaceful sleep.

We went home an hour later, exhausted. On the bus, I told Joe what had happened. "Mom," he said, "that was an exorcism." I shuddered and turned to look out the window as the sun set. It cast a red glow over Boeung Kak Lake, filled with lily pads and ringed with morning glory. I had something to offer that afternoon. And for today, that was enough.

Weeks later, I heard from Amy that the man died the day after we left. My feeble attempts at language and my noble attempts at prayer brought peace to a dying man. I didn't have to be a teacher, nurse, or project manager. I needed to follow where God would send me and give him what was in my hand. On that day, in my hand, was prayer, presence, and faith. The same things I offer my family daily. The same things that comforted me when I was suffering. It was time for me to share that with others. It was time for me to leave the green gate and become a missionary.

UNMOORED

Months after visiting the AIDS hospital, I held a tiny baby. I could see her heartbeat through her translucent skin, her veins visible like bloodied spider webs. She breathed laboriously while her eyes fluttered opened and closed.

Her name was Rena. She was a premature AIDS baby, unwanted by anyone except the Maryknoll Catholics who had taken her in. This was one of the many orphanages we visited to expand our understanding of orphan care in Cambodia.

As I stared down at baby Rena's helpless, fragile little body, my mind wandered to the many other types of orphanages that we had encountered in our time here, and the secrets held behind their closed doors.

Before we left America, our mission organization had tasked us to start an orphanage. We were all on board after seeing endless photographs of orphaned children passed around at church by Matt and Jean. Was there a nobler box to check on the sanctification ladder to heaven than feeding the widow and orphan? We were all in.

We raised money from other dreamers, and we believed, because of what other missionaries had told us, that many orphaned children were waiting for a home. Waiting for us to give it to them.

When we landed in Cambodia a year and a half prior, we realized that the truth was more complicated. We didn't visit many orphanages at first. We were too busy learning the culture and language and trying to assimilate and acclimatize our family into this incredibly challenging environment.

But as time went by, we did our own research on the needs of orphans in Cambodia. We were already involved with Ponlou Home and had spent many hours getting to know the children. They were friends with our children and the mission teachers at the Svay Rieng Bible Club, which had started in Monee's village months ago.

Matt and Jean's model was isolationist, Western, and developed to eliminate the children's cultural ties to Cambodia. We knew this would put the children at a disadvantage, so we attempted to help by taking the older teens to Svay Rieng and the younger girls to the Maryknoll Orphanage so they would not be cultural misfits. Ponlou Home was not a model we wanted to emulate.

We knew of other orphanages, so we went to find them, one by one. We traipsed in and out of dozens: a large one in Kampong Som, smaller ones run by a single missionary or an American family, some run by Cambodians and others by Koreans. Each one had its flaws. Each one had its secrets. The biggest secret? A large majority of the children in these orphanages were not orphans.

We didn't believe it at first. We asked staff members, administrators, and even the children themselves. Everyone gave us the same answer: "Oh, yes, they have parents or family in their villages." Shocked, we felt betrayed by our mission organization, who had sent us to Cambodia under the assumption that it was swimming with true orphans. But these children were in the orphanages because of AIDS, poverty, and dismantled local support systems, but not because they were without families.

The secrets ran deeper the harder we looked. After basic needs were met—food, clothing, shelter—there was often utter deprivation. They lacked true attachment figures, sound, present and attuned caregiving, and had minimal education. In an extreme case, threats of corporal punishment prevented the children from engaging in their own culture and language. We found that teenagers leaving the orphanages were at a loss in a culture that leans heavily on societal networks for jobs.

For children in families, the villagers, extended family, and elders would have taught these children, passing on skills and knowledge from one generation to another. One mission director noted Khmer employers were hesitant to hire young adults raised in orphanages. He said they often lacked work ethic, efficacy, and drive.

The more we heard, the more confused we got. Our mission organization had misled us, making us believe Cambodia needed us, that every corner held orphans, and that these children would die without our help. None of this was true. In fact, they did not need us.

Our conscience told us we could not start another children's home. Our mission to start an orphanage became a dead dream; its inception would have been a nightmare.

It was a few weeks after coming to this decision that we wrote to our mission board and told them we, in good conscience, could not continue working towards opening an orphanage. We proposed other alternatives for our work in Cambodia, places we saw needs we could fulfill. We could continue to run the Bible Club in Svay Rieng, teach the teenagers at Ponlou Home, or work with Panha in the provinces, helping poor single mothers so they could keep their babies. We laid out alternatives, plans, timelines, and resource allocations.

Then we received an email. "Thank you. You are fired." No discussion. No dialogue. We did not fit their vision of what Cambodia needed, even though, except for one, none of the board members had ever lived there or spent the time or resources to investigate the Western narrative of how to care for Eastern children.

According to the board of directors, since we were now fired, our monetary support would stop at the end of the year. We would no longer have them as a foundation under us in this hard place.

We also lost Panha as our Cambodian link and our partner. He belonged to the mission. They paid him. They had other plans for him. He was going to move to a beach town in southern Cambodia with another missionary family and start an orphanage. Their mission would carry on without us. We, in one fell swoop, did not have a mission organization, monetary support, or leadership to lean on.

I looked desperately at John after I read the email. "We moved our family across the world. What are we supposed to do now?"

His jaw tightened. "Not sure. I need to talk to some people. But . . . screw them." He clicked the mouse and closed the program. Grabbing his motorcycle helmet, he marched out the door. I heard him jump the kick starter once, twice, and the engine roared. The gate clanged shut behind him.

I heard Ly's flip-flops padding back to his room. John's motorcycle roared down our street, gears shifting, the distinctive mechanical whine disappearing in the distance. Leaning over the handlebars, face set in flint, my husband was hell-bent on keeping his family in Cambodia. He set out to find some answers.

The whine of the motorcycle faded in the distance. The whoosh of the washing machine and some laughter from my girls playing under the glossy leaves of the pomegranate tree impregnated the silence.

The truth we had uncovered about orphanages—a truth no one in America wanted to hear—left us abandoned, stuck, and desperate on the side of the road. But our troubles brewing in our home country were not over. New information came to light that would leave us even more isolated and rudderless.

A Tuesday afternoon, a few weeks after receiving the email, John and I rode to Matt's office on his motorcycle, leaving the smaller kids at home with Ohm and Maiy.

John and I glanced at each other as we got off the motorcycle, unbuckled our helmets, and hung them on the handlebar. Matt, as principal of the school, had a large, bright office with windows that looked out on the schoolyard, pool, and front gate. Nothing escaped his gaze. We entered through two large glass doors into the tiled cafeteria and then into his office.

A couple of Ponlou Home girls who were sitting behind Matt's desk scuttled out the door. Other missionaries from our home church in Colorado arrived after us. I sat down while John stood with the others in the back. Matt rubbed the back of his neck and cleared his throat. "I got off the phone with Pastor Greg."

He hesitated. I looked at John.

John shrugged and crossed his arms. Greg was the pastor of our home church and on the church's mission board, which divided up the tithe among the foreign missionaries, including us. It was then funneled to our mission organization . . . which had just fired us.

Matt's short, stubby fingers fidgeted with his computer mouse. "Our church, Pastor Greg's church in America, is dissolving. It will cease to exist by the end of the year. Our funding will dry up."

John stiffened. "How did this happen?"

Matt shook his head, looking down, his dark brown eyes bored holes in the floor. "Remember all those, umm . . . moral infractions among the parishioners?" The other men were looking out the window. "They could never recover. Greg is resigning and going to teach at a Christian college. Everyone is finding other churches to attend."

I felt my heartbeat in my throat. Our sending church was our foundation, financially, relationally, emotionally, and, we thought, spiritually. They were our lifeline back to America. Without them and our mission organization, we were completely unmoored.

The men talked quietly under their breath while I stared out the window. With nothing more to say, we stumbled out to the school grounds. I spotted Seth playing soccer with his friend on the small field. Joe and Tim were in the gazebo with other high school students and their classics teacher, talking about Augustine's *Confessions*. Joe caught my eye and waved briefly before turning back to challenge a remark made by a classmate.

In one month, we had lost our mission organization and our sending church. We lost our foundations. But our children were so happy here. They were thriving in this environment, and I worked hard to create a home for them. I didn't dare rip this life out from under them. I didn't dare turn and steal and rob them of the life we had painstakingly created here. It wasn't fair to be drifting without an anchor. It wasn't how I pictured God's plan.

Seth spotted us, abandoning his game to run toward us, his smile untouched by the weight crushing my chest.

"Mom! Did you see my goal?" he called.

I caught him in my arms. Over his shoulder, I watched Tim gather his books, noticing how easily he fit here among the international students, how completely we had failed him.

"Yes," I lied, holding my son tight. I had the printed email from our mission board in my pocket; I had been hoping to discuss it with Matt after the meeting. *Pulling all funding by the end of the year.*

John pulled up on his motorcycle, dust swirling around the tires. Now there were bigger things to worry about than our lost mission. Without a word, I kissed Seth's sweaty head and climbed onto the back, wrapping my arms around John's waist. He nodded once and gunned the engine.

We sped away from the schoolyard, weaving through the chaotic afternoon traffic. The children's laughter faded behind us. Wind whipped my hair as we navigated narrow side streets and dodged fruit carts and tuk-tuks. Clinging tightly to my husband, I buried my face against his shoulder, letting the blur of the city wash over me.

We arrived at home.

John cut the engine, and in the sudden quiet of our courtyard, I pulled the email from my pocket, staring at the words until they blurred. With trembling fingers, I tore it into tiny pieces, watching them scatter and fall onto our tiled courtyard.

THE AIDS ORPHANAGE

The days blurred together after that. We sold what we could spare, reached out to personal contacts, and stretched every dollar. John and I lay awake at night, reworking budgets and contingency plans. Our supporters in America let us know that they would stay with us into our next mission organization. John stayed after Monday night basketball to talk with other missionaries. He searched for another organization we could apply to. I woke each morning determined to live as if we were going to stay in Cambodia long past Christmas.

Four months after our initial visit, the kids and I returned to visit baby Rena and the others at the Maryknoll AIDS orphanage. It was a quiet Wednesday afternoon in November when I stopped at Ponlou Home to gather a few of the teenage girls and continued to the far end of town.

This orphanage differed from all the others. In an old but spacious home, the Maryknoll missionaries had created a place for the palliative care of children dying from AIDS with simplicity, dignity, and unexpected joy. The children's laughter, not sadness, filled the halls, and the Khmer staff treasured each child for their remaining time.

This was the same orphanage that Pastor George, the Southern Baptist preacher, told us was run by Catholics.

Those Catholics, he'd said, "were not Christian and worse than Buddhists." Well, these Buddhists or Catholics—I did not ask—were kind, generous, and patient with the dying children. Some women nursed the sicker children while others dished up bowls of rice and ladled a meat, ginger, and morning glory broth over the top.

They invited us to eat lunch with them at the long table outside under the banana tree. The little children would climb into our laps as we ate. We sang and told them silly stories about monkeys, snakes, and elephants, and their favorite, clever rabbits who had the last word.

Rena, as big as my hand, stayed at Maryknoll for two more months. Then that day in November arrived. I searched everywhere for her. I met one of the staff's eyes and asked, "Where's Rena, Srey?"

She stared down at her feet and motioned for me to follow her inside.

Rena was lying on a reed mat in the corner of the stuffy room. She was gasping for air, and her skin was pale and clammy.

"She's dying." Srey bent forward to touch her forehead.

"Can I hold her?"

Srey nodded. I reached down and picked up Rena and found a spot in the corner against the wall to sit with her. Her breathing was laborious, and her eyes stayed shut. I stroked her, kissed her, and whispered a song into her tiny ear. I stayed that way until the Ponlou girls found me. "Miss Sheryl, it's time to go home for dinner."

With an empty stare, I laid Rena back on her mat. With great love, each girl kissed her tiny forehead. As I got up to leave, Srey grabbed my hand and gave it a squeeze. Her eyes were weary. She was much too young to carry this burden. My heart hurt for her as much as Rena.

The drive home was heavy. The girls, usually chatty, were noticeably quiet. I weaved our van through rush hour traffic, eager to get home. We stopped at a red light behind six motos. In the lane next to us, a shiny black Lexus pulled up.

Emma was in the passenger seat with the window down since our air-conditioning had stopped working weeks ago. I watched the tinted window of the SUV slowly wind down. The driver, muscles straining in his neck, glared at the mass of motos in front of us. There was now at least a dozen of them weaving their way to the front. I kept my eyes on the driver while silently motioning to Emma to roll up her window.

In a split second, I was staring at a handgun. The driver swung a revolver over my car and pointed it down the street. He pulled the trigger twice. Clenching the steering wheel, I pushed Emma's head to the floor.

The driver's eyes focused straight ahead. He waved his gun toward the mass of motos ahead of us. Panic flooded through the masses. They bolted in all directions. When he got the result he intended, the driver gunned his SUV and peeled around the corner, leaving a swirl of dust.

The younger Cambodian girls whimpered in the back. Emma didn't blink; lifting her head, she stared straight out the front window.

With Rena's small dying body still imprinted on the palm of my hand and gunshots ringing in my ears, my shaking foot stepped on the gas pedal. I spotted another black Lexus coming towards me in the opposite lane. A cry caught in my throat. He flashed his lights, which meant to everyone, "I'm coming. Get out of my way." He swerved into my lane to go around a dilapidated Camry while I swerved and nearly missed a tuk-tuk creeping alongside me.

I slowed down and kept to the far right. Another black Lexus pulled out of a side street and turned right. He lumbered beside me. They were everywhere, like ants infesting and tyrannizing their way through Phnom Penh, dictating the traffic, controlling the police. They were the ruling elite.

Back at home, I struggled to get out of the car. Olivia ran up to me with a huge mango seed in her hand that Ohm had given her for a late afternoon snack. She grabbed my shaking legs with her slimy hands and looked up at me with her large green eyes. "Mommy home. Eat rice."

"Yes, my sweet." I scooped her up in my arms and held her strong, healthy body next to me. I felt her steady heartbeat pounding with life and vitality. We moved into the dining room. Clara and Emma ran ahead to tell everyone how a man in a black car almost shot us.

John jumped up from his seat at the head of the table. "What happened?" His eyes burrowed into mine.

"Sit down. I'll tell you all about it. It's been quite a day."

TWO BABIES

Months later, I found out that I was pregnant again. I scheduled an ultrasound at Michele's international medical clinic to check the status and age of the new baby. Clara and I met Michele at the clinic on the southern side of the city. The clean waiting room was a welcomed change from the stuffy, dirty medical clinics near our home. Michele came out in her blue scrubs and dark wavy hair, chatting while she took us back to the ultrasound room.

Clara crawled up on the table, lifted her shirt, and pretended to be a patient while Michele rolled the ultrasound recorder on her stomach, asking if she was going to have puppies or kittens.

Clara giggled and said, "Puppies. Three of them."

We laughed.

I sat down next to Clara, and she curled up in my lap as we waited for the ultrasound tech. A young Khmer man with kind eyes and large hands came in while we were discussing names Clara wanted for her three puppies.

He greeted us in broken English and turned on the machine, which was many generations older than ultrasounds in America. Clara moved to the end of the bed, and I lay down and lifted my shirt for him to begin the procedure. The machine hummed and Michele chatted with Clara while the tech moved the receiver with its cold jelly across my belly.

He mumbled, clicked a few buttons, and furrowed his brow. "Oh, two baby."

"What?" I tried to sit up.

Michele jumped to the monitor. "Let me see."

He turned the monitor towards me and moved the receiver back and forth.

"See"—he pointed—"two baby."

Sure enough, in full sight were two little beans kicking and moving, full of life and vigor.

I bit my lip. "Are they okay?"

"Oh, yes! Two baby healthy."

Michele and I looked at each other. Clara jumped up and down with excitement. "Two babies, two babies."

Two babies! The tech told us they were due late spring.

Where would they be born? Who would give me adequate prenatal care in Cambodia? What did this mean for my mission work?

I knew the answer to that. Two more babies meant my mission was home, once again, as it has been and would be if there were young children in my house. I knew that. I had always known this. It was insecurity that had told me otherwise. Home was my mission field.

It was an hour before we made it back behind the green gate. I told Clara that the twins were our surprise until dinner.

She put her finger over her mouth and smiled. "I keep a secret."

I found John studying Khmer on our king-sized bed. I crawled in next to him and peeked over at his Khmer language book. He turned suspiciously. "You're home."

"Yeah."

"So, how's the baby?" He turned back to his textbook.

"The babies are fine . . ." I tried to hold back a smile.

The book dropped into his lap. He stared at me. "Babies?"

"Yes. Twins. Due May 18." I could not contain my excitement and jumped off the bed. He looked at the ceiling as if counting in his head. "Wow, we have some work to do, huh?"

"Yes. I am already exhausted." I moved towards my armoire and turned side to side, looking in the full-length mirror. Twins! My baby pouch showing and my eyes bright, I tried not to consider all the complications. I only stood there gleaming with joy and congratulating myself. Twins.

～

Dinner was a roar of excited yells and exclamations after we told the kids about the coming babies.

"I can't wait to tell my friends," Tim said, while taking the last piece of sliced watermelon off the plate.

Emma bounced in her seat. "Can I help with the babies, Momma?"

"Of course, sweet one." I pushed her wispy blonde hair out of her blue eyes and behind her ear.

Olivia clapped and shrieked, "Baby, baby!"

"And this means we will return to America in the spring to have the babies," John announced.

"America?" Joe blew out a long breath and smiled. "We are going back. That's great." In another explosion of discussion, the kids rattled off all the things and people they could not wait to see in America.

Seth toppled his chair, trying to stand up. "Can we stay with Grandma and Grandpa at the lake house? And ride the horses?"

Clara bounced and chatted about baby goats at Grandma's farm. Emma wanted to make sure she could spend the night with her cousin Erica. Stephen wanted to see movies and eat popcorn. Joe and Tim left the room to email their friends in Greeley to plan a visit to make home movies and float down the South Platte River on inner tubes.

I cleared my plate and looked at John. "Well, that was a hit. Two babies and a trip to America. They were excited." He chuckled, gave me a kiss, and left the room, hollering at the boys to come back and clean up the dinner dishes.

Checking on the girls after their shower, I found Emma curled up with her face in the pillow. Clara was sitting next to Emma with her legs crossed and playing with her doll. "She sad, Mommy." I dropped beside Emma and leaned over her to kiss her wet head, smelling of pink shampoo with jasmine flowers.

"What's up?"

Her muffled voice came from the pillow. "We don't have a home in America anymore. And we don't have a home here either."

I smoothed her tangled blonde hair. "We have a delightful house here, and we are making friends." My heart pounded in my chest. I knew I was lying to her and to myself. She sat up to look me straight in the eyes. "I don't have friends. This house smells funny. I want to go home."

She flopped back down, sniveling into her pillow, trying to keep her breath steady. I stroked her hair, but I could not console her. I could not reassure her it was going to be alright. I did not believe it myself.

Now with two more babies coming, how could I take emotional care of my seven other children, create a home from a house that smelled funny, and prepare to return to America in six months? I knew I needed to fight the urge to pack up and never come back here.

The weeks passed, and Emma was still somber and sad. She stuck close to Ohm and Maiy, helping them cook and fold laundry. She spent the evenings in the garage with Hok and Ly, watching movies on their computer and eating their leftover rice and fried fish. She avoided me.

The holidays were coming. In between bouts of pregnancy fatigue and morning sickness, I planned for the perfect family holiday season. I unpacked several scented candles of pine and apple pie that I brought from America smelling like our cozy farmhouse on crisp fall mornings.

I commandeered Ohm and her sewing machine to make nine Christmas stockings to hang on the upstairs railing. I scoured the

Western markets for cocoa, butter, and pecans to create all our favorite pies and cookies. I found small and rather tasteless pumpkins in the local markets for both pumpkin pie and table decor.

When a turkey was nowhere to be found, we roasted two small chickens stuffed with homemade bread stuffing and lots of herbs, and I conjured up recipes on the internet for eggnog. We decorated our green wire and plastic Christmas tree with cheap ornaments found at the Chinese store.

If we closed the shades, blasted the air-conditioning, and played Christmas carols on the highest volume, we could drown out the Phnom Penh traffic, the yipping dogs, and the grinding of the construction saws and believe, for one moment, that we were celebrating Christmas in Colorado.

But the holiday was a cheap imitation. The heat spoiled the eggnog. The chicken tasted like chicken. The Christmas cookies burned.

But we found a copy of *It's A Wonderful Life* on a compact disc at the Russian Market. And we could sing. John brought out his guitar. We handed around copies I had printed of our favorite Christmas carols. We sang in our tank tops and shorts, fighting for the best seats next to the fans as we sweated on our songbooks.

It was late that Christmas afternoon when I walked down to the internet cafe at the end of our street.

The front room was filled with computer screen glow as the ceiling fans turned lazily overhead. The owner gestured to the back where a row of plywood phone booths lined the wall, each barely wider than a shoulder span, with sliding doors that never quite closed. Inside each booth was a small shelf with a phone, a plastic chair, and, taped to the wall, a grimy chart showing international phone rates.

I shut myself inside. And with a dirty phone receiver smelling like dried saliva tucked under my ear, I called my family waking up on Christmas morning. From the tiny wooden booth, the phone's ring scraped across the continents, sounding alien and harsh, like a metal rake being dragged across sun-softened asphalt.

Homesickness rolled through me, hot then cold, with a hollow ache that started in my stomach and rose until I could taste it. I died inside when my mother's sweet voice picked up on the other end a hemisphere away.

"Hello?"

"Momma . . ." My voice cracked. "Can I come home?"

SIX MIDWIVES

Six months later, when spring was in full bloom in Colorado, I saw my mother's face again. The flight had been long. My ankles were swollen, my face puffy, and my belly bursting with the twins. After gathering our twenty-three almost empty totes at the baggage carousel, we loaded the children into my mom's car and my dad's truck and headed off to my parents' lake property in the green foothills of the Rocky Mountains.

My heart, bursting with joy to be back in Colorado, drank in the crisp, cool air, the large open highways, and the beckoning mountains. I had been pining for home since my tearful Christmas phone call six months earlier. My mother's voice rang in my ears. "We would love for you to come back, but Cambodia is your home now." Her response made me feel orphaned. Severed from my roots, I yearned for my feet to touch American soil. I would find that feeling of belonging again once we got settled.

As spring moved into summer, the air warmed. I smiled at my children playing with the baby goats, riding the tractor with John, and, with all the cousins, helping gather the hay into the barn. I breathed a sigh of relief at our freedom here. There were no high walls with razor wire or barred gates. But something was different. Something changed, or maybe it was me.

I watched the children from the kitchen window one day in June as I rinsed the last of the lunch dishes. Afternoon light filled the farmhouse. My mother-in-law, Judy, kneaded bread dough with practiced hands. The scent of yeast hung in the air.

"The co-op got the winter wheat in," she said. "Makes all the difference in the texture."

I nodded, my fingers tracing the porcelain of the kitchen sink. "In Cambodia, Ohm made us rice porridge. I like the texture when she adds palm sugar." My memories echoed with the sound of Ohm's wooden spoon against the pot. I looked out at the cloudless Colorado skies.

Judy smiled politely before turning to check her goat cheese draining in the colander. "Did you hear we are finally getting a storm this week? We need it so badly. The drought has been horrible the last few years." She brushed her hands on her capris and threw a dish towel over her shoulder as she leaned to look out the window at the northern sky. I fell silent, hearing monsoon rains on a tin roof.

Later, I sat on the back porch watching the children play in the distance. The golden hour light bathed the farm in warm hues. Stephen, nine years old, helped Uncle Mark repair the goat fence, while Emma, seven, surrounded by cousins, fed the cow long stalks of grass over the fence.

It was beautiful. It was home. And yet.

I looked at my watch, calculating the time difference. Fourteen hours ahead in Cambodia.

That night, after the children were asleep in beds that no longer felt foreign to them, I sat alone in the kitchen. The house was quiet, save for the occasional creak of settling wood.

I thought of the email we received from Ly earlier that day. Ly told us of monsoon rains flooding the yard, of his niece's fever that had broken, and of the new checkpoint that had appeared on the road to the market. I felt the distance between worlds collapse. For those precious minutes, I was there again—the heat, the smells, the constant chorus of insects, the weight of responsibility.

"*Khmnon nuk, neak srok Khmer robah khmnon,*" (I miss you, my Cambodia) I said in Khmer to no one, in a language that now felt as intimate as my mother tongue. Outside the window, America slept peacefully, unaware of the other world I carried within me.

The next morning at breakfast, Mark discussed the upcoming town meeting about ditch water rights. All I wanted to talk about was babies dying of AIDS, villages with ransacked churches, and our beloved Khmer family—Ohm, Ly, Hok, Sothea, and Maiy—that we left in Cambodia to tend to our home and animals.

Tim caught my eye across the table and held my gaze longer than usual. At thirteen, my son understood what it meant to live between worlds. I saw in that look both recognition and fear—recognition of our shared experience and fear of the isolation it created.

That night, I dreamed of the red dirt roads of Cambodia, of Ohm's weathered hands showing me how to select a pineapple, of Maiy's laughter as we failed to communicate across the language barrier. I woke before dawn, the phantom scent of incense and tropical flowers lingering.

Breathing in the cool morning air, so different from Cambodia's perpetual humidity, I reminded myself that this was home too. But it was also clear that the me who had left two years earlier no longer existed. The me that returned carried multiple worlds inside her. Worlds I couldn't integrate.

The children were becoming exceptional at entering America as chameleons, changing colors with the different homes or events they entered. But I knew they missed Cambodia, too. They wanted to hear us speak Khmer, wanted to buy mango in the Boulder grocery store, and wanted to talk about their tropical home late in the night as I put them to bed.

I didn't have time to wallow in these changes. The babies were coming. We had planned for a home birth at Grandma's farm, so I stayed in the back room of the farmhouse waiting for my babies to be born. Then one bright day in June, my body labored slow and gentle.

The midwives arrived. One by one, they came in to introduce themselves. Six of them, puttering about setting up the two oxygen tanks, laying out the medical supplies, and putting fresh chicken soup to simmer on the stove. It was early that afternoon when Pam slipped in and perched herself at the end of my bed.

"Sheryl. Hi. I'm Pam. I will be one of the twins' primary midwives."

I sat up, using my free hand to shield my eyes from the sun coming in behind her.

"I am excited to help you out. Also, I am so interested in Cambodia. Can you tell me a little about it between your contractions?" Her hand rested on my leg and her eyes were warm with curiosity.

I shared what I missed and the people who meant the most to us. Her gentle prompting of my memories made the time pass quickly. Labor intensified to the point I could no longer articulate memories, and with Pam's help, I focused solely on my labor.

Late in the evening on June 10, Mary and Christina, twin girls, were born an hour and forty-five minutes apart. They were healthy, strong, beautiful.

One was dark, and one was light. They represented the dichotomy of our two lives. Cambodia and America. Both loved, yet so different from each other. As they grew and their personalities flourished, this difference in them became even more apparent. How can two girls and two places be so different and yet so equally loved?

The summer flew by in a haze of simple joys. One evening in July, I watched from beneath the spreading ash tree as my children darted between garden rows, their excited voices carrying across the yard.

"Mom! Look what we found!" Seth came running, cupping something in his hands, siblings trailing behind him.

He opened his palms to reveal a tiny toad, its skin glistening in the Colorado sunshine. "Grandma says they're good for the garden. Can we keep it?"

"For a little while," I laughed, adjusting the baby at my breast. "Then back to its home in the vegetables."

The children raced away, and I leaned back in my chair, the warm breeze rustling through the ash leaves above. These quiet moments nursing my babies while watching my children experience farm life had become my sanctuary.

Later that evening, John brought out two glasses of iced tea and settled beside me on the porch. The sun was setting over the mountains, painting the sky in brilliant oranges and pinks.

"I spoke with Pastor Michael today," John said, passing me a glass. "The Anglican church is officially bringing us on as missionaries."

I clinked my glass against his. "A far cry from where we started."

"I remember our first Sunday there," John said. "I hadn't realized how much I missed liturgy."

"I know exactly what you mean," I said, watching the gathering dusk. "When everyone recited the prayers together, it felt like coming home."

The ice clinked in John's glass. "I spoke with the new mission organization again. They've got three families in Phnom Penh who are eager to help us settle into the new organization. Their director has twenty years of experience in missions."

A shout from the barn interrupted us. The children were helping Grandma bring in the goats and chickens for the night, their small figures silhouetted against the fading light.

"We should probably rescue your mother," I laughed, standing and stretching.

As we walked toward the barn, each holding a baby, the evening air filled with the sound of our children's laughter and the gentle bleating of goats.

A month later, eleven of us boarded the plane once more, loaded with our twenty-three pieces of luggage filled with coffee, new schoolbooks, new toys, and gifts for our Cambodian friends.

John once again cared for the passports, customs forms, and immigration papers, while each of the older kids had a travel buddy they were responsible for. I tandem-nursed the twins, only six weeks old, across the ocean for twenty-six hours.

It was during a long, dull stretch over the Pacific Ocean that I realized that when I was in Cambodia, I had never forgotten the aromatic fragrance of Rocky Mountain spruce and pine under the noonday sun. But, since I boarded the plane this time, I could no longer recall the feel of the luscious mountain air, the sound of the cold Big Thompson River cascading over brown rocks as large as elephants, or the smell of Weld County's tasseled corn ready for harvest.

These were already gone. In their place was an ever-growing excitement for blunt shadows under waving palms, the sweet smell of jasmine, and the feel of sweat dripping off my body the moment the sun came over the horizon. I couldn't wait to get back behind my green gate and the yellow wall. As crazy as it sounds, even with all its warts and worries, I was excited to go home.

LITURGY

The morning was cool for August in Cambodia. I sat on the front veranda on the rosewood bed with my journal, Bible, and a lovely collection of pens that I brought back from America three weeks earlier. I journaled during this rare moment when both babies were happy and cooing next to me. I wrote of the happiness that we found in the Anglican Church:

Oh, the beauty of Christ's blood. Oh, the beauty of the Liturgy of the one catholic church of the religion of the heart! Oh, how happy I am at this moment to be in the faith of my childhood – the faith that speaks to me from the heart and draws me into the heart of God.
– journal entry, August 12, 2005

Since our return to Cambodia, we attended the local Anglican church, housed in the first home of the American ambassador to Cambodia. The church boasted an outside narthex under the shade of a bougainvillea, which bloomed all year with blood-red flowers.

Years before, parishioners had transformed the home by building an altar, constructing the transepts, and designing a baptismal font behind the church under two banana trees.

This became our home away from home and our place of peace and joy. John jumped in to serve the youth of the church, visit the sick in the provinces, and lead the music every Sunday. Our children were involved in Sunday School, making new friends, and playing all the parts in the Christmas pageant.

Days melted into a rhythm of tropical life—rocking twin babies, guiding four students through their lessons, and devouring books brought from America like they were water in a desert. The mantle of "missionary" that once weighed so heavily on my shoulders had slipped away. I saw how I'd been dancing for an audience across the ocean, trying to justify my place in Cambodia through a frenzy of doing rather than being. The seed that was planted after finding out of the twins' pregnancy bloomed in confidence and conviction. Home was my mission.

Not just a house, but a haven. Each day of prayer from the Anglican prayer book, each story read aloud to children, and each meal shared peeled away another layer of pretense. The mission wasn't out there in some imagined field—it was here, in the quiet conversion of my heart, in creating a sanctuary where weary souls— Khmer, American, expatriate, local—could lay down their burdens and rest. My mission now spoke in the language of open doors and welcoming chairs, of quiet spaces and sanctuary gardens.

One rainy afternoon, I drove gingerly over the bump at the front of our driveway so as not to disturb the thirty-four plants I had stuffed into the back of my van.

A week earlier, I had stood at the far end of our front veranda with my hands on my hips surveying the long terra-cotta-tiled porch hidden away on the far side of the house above the garage. As of now, it was a forgotten, bare space.

I had a new vision. I took thirty-four plants, with the help of Ly, Hok, and my boys, up to the forgotten porch. Then, I placed two white benches facing the blooming tropical plants and the water fountain brimming with lotus, duckweed, and koi. It became our refuge and escape. We called it the serenity garden.

John and I began weekly date nights in the serenity garden. With candles, wine, and some special treat from America (usually involving chocolate), we would spend a couple of hours every Monday there after the kids were in bed. This became a weekly tradition. It all started with a need for connection, peace, and a place of serenity.

After our return from America with the twins in 2005, our days fell into a steady rhythm of work, school, and mission. Time flowed faster, and events came and went rapidly as I managed our large household. I remembered those early days in Cambodia, when each day stretched out so that the time between dawn and dusk felt like eternity. Each new experience needed a chapter of its own as we learned to navigate our new land.

Now, time moved too fast. Novelty had worn off and days ran over each other. But within that, I found new energy, time, and mental space to reach beyond our green gate yet, at the same time, keep home and mission inside.

My mission became hospitality. That fall, they came. All the new teachers arrived to teach from all over the world with hearts full of dreams and fear. The international schools were demanding their time, and Cambodia was draining their souls. It was a struggle for them to buy furniture and household goods, avoid getting lost around town, and learn a few phrases in Khmer, all the while navigating the demands of an international teacher.

I would see them looking dazed and frazzled after a long day setting up their classrooms, then leaving to find food for dinner and sheets for their beds. I had pity remembering my first days. I reached out to them and asked if they needed help to get settled; mostly, they needed a place to vent, cry, scream into the void, and find comfort.

This began my Bible study for the new teachers and missionaries looking for a place to belong, away from their school or mission organization. A place for prayer, presence, and much-needed grace for the weary. We would meet weekly in my living room, studying books from the Bible, sharing our prayers and praises, and drinking Maiy's delicious iced coffee made with love every week.

Maiy, unhappy working for her missionary family, and I, needing more hands around the house after the twins were born, forged a happy alliance. She needed us, and I needed her. Her commute became two steps outside the bedroom she shared with Ohm instead of across town. She weaved her way into the rhythms of our life helping Ohm with cooking and cleaning, watching the twins during my homeschooling hours, and teaching the older girls Khmer traditions.

Chbap srei, the Khmer women's rules for living, was a moral code passed down through the generations and used to guide moral behavior. These rules were transmitted orally and written as didactic poetry. Ohm and Maiy shared these with my daughters. They stressed feminine ideals of modesty, obedience, domestic skills, respectful behavior towards elders, and maintaining family honor. Virtues of gentleness, patience, and devotion to family duties were highly prized.

As I watched the blossoming affection between Ohm and Maiy and my girls, a contentment and peace settled into my bones. They were being well cared for, and I could spend more hours devouring my newfound love for Anglican theology and liturgy.

My journal expressed my joy:

I am so excited – I am really feeling the depth and breadth of God in the ancient church. NO MORE strivings because before (we found the Anglican Church) right doctrine was what mattered. I was not interested in intellectual striving after the truth. I wanted it to be given to me to eat – not to have to seek it. SO MUCH comfort in the ancient church. I have FOUND MY REST! My soul cannot contain the joy I feel at this. I will drink out of this endless well as I continue to plunge into the ways and movings of the ancient church. OH, THE RICHES! My soul cannot hold it all! I have found my true love again!

And in all the seeking, I was found.

Let me seek Thee in Longing,
Let me long for Thee in Seeking, Let me find Thee in Love,
And Love thee in Finding. – Saint Anselm
– journal entry, August 14, 2005

. . .

I thought that this new season of our life in Cambodia would take a gentler turn. We could lean into our new community, strengthen our children's friendships, and settle into a ministry. But after returning from America in 2005—two and a half years, two pregnancies, and two mission organizations since we landed—John's ministry took yet another turn.

∼

Months earlier, before leaving for America, I was catching up with Jean at a local coffee shop.

She stirred another sugar packet into her ice coffee. ". . . I was on the roof hanging laundry. I reached out to pin another diaper on the clothesline"—she stopped, her hand poised as if clutching a clothespin—"and the whole wall crumbled and fell into the court-yard." She stopped to breathe. "It was terrifying. Luke was right there. I had to swish him behind me." I pictured her youngest tottering behind his mother two stories high and shuttered.

As she continued to stare out the window, my phone pinged. I noticed a text from John.

He wrote, *One of the girls wants to leave Ponlou Home and go home to her parents. Matt is resisting her leaving. We will talk later.* I glanced at Jean as I put my Nokia phone in my lap.

"That sounds really scary. I guess I am glad my clothesline is in my courtyard and not on my roof." I knew this was not very empathetic, but I was still trying to figure out what was going on with Matt. "So, have the Ponlou kids been really busy lately?" I asked.

Jean looked back at me. "Yeah, lots of studying, and Matt has them staying home for chores and projects . . ." Her voice trailed off. Matt was keeping them close.

Jean and I parted that afternoon, but soon we were seeing less of each other. She, also, seemed to be busy. And sad. Her tired, distracted eyes would meet mine occasionally across the room. Something was up, but she was a vault.

Now that the summer had ended and the new school year had started, Matt told the kids that they were no longer allowed to go out to Svay Rieng with us for the children's ministry. They were going to be too busy, he had said. Now not only was he keeping them close, but he was keeping them from us. Soon after school started, Matt and Jean left for their yearly trip to America.

Without the Ponlou teens as Khmer teachers, we did not have a ministry in the village. We took a final few trips out there and said goodbye to the children and their families. Another dead dream of ministry in Svay Rieng. And strange behavior from our friends.

Meanwhile, we were finding our niche in the Anglican church. We worked regularly with Pastor Jun Hao and his wife, Wan Tang, both from Singapore. John helped Pastor Jun Hao by teaching the Bible to Khmer young adults, some garment factory workers, and other students from the province. Even with this meaningful work, John was still restless. He missed the work in the province. He missed Svay Rieng.

That was when he met up with Jamie, another missionary from America. Together they rode motorcycles out to the provinces every other week to teach the Bible to village pastors. Jamie and John became like brothers, similar in temperament, personality, and interests. We called them the Sons of Thunder, like James and John from the New Testament.

John began to smile again each week when he drove his motorcycle out of our driveway and away from the busy city, but the other nights of the week, I noticed that something was still off.

We talked for hours in the serenity garden Monday nights. There, among the potted plants and whispering leaves, he would unravel his concerns about working with the Khmer pastors and students.

His voice would grow soft, thoughtful, as he wrestled with the weight of being Western in an Eastern world, wondering if his American perspective was a bridge or a barrier. The curriculum he taught haunted him. Even translated into Khmer, did its Western roots reach deep enough into Cambodian soil? Did its theological branches spread in ways that made sense in a Buddhist landscape?

"I'm too new," he said, watching the gecko shadows dance across the garden wall. "Am I planting truth or transplanting my own cultural assumptions?" The fear of teaching false doctrine in the province sat heavy in his words, while the shadow of Ponlou Home and its children haunted him. We had lost any influence there. Matt cloistered the children back into his Western bubble.

Then one day, John got a phone call from Wan Tang. A bombshell dropped.

LOST INNOCENCE

I t was October and even though the rains were letting up, I still fought the occasional monsoons to get the laundry in before another deluge. I was folding yet another load of laundry on the veranda when John called my cell phone.

"Hey, what's up?" I pressed the phone into my shoulder while I finished folding a pair of Olivia's jeans.

"I have some bad news. Are you somewhere where the kids can't hear us?"

I shifted the phone and looked around. The girls were riding bikes in the courtyard, and the boys were still at school. "Yeah. I'm here alone."

"Wan Tang called me. There is some disturbing news coming out of Ponlou Home. It's possible that Matt has been sexually assaulting at least one of the kids over the last two years."

"Matt! How could that be?" I dropped the pile of laundry on the nearby chair and glanced at the girls in the courtyard. I frantically tried to remember if I had ever left them alone at Ponlou Home. Did I need to talk to them? My boys? I thought of the hours we'd spent there with this happening right under our noses.

"I know. I'm as shocked as you are. Things aren't what they seem, Sheryl. There are dark things happening over there." He paused, and I could hear his labored breathing. "Now we've got to do some kind of investigation."

"We?" I thought about the years John put in at the Greeley Police Department, his training in interrogation and investigation, and his experience as an undercover drug officer.

"I'm afraid we're going to do this on our own. I have a bad feeling that the Ponlou mission organization in America will not pull the American or Cambodian authorities into this. We're reaching out to the mission today."

"What can I do?" I was shaking as I walked back into the house from the veranda and past our desk with the clunky computer and piles of unfinished Khmer lessons and partially written mission letters.

"Pray. I need to go. There is a lot to take care of. Luckily, Matt and Jean are in America right now. The kids at Ponlou Home are safe for the moment." The phone went dead.

How did we not see this? I thought as I stumbled downstairs, walking past Olivia and not even seeing her. I sat down on the swing in the courtyard and stared at the leaves on the mango trees, twisting and turning in the breeze.

The pieces came together. Small, little details I had thought little of individually, but in context, they were all beginning to shape a different picture. The affection Matt would show the orphans seemed excessive. When confronted, Matt would say that he needed to give them "fatherly love," which included physical touch.

Chills went down my spine. I shuttered.

I remembered how Matt would preach on Sundays about male headship of the home, male leadership in the church, male authority to rule his home without intrusion, and his right to discipline his children, including the orphans, as he saw fit. This was not an uncomfortable teaching for me. We had received these same messages from our Grace Community Church in America. But now they rattled me to the core. This isolation hid hideous secrets.

But Matt was an upstanding missionary in this community, renowned for taking in orphans and providing them with a home and an excellent Classical education. Evangelical conservative books rattled in the school's library, preaching a framework that presents marriage and family as strict hierarchies in which wives and children exist under complete male authority. Teachers of this ideology preached complete female submission, the breaking of children's wills through discipline, and paternal authority over daughters until marriage transferred that authority to their husbands.

Controversial in the missionary community, yes, but Matt had devoured these books. I could see now that this created a closed system at the Ponlou Home where abuse could flourish.

No wonder Matt had shut us out months earlier when he forbade the Ponlou children from going out to Svay Rieng or Maryknoll Orphanage. We were a threat to his closed system.

I brushed the cool raindrops off my cheeks, wiped the tears from my eyes, and wandered back into the house just as the sky cracked open and the monsoon rains deluged our courtyard as the girls shrieked and ran inside. This rocked our world. A child's life shattered, a missionary brought shame to the Christian religion, and we would find out later, it would be covered up.

The news divided the community. Some thought that Matt was one of the best missionaries in Cambodia. He wouldn't have abused anyone. It must have been consensual, adultery, an affair.

Others believed the victim. Why would the victim come forward if it wasn't true? You can't have a consensual affair if the victim is underage, and the perpetrator was an authority figure. The hushed talk rattled closed doors, everyone taking sides.

Within days, the director of the Ponlou Home Mission in America came out to squelch the talk and decide the fate of Ponlou Home the school. John picked him up at the airport. A former police officer and investigator, John was adamant: "We've got to do an investigation. Not just here, but in America. He's been alone with other Ponlou children in the United States on their trips together. We've got to investigate this immediately."

"Hmm," said Douglas, the director. "We don't need to jump to conclusions. This happens all the time."

John's mind was racing. *What do you mean? It happens all the time, sexually molesting minors in an orphanage? This does not happen all the time, not in my world.*

Douglas, yawning from jet lag, calmly went on, "Well, we'll see what we can do. Probably, we can get this thing figured out and restore Matt back to spiritual health to get him and Jean back here again."

Hell no! Over my dead body is he going to come back here. John glared out the window, his mind churning.

Weeks later, there was an investigation—not an official one conducted by a government entity, but an investigation done by a small human rights organization. John was one of the few to whom they sent the final report.

John read the report to me one evening months later. "Well, it's seems to have been determined that there was abuse."

My heart raced. John went on, "After interviewing all the kids, many teachers, and other missionaries, it seems that they found out that Matt not only broke Cambodian law and American law, but together they violated multiple articles from the United Nations Convention on the Rights of the Child, which was ratified in Cambodia in 1992." He stopped and looked out over our gate. He looked at me, and in his eyes, I saw his heart burning for justice and for mercy for the children in Ponlou Home.

Pushing the laptop aside, John turned in his chair. "I'm glad that someone seems to have acknowledged the abuse. But I heard today, even after receiving this report, it seems that their mission organization won't conduct an American or Cambodian investigation. They won't pull the proper Khmer or embassy authorities into this." John stood up and ran his fingers through his graying hair. "I told the mission that because of the PROTECT Act,[1] Matt has potentially

---

1. The PROTECT Act (Prosecutorial Remedies and Other Tools to End the Exploitation of Children Today Act) is a US federal law enacted in 2003 during the Bush administration to strengthen protections for children against exploitation and abuse.

committed a crime in the United States as well as Cambodia."

I stared out into the dark night. "Really? What is the law?"

John replied, "A US citizen who has committed a sexual offense against a minor in a foreign country has committed a crime." He turned to look at the printer that churned out the confidential seven-page report. "We can and should prosecute this crime in the United States. But the mission will only have an in-house investigation in America using untrained professionals.

"Interviewing possible sexual abuse victims, like the Ponlou kids here or who are living in America, takes years of practice and training." He stood up and grabbed the pile of papers from the printer and left.

Swift changes happened overnight. The mission organization installed new houseparents for Ponlou Home and a new principal for the school. Quietly, Matt and Jean settled into life with their children back in America.

In another devastating turn of events, we realized that we had become the enemy. We had heard that Matt and Jean had spread misinformation not only about the victim but about us as well, claiming we had broken up their family and destroyed their home.

We had to accept that, despite fighting for all the children in that home, they now considered us the villains. Someone had to be blamed, so instead of Matt, it was us.

I grieved the loss of friendship with Jean. But I also saw that she was as trapped as the children. I could not rescue her. I spent nights wondering what I could do or say. One afternoon, she came back to Cambodia to gather her belongings. I knew I needed to call her, even if it was for one last time.

"Jean, it's Sheryl . . ." There was an uncomfortable silence. "I wanted to say that I am sorry for how you had to leave Cambodia. I want you to know that I am here for you. I love and care for you. If you need anything . . ."

Silence. I could hear her breathing. She swallowed after a bit. "Okay. Thanks. Ummm . . . I have a lot to do."

"Sure. Just wanted to let you know that. I am not sure when I will see you again. Maybe in America?"

"Maybe . . . so, umm, goodbye." The phone went dead. That was the last time I ever talked to her.

But the smoldering shadow of the Ponlou Home scandal would not be the end for us. What started as a spark that dark September flickered for years. Nearly a decade later, John channeled his anger over this broken system—where nonprofits covered up their missionaries' sins—into rescuing Cambodian women and children from sex trafficking.

But until then, he burned inside.

FRACTURED UNITY

W e were still mired in the Ponlou Home aftermath. Emails were flying back and forth, meetings called, the teachers had to be debriefed to support the remaining orphans.

Both John and I became cynical about all mission organizations, including our own. We needed them, but we kept them at arm's length. Meanwhile, we leaned closer into the Anglican Church. The vastness of its reach, the depth of its history, felt safe. It felt safer than the fly-by-night nonprofits that came and went with every prevailing wind and had no courage in the face of crisis. So, John poured his time and energy into the church's ministries.

Months later, after being approached by Singapore's Anglican Archbishop John Chew, John decided to enroll in seminary to find answers and a ministry path. Late one afternoon during cool season, I found John typing away on our ancient laptop, muscling through an essay on the early church fathers. His seminary books tottered on the corner of his desk and a cold cup of coffee perched on the edge of the bamboo side table.

"Sheryl, listen"—he turned in his chair as I walked in—"did you know that in 1517 after Luther nailed his ninety-five theses to the door, he had an audience with Charles V of Germany? Charles said to Luther, 'If every man can follow his own conscience in regard to the correct interpretation of scripture, how will we ever know what truth is . . .'" He paused and looked out the window. "Of course, it would have led to schism, and now we have forty thousand Protestant church denominations. Charles V was prophetic . . ."

I had to recall from my college world history classes who Charles V was and why this mattered. I remembered that Charles V, Holy Roman Emperor, initially sought to address Martin Luther's challenges to Catholic doctrine through dialogue, most notably summoning Luther to the Diet of Worms in 1521, where Luther famously refused to recant his teachings.

Later, when Luther failed to submit, Charles declared him an outlaw and heretic, but was unable to effectively suppress the Protestant movement due to political distractions from wars with France and the Ottoman Empire, ultimately allowing Lutheranism to spread throughout his territories.

I paused, considering the fallout since 1521, especially how it had influenced my life. All the churches I'd attended since my youth stemmed from this moment. Charles V's call to "follow our own consciences" explained why I found only disunity, never unity, among those churches.

John went on, "And, it says here"—he pointed in his book—"the early church, according to church fathers, celebrated a liturgy, an order of a corporate worship service, which included the Eucharist, communion. They did not gather to eat a meal together like we have been told all these years. This stuff is so fascinating. This"—he shook his head—"is changing the way I see church."

I nodded and picked up one of his textbooks. I sat down on the edge of the bed and flipped through the pages. "What are you going to do with all this knowledge since you don't think you have the temperament to be an Anglican priest?" Smiling, I tossed the book at him playfully.

He laughed. "Yeah, that might be the truth. This stuff will be useful in understanding the concept of church by looking at the form of the ancient church that Jesus established. The growth of the church, doctrine, liturgy was happening way before the Bible's canonization in 382 AD. This is kind of rocking my world." He paused as we both listened to the whir of the fan overhead.

I laid my head on the pillow and shimmied over to where I could feel the full blast of the air-conditioning. John put the book down and laid down beside me, both of us watching the overhead fan spin and shake, thinking of old ways which were becoming new to us.

John decided after two semesters of seminary that he was not called to be an Anglican priest. But his classes had an impact. John continued to read and wrestle with deep theological questions, especially the conflicting views of Cambodia's missionaries on baptism, Eucharist, church history, and salvation.

One dusty afternoon in the middle of the hot season, John had a chance encounter in an open-air gym which brought this into sharp focus.

I had visited there myself and felt the heat rising from the dusty floor when John described a young Khmer man wandering over to him. The young man made small talk in halting English.

After a moment, he asked John, "Why are you here?" He looked him straight in the eye, an unusual posture for Cambodians. "Why are you in Cambodia?"

He told the man, Savoen, that he was called to be a missionary. He had left police work and our farm in Colorado to come to Cambodia. He did not tell him how our mission had changed multiple times since we had arrived and that it was still not settled.

Savoen leaned in. "I have a question for you, then."

"Sure." His boldness surprised John.

"Why can't you Christians agree?"

John felt his gut tighten. This was the same question he had been struggling with since we stepped off the plane and onto the tarmac three years earlier.

Savoen sat down on the bench next to John. "I mean, I know one missionary down the road"—he waved his hand to the left, motioning to the other side of the moto parking—"telling me one thing about a Bible passage. But then another missionary that way"—his hand changed direction, and he flicked his wrist towards the guard gate at the entrance to the gym—"tells me that the same passage means something different. Then, when I told him what the other missionary said, his face got red and he told me that the other missionary was . . ." He struggled with the English word. ". . . *at thom trov.*"

"Not correct," John translated. Savoen nodded.

"What were they disagreeing about?" Intrigued, John leaned forward.

"Baptism."

John sighed, leaned back, and then became angry. He often heard those same conversations among missionaries. This was a scandal, he thought.

Savoen stood back up and smiled. "Wondering if you had an answer."

"I don't." John stood also. "But I need a spotter. Do you have a minute?"

John's voice trailed off while the rest of us took our last few bites of Lok Lak, and the boys stood to clear the dining room table. Maiy took the twins outside to the spigot and blue tub and gave them their evening bath. I stared at the pale, cream-colored cement wall where the cracks melted into a maze. Savoen's question plagued me.

The missionaries' conflicting biblical interpretations created a maze of confusion for the locals. And to be honest, for me as well. Each denomination, short-term mission team, or fly-by-night missionary espoused a different doctrine. Was baptism only for those who consent with their minds that Christianity is the truth? Was it part of the covenant that God made with his people? Did it imbue one with salvation? Was it only a symbol? Can infants be baptized? Why were there so many schisms and factions within Christianity?

We were part of the problem. I knew we didn't have the authority to interpret those verses on baptism either. It made me wonder who did. Over the months, we masked the doubts and pushed through our skepticisms to keep working in our little corner of the very-crowded missionary world in Phnom Penh. But Savoen's question continued to haunt us for years to come.

FLOODING

T hough my soul was filled morning to night with prayer, the struggles of living in Cambodia increased. The sheer amount of energy it took to live there blunted the excitement of our noble aspirations. Cambodia was an abusive lover. It wooed you in and then twisted the knife.

After months of construction, as our neighbors built monstrous homes and dumped loads of concrete-filled water into the sewer system, the flooding was bound to happen.

It was the rainy season, and 2006 had some unusually powerful storms. Early one Saturday afternoon, when John and I were resting in our bedroom and the kids were playing in the courtyard, a storm blew in.

"Mom, Dad! The rain waters are coming in from the street and filling up the courtyard." We raced downstairs, the children's yells drowned out by torrential rain.

We found the little ones sliding around in the flooded courtyard, while the older boys, along with Hok and Ly, had grabbed empty totes from the garage. In their shorts and bare feet, they bailed the water flooding in from the street. It was futile. The sewer drains could not hold the rainwater. Our courtyard, the lowest on the street, was flooding.

I watched as the water crept closer to the double front doors going into our home. I called Maiy and Ohm to grab brooms, buckets, and anything they could find to fend off the beast. The water came into the Great Room and crept towards the homeschooling materials and books scattered about the tile floor.

"Kids!" I hollered over the rain into the courtyard. "We need your help."

Racing in, they grabbed their schoolbooks, papers, and pillows resting against the couches. The water continued to move and rise steadily. We moved to the bedrooms, throwing clothes on the beds and fishing CD players and school backpacks from the floor as the water followed us in. It was in relentless pursuit of everything in its path.

Two hours later, the rain had stopped. We gasped for air. The first floor of our house had been claimed by the flood. All our efforts to stem the tide had failed. The mess, smell, and dampness lingered through the evening and into the night. We sat on the upper floor of the house and waited.

I was terrified of what was in that water—sewer runoff, feces, trash, parasites, bacteria, worms. It was now in my home. We spent hours wading through it barefoot. That night we scrubbed ourselves raw in long, scalding showers, desperate to wash away the filth.

The streets slowly drained, and the floodwaters in our home and courtyard receded. We mopped the now-damp floors with bleach water and wiped down the legs of all the furniture. I worried it would only happen again.

And it did. We called the landlord, who built a concrete berm at the front of the driveway and a six-inch concrete lip in front of the Great Room doors. It worked for a while, until the sewers clogged completely. The rains coming from the street grew high enough to pour over the top of the berm and stay trapped in our courtyard for days, breeding mosquitos and bringing in baby frogs and crabs.

We called the landlord again. He came back out and installed a water pump near the front gate. Most of the time, the pump kept the courtyard clear of water. But it often malfunctioned. We were constantly on guard listening to any changes in its whirring rhythm.

Finally, the rainy season stopped, and the pump sat idle. We breathed a sigh of relief and put more creams and ointments on the skin infections.

The natural world was fickle. A quiet, gentle rain could cool and clean or turn into a monsoon that flooded our house. Cambodia was fickle as well. It had wrapped its warped embrace around our hearts only to break them open again. I was not sure how or if we could ever escape the whiplash. After this many years, I was not sure I wanted to.

SILENT CURRENT

The monsoon season had given way to drier days, a short reprieve which we called "the mini-dry season" before the rains started again. After weeks of being confined inside our gate, watching water rise around our home and listening to it drum against our roof, even the smallest reprieve felt like a gift.

The moments of normalcy, like a trek to the school's swimming pool, were precious islands in our expatriate lives. The contrast was there: cockroaches in the morning, swimming lessons in the afternoon. At least in the chlorinated pool, we could pretend that we were not at war with the elements.

One afternoon in August, I gathered the kids' clothes, towels, and flip-flops that were scattered around the pool deck.

"Everyone out of the pool!"

Mary, fourteen months old, sat on the step with her pink floaties around her arms, keeping them slightly akimbo, kicking water into her brown eyes. She blinked twice at me when I yelled.

Her twin, Christina, sat next to her in blue floaties, with her first two fingers in her mouth, and watched the kids splash and play Marco Polo at the far end of the pool.

"We need to get home for dinner. The boys are done playing basketball." I glanced over the pool gate at the concrete basketball court where the high school boys were finishing their scrimmage and taking sips from their water bottles. Joe and Tim looked at me and waved.

I smiled back and tried to hustle the rest of the kids out of the pool so we could all pile in the van and go home. I hadn't eaten since lunch. I looked at the pile of snacks I brought for the kids: dried mangos, fish crackers, and strips of seaweed.

Though I was hungry, none of it looked appetizing. In fact, I felt nauseous. It was not uncommon for us to come down with a stomach issue every few months. We ate street food, at our Khmer friends' houses, and at random restaurants on the side of the road when we traveled. We were far from cautious when eating, and we paid for it. But over the years, our stomachs became more accustomed, and we got sick less often.

But today, it was my turn to feel sick. I was impatient and irritable. The kids were slow to respond, and gathering the twins and getting them dressed was like corralling cats. Emma came to help me while Stephen tried to get Olivia and Clara out of the pool.

"One more cannonball," they insisted.

I snapped, "Get out now. I am getting angry." I bit my lower lip to keep from yelling.

Living in Cambodia these last three years had changed me. I dressed modestly, danced in circles with Khmer people at weddings, scarfed down street food, ate rice every day, and never yelled at my children anymore. But my kids know my lip bite means I am really getting worked up.

Clara and Olivia slinked out of the pool, gathered their things, and tried to keep up with my fast pace to the van.

The older boys followed with their school backpacks flung over one shoulder. Joe and Tim, in their basketball uniforms, reeking of teenage boy sweat, crawled in the van last.

"Make sure those uniforms go straight into the wash," I snapped at them. "I'm tired of your bedroom smelling like a locker room." I bit my lip again as both anger and nausea coursed through my body.

I stopped by the small local pharmacy, left the kids in the car, and asked the pharmacist for ten boxes of worm medication and one pregnancy test.

Maybe that was it. Another pregnancy.

The afternoon and evening wore on. After dinner, the kids stomached down the nasty-tasting worm medication, cleaned the kitchen, and put away the laundry. Then, everyone went to their rooms to finish homework, read, or listen to music. I got the twins to bed after I nursed them and went to read to the younger kids. I was so tired.

I grabbed a book that I knew by heart. "We are reading *Ferdinand the Bull.*"

"Not again. We read that last night," they whined.

"I don't care. It was on the top of the pile." I turned on the fan while the younger kids fanned out around me in the giant papasan chair. I read *Ferdinand* and then got talked into reading another chapter of *By the Shores of Silver Lake.* With kisses and prayers, I settled the girls.

I wandered into Stephen and Seth's room to find them both reading on their bunk beds. I kissed them both, and we prayed.

Then I visited Joe and Tim downstairs. They were working on their homework while listening to music on their CD player. I waved good night to them, and I grabbed my water glass for bed. Another wave of nausea passed over me. I swigged the cold water from the cooler.

Upstairs, I took the pregnancy test to the bathroom and, knowing the drill, I put the stick in a cup and put it aside while I brushed my teeth and washed my face. Glancing briefly at the stick, I saw it. Two pink lines. Pregnant again.

I sighed, one hand resting on my stomach. "I know I will love this baby, Lord," I whispered. "But I am exhausted."

Later when John came from his evening shower, droplets still clinging to his hair, I told him the news. His eyes crinkled with delight.

"Really?" he asked, his voice soft. "You're sure?"

I nodded, managing a tired smile. "The test was positive."

"Another one," he repeated, wrapping his arms around me from behind.

He didn't notice my hesitation, or perhaps chose not to. John was always thrilled at the announcement of a new baby, his joy uncomplicated by the reality of swollen feet and morning sickness.

We settled into bed, the sheets cool against our skin. Outside, the tokay geckos began their nightly chorus, their distinctive calls echoing off our garden walls.

I nestled close into his embrace. Within minutes, we both fell asleep to the rhythmic gecko trills and chirps.

One afternoon, a few weeks later, I finally had a quiet moment to myself. The babies and Olivia were napping upstairs. Stephen, Emma, and Clara were reading sprawled out on the couches downstairs, their legs sticking up in the air or draped over the back of the couch.

The hum of the wall fans soothed as they moved back and forth across the room, ruffling papers and hair as they passed. I was working on my latest missionary update letter when I noticed that the computer kept losing power.

I wiggled the cord on the back of the computer, but nothing happened. With my fingers, I traced the cord down to the power strip under my desk. I wiggled the plug and looked up. Nothing. I continued to trace the power strip cord to the plug in the wall.

Like most of the other sockets in the walls, it was loose. My computer power strip ended in the typical European two-prong round end. Not realizing that one finger rested on the metal prong, I grasped the plug, pulled it out of the socket, and tried to place the plug back in the wall.

Tingling. Then my hand froze. I felt 220 volts of electricity surge through my body. With my other hand, I pulled my hand off the plug and sat down hard on the tile floor. My heart pounded and my eyes swam. I put my hand to my heart and tried to breathe. My eyes swelled with tears, and I could not move for what seemed like an eternity.

The fans hummed, and my kids turned their pages slowly. No one noticed my electric shock. But I was too terrified to move.

"Mom, why are you on the floor?" I looked up to see Clara come over to show me a picture she'd finished drawing. The paper waved in her hand as the fan blew it from side to side.

I watched the paper move back and forth, not knowing how much time had passed. "I was looking for something," I lied, not wanting to scare her.

Getting up slowly, I took her picture from her hand and praised her. I placed it gently under my computer and kissed her on the head.

"Mommy needs to lie down for a nap. I'll be back in a while." I turned to go upstairs, my heart still pounding out of my chest. I laid down, turned on the air-conditioning, and slept.

INTERRUPTED CIRCUITS

I n the weeks that followed, life settled back into its familiar rhythms, the electric shock fading into memory like so many other close calls. Dry season was here. The rains stopped, the weather cooled, and the rice farmers were reaping the last of their harvest.

I sat on our veranda, watching the evening breezes brush through the mango trees, waiting for John to return from his Thursday night hockey game.

My cell phone rang

"Sheryl, this is Peter . . . Something's happened . . ."

I shifted the phone to my other hand. "Yes . . ."

"Well, um . . . we were playing hockey and . . . well, I hit a slap shot."

"Go on . . ." My hands shook.

". . . and . . . John didn't see it coming . . ."

A street hockey ball, a slap shot. I was still struggling to imagine what could have happened.

"The ball hit him in the eye. His eye . . . it's full of blood . . . He says he can't see anything. Nothing. You need to come down to the medical clinic right away."

The next morning, we left for medical evacuation to Bangkok. The flight to Bangkok was only forty-five minutes long, but it felt like forever. The romance of handling our own medical issues via that silly book had worn off long ago.

The plane landed; an ambulance took us straight to Bumrungrad Hospital. There was a series of tests, X-rays, and drugs administered. John napped in the afternoon before we met with his charge doctor, a renowned eye specialist.

Later that day, we scuffled down to his office. The large Thai doctor in his starch-white coat peered over at us. "We can't guarantee that we can save your eyesight. The eyeball is full of blood. We don't know whether the optical nerve is damaged."

He pointed to John's skull on the X-ray. "You also blew out your eye socket. The impact shattered the bones. You need to stay here until we know what is going on."

I sat staring at the image, trying to put the bone shards back together. John sat silent.

"It could require surgery. If it does . . ." The doctor paused, then continued, "We would have to go in through the brain."

My hands shook, and John looked pale.

"Is there anything we can do?" I leaned in.

"No, we need to wait."

We waited.

Days later, the swelling subsided, and the body reabsorbed most of the blood. But there was damage to the retina. Vision loss, severely dilated pupil, shattered orbital bones.

I looked out on the smoggy skyline and thought about the last time we were in Bangkok, when I was nursing a feverish husband in a posh hotel room. I looked over at John watching sports on the hospital TV. Thailand had lost its romantic qualities long ago.

But John adapted. He found humor in the hospital's rules, which he broke repeatedly, made friends with the nurses despite the language barrier, and treated his injury as an inconvenience rather than a catastrophe. His resilience never ceased to amaze me. When John's vision stabilized, we headed back to Cambodia.

I was terrified of another trip to Bangkok. The city became a trigger, each mention of it sending my heart racing. Back in Phnom

Penh, I'd wake from dreams of sterile hospital rooms and emergency flights, the scent of antiseptic lingering even after I opened my eyes.

John continued life as before despite losing vision in his right eye at the focal point. He continued to work, to drive his motorcycle, and to play hockey.

~

Hot season moved into rainy season, and soon our favorite season arrived—cool season. While the gentle breezes and milder temperatures brought comfort to our daily lives, I still carried medical fear within me like a phantom pain—present even in its absence. Then I had one more medical incident blow in with the wind, and with it guilt and grief.

It was the last week in November, the day before my fortieth birthday. I was standing stiff on the veranda, staring out at the house across the street, my hands clutched, hanging at my side. The movement of the power lines swayed and sizzled in the afternoon breezes.

The power lines, a huge, tangled mass, joined to multiple power boxes high on wooden poles, lines strung between houses and the street. One line bled into another.

"So unsafe," I whispered. I could not bring myself to believe what I knew to be true.

I lifted my hand and looked at it again. A speck of blood was still on my finger, and I picked at it desperately.

In the bathroom trash can was a crumpled-up wad of bloody toilet paper. The cramping had started a few days ago. Now the blood. I knew this routine. I was losing the baby.

My baby died. I killed it. Cambodia killed it. We had electrocuted my baby.

One morning a few months later, I snuggled with Clara in one of the large papasan chairs on the front veranda watching the sky grow from pink to blue. Grief hung between us like a mist.

"This was going to be my baby, Mommy." She looked at me with her huge, round eyes brimming with tears. "You said we would be birthday twins." She knew how special birthday twins were in the family.

Kids whose birthdays were within a few weeks of each other were called birthday twins. For their birthdays, they got to go to a special dinner with Mom and Dad to a restaurant of their choice in Phnom Penh. It created a special bond. Clara's birthday twin died two months ago.

"I know, baby girl." Stroking her blonde hair, I stared at the brightening sky.

We sat together under the blanket and watched the sun fill the sky with light. "Let's go make some breakfast, shall we?" She perked up and nodded. Jumping out of the chair, she pattered downstairs in her fleece socks. I followed her. The electrical lines sizzled behind me.

THE SAGE HOUSE

The months after the miscarriage blurred together. Clara bounced back with resilience, though I'd sometimes catch her staring at the twins or asking questions about heaven. I envied her ability to process grief so openly, while mine lingered beneath the surface, bubbling up at unexpected moments.

Cool, dry season was here, but not before we got one final, huge rainstorm. With the storm came my frustration with our living situation. The dampness seeped into my clothes, my furniture, my spirit.

I stepped through the flooded courtyard, my flip-flops submerged under an inch of murky water. "I can't do this anymore," I whispered to myself, wringing out the hem of my pants. "We deserve better than this."

That evening, after putting the children to bed, I found John in our bedroom, paging through a book while the ceiling fan whirred against the humidity.

"John," I said, sitting on the edge of the bed. "We need to talk about the house."

He looked up, noting my serious expression. "The flooding?"

"It's not just the flooding," I said, my voice rising before I caught myself. "It's everything: the mosquitoes breeding—any of which could carry dengue—the cockroaches multiplying in the wet wood, the hours I spend mopping the floor instead of being with the children."

John closed his book. "Yeah, it's been a pain."

"It's become impossible," I continued. "The twins are constantly fighting skin infections. I can't get Christina to stop sucking her fingers while she is playing in the muddy courtyard. I found mold growing in the boys' closet yesterday. We need to move before rainy season hits hard next year."

John was quiet for a moment, his eyes on the spinning fan.

"You're right," he said. "This place is too much now."

Relief washed over me. "So you agree? We'll start looking for another rental?"

"I'll ask around tomorrow." He nodded. "See what's available in our price range."

"Thank you." I squeezed his fingers. "I know moving is a hassle, but I can't keep watching our children wade through sewer water every time it rains."

"Bailing out water every monsoon has definitely gotten old," John admitted with a wry smile. "You might want to do the bulk of the research. You know what we need better than I do."

I nodded, already mentally cataloging our requirements: proper drainage, elevated foundation, no visible water damage. A fresh start.

"We'll find something better," I promised, more to myself than to him.

A few weeks later, a friend mentioned an empty lot next door to her. She had built her own house a few years before and raved about being able to design the perfect house for her family.

I mentioned this to John, and we were both intrigued. Maybe we would take the risk so that we could own a home built to our family's unique needs.

Months passed as we worked with a Cambodian real estate expert who helped us buy the piece of property in Ly's name since we could not own land in our own. We trusted Ly with our lives and our investment.

We were not sure we trusted the rest of our team. The real estate agent, the builder, and the overseer were all related. Our overseer was necessary to make sure that the builders were not skimping on the size of rebar, using less concrete and more sand, or buying cheaper materials than what we agreed in the contract. This was a recipe for corruption with the naïve foreigner in the dark.

Then there was the problem of wiring the money from America to Cambodia and trusting that it would make it into our Cambodian bank account. Banks in Cambodia were new institutions, and both Cambodians and expatriates eyed them suspiciously. It took publicity and promotion on behalf of the banks to get anyone to even trust them with a weekly paycheck, let alone the sum we needed to buy land and build our house.

Then there was the question of property deeds. Since the end of the civil war in the seventies, many Cambodian people had scrambled to return to their family land, or they squatted on land that was not theirs. All land was up for grabs. Lost titles, dead owners, and general confusion reigned.

Over the years, people wrote makeshift titles to protect their few remaining rights. Many times, over the years, someone who had more power and influence would swoop in and claim that a property was theirs, bribe a judge for a new title, and evict the long-term tenants.

This was a risk we took when we signed the documents and handed over large amounts of money. We had no guarantee that someone more powerful than us would not confiscate our property.

I lost sleep over these risks. I asked myself why we were doing this. *You need to put down long-term roots, you trust Ly, you need a home that will sustain you for the long haul, and you crave an oasis in this foreign land.*

We prayed, hovered, worried, spent money, and hoarded time to get this house built. My Khmer language abilities grew by leaps and bounds as I worked with the contractor. I learned how to discuss concrete, foundations, paint colors, rebar sizes, and plumbing. I could also discuss receipts, accounting, and holiday breaks. I traveled daily to check on the progress. Curiously, I found my job of general contractor more fitting than a missionary. Six months later, the project was complete. The final touch was a fresh coat of paint—sage green, my favorite color.

Moving day, May 1, 2007, was exciting. The children had not moved in the four years since we left America with twenty-three pieces of luggage. This time they rode in the backs of trucks over-loaded with wicker furniture; totes of schoolbooks, clothes, kitchen items, bikes, computers; and a few small boxes for Ly, Hok, and their youngest sister, Sothea.

We built them two rooms and a bathroom so they could join us at the Sage House on Street 564. Ohm and her nieces, including Maiy, had moved out months earlier to a house on Street 576. Ly and Hok were both working in Phnom Penh after graduating from college, and Sothea was finishing her bachelor's degree in math with a plan to teach high school. They were our family. We would not move without them. So, they loaded up their own belongings, excited to move to the new house with us.

The house offered what we needed: a schoolroom, open floor plan, lots of windows, five bedrooms including a guest room since we hosted dozens of guests every year, an ample kitchen, a front veranda, and to my insistence, a grassy yard with a play set, basketball hoop, and cement pad and a serenity garden in the back.

This garden boasted a koi pond with a rock fountain, bamboo hedge, and a terra-cotta patio with a thatched shade shelter. It was lovely and soothing to my soul. I spent mornings out there with my coffee, my journal, and my Bible. It was my sanctuary.

I continued to host my women's Bible study that was now four years old. My younger children were still homeschooling, but I was starting to feel isolated as a homeschooler, plus the juggling to find friend dates for my younger kids among the international school students was getting exhausting. I knew we needed a homeschool community. I guess I was the one to build it.

I started by asking other mothers if they knew any homeschoolers in North Phnom Penh. There used to be a homeschool co-op south of town, but it was starting to splinter and die off as missionaries moved back to their home countries. A few strays from that group and others hidden away in our neck of the woods heeded my call.

We called ourselves Shaping Hearts Homeschool and even made a banner with all our children's handprints covering its stark white surface. An oasis in the storm, each of us used our gifts to teach and mentor an eclectic group of students from around the world. I was the director of the group, taught English literature and grammar, and made sure there were snacks for hungry kids. We had a variety of other teachers: a medical doctor who taught science, a college professor of art who taught art history and creative design, a mother from Singapore who taught Chinese, and a professional dancer and theater owner from England who ran our theater program. We found each other, and our children found friends, cross-cultural travelers, and confidants.

The Sage House, my routine, and my new community was the answer to my increasing anxiety. Change locations, build the optimal oasis, hunker down in my perfectly created nest, create community. But I should have known. There was no place to hide. The Sage House would have its own demons.

BURNED

At first, the house felt like salvation. We settled in quickly, the children claiming their spaces with excited chatter. My anxiety eased as the rainy season came and went without a drop of water flooding our courtyard. The garden became my refuge —a place to breathe when the weight of Cambodia pressed too heavily. John was more relaxed being free from the constant battle against floodwaters and mold.

For three blissful months, I convinced myself we'd found our haven. The children thrived in their new bedrooms. The schoolroom bustled with activity each morning. Even the kitchen, with its ample counter space and reliable appliances, became a place of joy rather than frustration.

But safety is an illusion when you're raising nine children in a developing country. No matter how carefully I designed our sanctuary, I couldn't control the risks. The dangers simply changed form.

One morning in September, the boys were getting ready for school. With three starving teenage sons, I needed to make large breakfasts—pancakes, German pancakes, or crepes. And loads of them.

Our family loved maple syrup, but it was impossible to find in Cambodia, even in the Western markets. I had guests bring me over small bottles of maple syrup extract, and I would make my syrup storing it in an old plastic bottle.

On that morning in September, I noticed we were almost out of syrup. I grabbed the extract and added it to boiling water and sugar. We were all late this morning. I did not have time to cool the mixture like I normally would.

In haste, I poured the sugary mixture into the empty plastic syrup bottle and set it beside Joe, who was carefully buttering each of the little kids' pancakes. Nearby, Seth and Tim stood at the sink washing dishes, their hands disappearing into soapy water. I returned to the stove to flip the next round of cakes, falling into the comfortable rhythm of our morning routine.

A piercing cry shattered the peace.

"It's burning her!" Joe shouted.

I spun around to see the sticky, boiling liquid cascading down Olivia's little face. Her eyes widened in shock; her screams filled the kitchen.

Seth moved with startling speed, pulling Olivia to the sink and dousing her face with cold water—once, twice, three times. With trembling hands, I scooped her up and rushed to the couch. Emma's feet thundered up the stairs and back down again, cold washcloths dripping between her fingers.

Olivia's whimpers transformed into deep sobs as angry red welts rose across her skin. My stomach twisted as I watched blisters bubble up on her cheeks, her lips contorting in pain. Her eyes, wide with terror, locked onto mine. The horrible truth crashed over me—the hot syrup had severely burned my daughter's face.

The kids were rattling in the kitchen. *What just happened? Why was she burned?* From the best they could discern, the melting plastic container had slipped from Joe's hand. As the container hit the counter, the hot syrup splattered out and onto Olivia's face.

In the living room, I could hear Joe's voice cracking with guilt. Without hesitation, I said, "It's not your fault, Joe. It's mine." My words echoed through the house as I cradled Olivia. "I put boiling syrup in that container without cooling it first. *This is on me.*"

I couldn't bear the thought of my oldest son carrying this burden into adulthood—the image of his sister's burned face haunting his dreams years later. No. This weight belonged to me. In that moment, even as I tended to Olivia's wounds, my maternal instinct extended to protect Joe, too. I would shoulder this guilt. I would absorb it, draw it away from him like poison from a wound. The blame was mine to carry.

Hearing her cries and my screams, John raced downstairs. We gathered her up in our arms and out to the van to the medical clinic across town. The van got stuck in traffic and the motos were driving way too slowly.

Anxious to move faster, my legs shook. I held Olivia whimpering in my arms, falling in and out of a daze, until we arrived forty minutes later. A German dermatologist was called in to meet with us.

He looked her over. "There is nothing we can do here. But thankfully it is only first- and second-degree burns. We need to give her some painkillers and get her on the next plane to Bangkok. She needs a burn clinic." Bangkok? Not again. I felt fear rising in my chest. I scooped up Olivia in my arms while the doctor dropped some cream and painkillers in my hands.

John was on the phone with Thai Airlines. He got tickets to leave that evening. He, Olivia, and Clara, who would keep Olivia company at the hospital, would leave in a few hours, and I would stay home with the rest of the children.

It was a long week while Olivia was at the Sumitiveh Bun Hospital in Bangkok. Luckily, a teammate of ours lived near the hospital. John and the girls stayed in their apartment. I waited at home, beating myself up for not cooling the syrup and dreading the thought that my beautiful daughter would be scarred for life.

John, Olivia, and Clara returned the next week. Olivia was cheerful and her face red and splotchy. "Mommy, they wrapped me like a mummy and only my eyes were showing."

John showed me a picture he had taken with our digital camera. My heart shot out of my chest. Her face was swollen and red. I put on my best smile and hugged her.

"You make a darling mummy," I whispered in her ear. Clara talked about Bangkok and the playhouse in the children's ward of the hospital, where they had spent hours of their time. I could not take my eyes off Olivia's face.

"She needs to put this cream on three times a day. Here is an antibiotic they need her to take for another seven days." John handed me a bottle of pills and a tube of white cream. "And she needs to stay out of the sun for at least a year."

I looked up. "A year! We live in Cambodia and swim almost every day!"

"Get her a hat." John carried the bags upstairs and went to catch up on emails.

Olivia hugged me again and told me stories of what she saw in Bangkok. We sat on the couch, and I fumbled with the lid on the cream. "Can I put some of this on your face?" I smiled gently.

"Okay, Mommy, then can I get a snack?"

"Of course." With shaking hands, I rubbed the cream on her red, swollen face, hoping she did not see the tears dripping into my lap. I fumbled with the medicine bottle, overwhelmed by guilt and trying to read the doctor's instructions.

Ohm appeared at my side. She studied Olivia's damaged skin, and without a word, she gently took the tube of healing cream from my trembling hands and began applying it to Olivia's face with the practiced care of someone who knew that healing required patience, not panic.

Olivia grew still under Ohm's touch. Those weathered fingers traced the edges of burn marks with infinite tenderness. When Olivia whimpered, Ohm began humming—the same ancient lullabies that had comforted our children for years. She settled Olivia on her lap, speaking in gentle Khmer as she worked. *"Kon-sreay s'aat,"* she'd whisper, *beautiful child*, reminding me the burns changed nothing about Olivia's worth.

Months later, the swelling subsided, and Olivia's little face healed, though tiny blood-red veins still spread across her cheeks like spiderwebs.

During the day, a floppy hat and good lathering of sunscreen covered her thin and splotchy skin. At night, after her shower, I would bite open a Vitamin E capsule and massage it into her skin. She loved this routine and our special time together. I would coo over her beautiful eyes and soft skin. She giggled and gazed at me.

We had many more medical incidents in those and subsequent years: stitches to the face at least two more times, a broken foot, shards of glass embedded in feet, sea anemone spines lodged in a big toe, even an emergency appendectomy in a Khmer hospital. Each incident, each time I had to take a child to a dirty, poorly run medical clinic, the pressure in my chest increased. I didn't know what was worse, a trip to Bangkok for a major medical emergency, or to stay close to home and take my chances with a nascent medical system.

Numb, I woke every morning and went about my day. The children were oblivious to the dangers that I was consumed by. They played happily in the bubble I created for them. I strained to keep them in that bubble. If it was up to me, they would never leave it.

KUHM

J ust as Olivia was healing, another crisis emerged—one that
reminded me yet again how fragile our safety was in this beautiful, unpredictable place. While I could meticulously control
some aspects of our lives—the medical supplies we kept, vitamin
regimens, sunscreen applications—I couldn't control the weather, the
local politics, our neighbors, and certainly not our sweet, not-so-
bright dog who found her own kind of trouble.

Our dog, Daisy, was a half-shepherd, half-golden retriever mix.
She was also black as ink, which scared Cambodians, who believed
black dogs were demon dogs. At least this guaranteed we would not
get robbed again.

It was only a month after Olivia returned from her burn treatment in Bangkok when we noticed Daisy was gone. Somehow, she
had ended up outside the gate. Maybe she went out to sniff around,
and no one noticed when the gate clanged shut.

It was around dusk when I asked if anyone had seen Daisy. It was
time for her to eat, and she was nowhere to be found. We searched
the house and the courtyard, but she was gone.

Desperate, we went outside where a few unfriendly neighbors sat
—unlike our old ones. We were mutually suspicious. When we asked

about our black dog, they said they'd seen her hours ago outside the gate before she ran down the street.

I was furious! How simple would it have been to knock on our gate and tell us that she was outside? That would have been the neighborly thing to do. But they watched our dog whine and cry to come inside and did nothing. She got spooked and ran off. Now we had little time. It was getting dark.

Joe, Tim, Hok, and Ly went to look for her at the end of our dirt road. The road ended at a small path which continued down to the railroad tracks next to Boeung Kak Lake—a very dangerous place during the day, let alone at night. But that was the direction Daisy had run. We told the boys to only go as far as the end of the road and no further. Forty-five minutes passed, and it was now pitch dark.

The boys had not returned, nor had Daisy. John called their phones, and we heard all four of them ringing in the house. John called Jamie to come help. Jamie arrived armed with an asp and an attitude.

John and Jamie planned to go down to find the four boys among the dangerous, drug-infested shanties along the railroad tracks. Terrified, I could only sit and pray the Lord's Prayer while I held Seth, who could not sleep until his brothers returned.

I knew that I needed to go with them. I couldn't stay home anymore. In the car with John and Jamie, I searched the blackened night as we drove to the end of the road. Shining the car's headlights on the dirt path that snaked past the dead end and between a few stilted houses, our eyes scanned the shadows. John and Jamie got out of the car and were about to walk down that path with their asp and butcher knife when all four boys came sauntering up.

In fear and relief, John shouted angrily. They hadn't listened to instructions nor found Daisy. Sheepishly, Hok told us they had been asking the residents if they had seen a black dog. The villagers had continued to point down the railroad track, farther away from our home. He looked at his feet. Ly, Joe and Tim lingered behind him.

Hok explained that they only stopped when an older woman warned them of a spirit-possessed man a few houses down who wielded his machete at night. That was enough to turn them home.

"I told all the local kids that we would give a reward to anyone who found our black dog," he said, giving us our first ray of hope that Daisy might be found.

We went home relieved the boys were back, but the boulder in my chest grew, and I could not budge it. I wanted to roll it down a hill, let it hit a landmine, and blow it to smithereens. Obliterated. I needed my anxiety obliterated. For my sake, for the sake of my children. I was already grieving the loss of our sweet dog, whom the children loved so much. I dreaded telling the young girls in the morning that she was gone.

The next day, Hok rode his moped down to the local meat market. There at stalls where sellers hung dead dogs, skinned and strung up, for sale to eat, he searched for Daisy. He did not see Daisy's rainbow-colored collar.

Later that day, three little boys came to tell us they had seen Daisy. They saw her tied up under a house near the railroad tracks. Ly and Hok went with the kids to bring her home and give the reward. Once they arrived and offered the reward, a large man with curly black hair and gray teeth told them that the ten-dollar reward was not enough. She was being held for ransom for twenty-five dollars because, he said, that was what he could sell her for in the markets.

Hok and Ly returned to tell John that her captors would not give up Daisy. John furiously marched out the gate and down the street with Ly and Hok sheepishly in tow. Walking straight up to the stilted house, he unhooked Daisy from the chain that held her captive.

"My dog is not for ransom," he spat. He turned to Ly. "Give him the ten dollars and tell him this is a reward, not a ransom. We are going home."

Kuhm is a Khmer word for revenge. To be specific, kuhm is a long-standing grudge leading to a revenge that is more damaging than the original offense. Kuhm was common in Cambodia when someone lost face. Daisy's captor had lost face. Hok and Ly believed we were going to suffer for it, that we would be the victims of kuhm.

Their fear of kuhm spread to me. I read in the news of people having acid thrown in their faces, marring them for life, for minor offenses. I had seen those people, mostly women, with their faces melted and their bodies scarred.

Besides my fear of kuhm, I was sad for my dog. Daisy was not herself for months. She cowered when the gate opened or closed, staying close to us. She and I were both afraid. Both of our fears rational. Hers faded away as her sense of safety returned. Mine never retreated.

THE BOOKENDS

As Daisy slowly recovered from her trauma, my anxiety found a new target. While I had been obsessing over acid attacks and neighborhood revenge, time had continued its relentless march forward. The children I had been so desperate to protect were growing up. The bubble I had worked so hard to maintain was stretching, thinning, preparing to burst in ways I hadn't expected.

While I was scanning the streets for threats, calculating escape routes, and categorizing dangers, my oldest son had been quietly transforming into a young man with dreams that would take him far beyond my protective reach.

I realized that an inevitable danger wasn't lurking in the streets of Phnom Penh—it was the natural progression of life itself. My children would leave. They would step outside the boundaries I had so carefully constructed. And the first departure was coming sooner than I was prepared to face.

I watched him out of the corner of my eye. My oldest son, with his brown hair cut short, imitating the marines he grew up reading about, would be entering his senior year of high school when summer ended.

His dream was to return to America and become a marine. His path to get there was the United States Naval Academy in Annapolis,

Maryland. He was eight thousand miles from Maryland, a high schooler at a small international school in Phnom Penh, Cambodia. How would he ever get an appointment or an acceptance to the Naval Academy? He was my child. It was his dream, so I was determined to help him.

We scoured the internet for applications and requests for senator interviews. Joe spent the summer hours perfecting his USNA essay and practicing for his Blue and Gold interview. He spent the summer dreaming of America, while I spent it managing my very busy household.

$\sim$

Early one morning, I was making yet another batch of pancakes. Between bites, Stephen, now eleven, bemoaned going back to school. "Do I have to go back to school?"

I flipped the golden-colored pancake onto Christina's plate and drizzled it with powdered sugar and lemon juice. "Summer just started. Why are you worried about this already? Is there a problem?"

"Yeah, he is always getting us in trouble." Stephen took another bite.

"Who?"

"Ji-hoon. He is so hyper and talks so much. Then when I sit next to him, I get into trouble too."

I smiled at my very talkative boy. "So sit somewhere else."

"It doesn't matter. I make faces, he makes faces . . ." He got up and stood waiting for another pancake.

I ruffled his hair and leaned in. "Then don't make faces."

"You don't get it, Mom."

"I guess not. I am sure he will turn into a nice boy. Try not to be tempted next semester, okay?"

"Okay . . . Can I have two more pancakes?"

"Sure." I plopped them on his plate and turned back to drizzle more batter on the griddle. My stomach churned at the smells of frying pancakes, melted butter, and freshly brewed coffee. Normally, these were smells I loved in the early morning.

After breakfast, I sat down. My limbs were heavy, and my eyelids drooped. Blinking slowly, I asked the younger kids to bring a book to the couch. Before long, with *Little Britches* resting on my lap, I was fast asleep.

That afternoon, I moved through the house with purpose, waiting for the children's nap time, when the house would settle into rare silence. I slinked into our bathroom. Weeks earlier, I had hidden the small pink box behind shampoo bottles in the bathroom cabinet.

The instructions were unnecessary. I'd done this before, many times, yet I skimmed them anyway, a ritual that provided the illusion of control. Three minutes. The box said to wait three minutes, though I knew the result often appears sooner.

I stared at the stick, watching as the second line darkened, confirming what my body had already been telling me.

Positive.

Twelve pregnancies. The number itself felt momentous, almost biblical. At forty, I knew the statistics, the increased risks. Yet I also knew the profound joy each child had brought, how our family had expanded not just in number but in millions of incalculable ways.

John was in America celebrating his mother's seventieth birthday at the family home in Colorado. I dialed the farmhouse number I had memorized since I was twenty-one years old. Balancing the phone between my ear and shoulder, I listened to the peculiar delay that marked international calls. Expecting my call, he picked up.

"Another baby on the way," I said after a pause. My hands never stopped their rhythmic folding, creating neat little stacks of the little girls' clothes snatched off the clothesline. Through the window, I could see clouds gathering, darker patches against the deepening blue of twilight.

Eight thousand miles away, John sat in the light of a Colorado morning, surrounded by the family farm's familiar comforts.

"Really?" John's voice traveled across continents, carrying his smile with it. The background noise on his end—family laughter, the clink of dishes—briefly intensified, then faded as he moved somewhere quieter. "That's wonderful news."

I knew he would say that, but at forty my body carried different messages than it had with previous pregnancies. The miscarriages and the twins' pregnancy had made their mark. And I could tell my body was tired.

I tucked the last pair of tiny shorts into the pile, my hand lingering for a moment on the soft fabric. Outside, the first heavy drops of rain struck the tin roof.

"Anything you want me to bring you from America?" he asked.

"A lot of prenatal vitamins, the kind your mom gives to her clients. And some good dark chocolate bars?" I smiled.

"Sure. See you soon. Love you." He felt so far away. The laughter echoed through the phone as the storm grew louder outside my window. The rain drummed against the metal overhangs, making any more conversation impossible.

"Bye, love you too!" I yelled into the phone over the storm. His voice faded in the distance. I hung up and watched the dark sky swirl and roar.

Later that fall, while I spent my mornings on the couch, the kids went about their days on autopilot. We sent Joe off to America to finish the last requirements for his Naval Academy application. In two weeks, he finished his physical fitness test, his senator interviews, and all the psychological testing. Then he flew home.

Later that fall, he received an email offering him an appointment at the Naval Academy. He was on his path to become a marine. He was gaining his future. I was losing my firstborn son.

The others had their own achievements to boast of. Tim was the school Head Boy that year; Seth excelled at four sports; Stephen and Emma went to international school and were busy with the theatre, sports, and their growing circle of friends; Clara and Olivia home-schooled; and Maiy helped me with Mary and Christina, who with their excessive energy needed constant redirection and creative outlets. Ohm, slowing down, worked only part-time these days.

I found a newly opened Thai hospital in Phnom Penh where I went for my prenatal visits. At every appointment, a different Thai doctor would look at my chart and click his tongue and shake his head. "Great grand multipara." I knew what he was saying: *too old and too many children.* "You are very high risk. But you are healthy and so is the baby. Still, you better plan on a hospital birth in Thailand."

That was out of the question. A Thailand birth meant six weeks away from my family. I had many friends who had birthed their babies in Thailand, and though the hospitals were state-of-the art, the wait was long for birth certificates, passports, and visas.

But having a baby in Cambodia was also out of the question. The hospitals were primitive and emergency care for babies and mothers limited. It was risky. My heart dreamed of another home birth. Like the six I had in Colorado, I craved the comfort of my bed, a slew of midwives to attend to me, and my children all gathered around right after the birth crawling onto my bed to snuggle their new sibling.

Thailand was too far away. Cambodia did not have the infrastructure for a safe hospital birth. Maybe I could have a home birth. Maybe I could get my Colorado midwife to come to Cambodia.

It took weeks of emails back and forth, but we settled it. We were going to fly Pam to Cambodia to be my midwife. I researched where to find oxygen tanks, birth supplies, and newborn clothes in Phnom Penh. My dream of having a Cambodian home birth was coming to fruition.

But we still had a problem. My babies were always late. This baby was due end of April, and we had tickets to fly to America on June 8, to take Joe to Annapolis for Induction Day at the Naval Academy. This would be the first and last time we flew with all ten children, and nothing was going to stop that flight from happening. We had drop-dead dates. There would be no wiggle room for error. This baby must come promptly.

CROSSING THE RIVER

Almost eight months later, Pam and her husband Edward arrived on the late flight to Phnom Penh on a sweltering, dark night in April 2008. We watched them exit the terminal. Pam's eyes were red and puffy. Edward, his hand outstretched and a large duffel bag swung over his shoulder, sauntered towards us.

It was the beginning of the hot season. Khmer New Year was one week ago, and the temperatures were climbing. John grabbed Pam's bags, one full of medical supplies and the other her clothes and gifts for the kids. She staggered to the van, wiping her forehead with her sleeve, and commented on the heat index at midnight.

We drove home talking about their flights and news from home. Pam glanced out the window periodically, her eyes darting, taking in the poverty, filth, and disorganization.

I pointed out the Thai hospital where I had my prenatal visits. She winced at the simple emergency room she could see through the glass windows. I breathed deeply, trying not to get panicky about her discomfort with the best medical facilities Phnom Penh could offer. Like the Cambodians deep in the villages, I also mistrusted modern medical establishments, preferring holistic care in the intimacy of home, with my *chhmop*, or midwife, to attend me.

She turned, smiling, and placed her hand on my round belly.

"Does the baby feel okay? Lots of movement?" Her thumb caressed the top of my uterus.

"Oh yes. Baby is doing well. Very active!" I tried to stay positive, but her discomfort caused me to catch my breath. "I also am very active. Trying to walk, even in the heat. And I can continue to home-school even though I sleep through most of it. Packing is very consuming right now. I need to organize the house and pack our bags for America before the baby arrives.

"And Joe needs to get all his belongings packed up. He can't leave anything here. I don't know what we would do with it if we had to leave Cambodia in an emergency. So, along with finals and graduation, he is sorting all his belongings." I bit my lip to keep from rambling nervously. She smiled and turned back to the darkened streets.

Once back at the Sage House, Pam and Edward got settled in their room, unpacked, and came upstairs to find us. Pam surveyed our bedroom, the place of the birth, and set down her medical bag on the bed. "Let's check that baby now, before we head to sleep, shall we?"

I nodded and lay on the pillow while she laid her doppler, stethoscope, and blood pressure cuff on the bed. She checked all my vitals, felt the height for the fundus, found the baby's heartbeat, and declared both of us in good shape.

"Now all we need to do is wait. Due date is in two days, right?"

I nodded again and reminded her I had late births. She packed her bag back up and gave my belly one last affectionate pat. "Yes, hopefully this baby is not too late."

John looked out the window. "We won't be able to get to the hospital in Thailand at this point unless we go overland. That will take two days. This baby needs to come in a reasonable time." We nodded at the gravity and headed to bed.

The days passed with packing and late-night conversations with Pam and Edward. The older kids continued with their studies at school, and the younger kids did the bare minimum of schoolwork at home— math, reading, and some writing.

I spent the days on the couch trying to stay cool or grabbing an early morning walk before the sun baked the city.

The due date came and went. John, Joe, and Edward took a motorcycle trip to Siem Reap for Joe's graduation present. They arrived back home dirty, exhausted, and exhilarated after 397 miles on Cambodia's lawless highways. The days passed slowly. Edward had to call the airlines to extend their flights. This baby was not going to come soon. Another week crept by. My baby was now two weeks overdue.

Pam started interventions with herbs, exercises, and positioning. Labor did not come. My Korean friend Eunice called in a Korean acupuncturist to help me get labor started. Late one afternoon, he shuffled in. His kind eyes reassured me. He shifted his Korean hanbok to find his small, tidy bag of acupuncture needles. I lay on the couch while he sat at my feet. His gentle hands were cool on my swollen ankles.

He mumbled under his breath and spoke to my friend. He looked concerned. My heart raced as I looked at Eunice. "What? What is he saying?"

She glanced at me. "He says that you have no energy to give birth. The body is tired."

"Well, isn't that why he is here? Tell him to use his needles and bring back my energy."

She translated, and he nodded, telling her he would try. He opened his worn leather bag full of long, thin needles. I lay still while he placed the needles: one for each foot, one under the ankle bone, and one near the big toe, and on each of my hands, in the fleshy part between my thumb and forefinger and on my forearm.

The needles waved and vibrated in my skin as I sat as still as possible. Time crawled as I watched him fuss and fiddle with the needles, then leave them to wave and vibrate. Occasionally, he would check my pulse on my ankle or wrist and cluck to himself. Longer and longer, I stayed there watching the needles dance.

When they had finished their rocking, he took them off, one by one. He checked the pulse again and shook his head. One side was better and stronger; the other was not. Still not enough strength to give birth. I sat up without using my arms, something I was proud of doing with all my pregnancies, to show him I was indeed strong.

Could he come back? He shook his head as if to say it would not do any good. I pivoted to look at Pam, my eyes searching hers. What other options did we have? If this baby did not come soon, we would need to seek help here in Cambodia. Not Thailand, Korea, or America. Our choices were slim and the medical establishments lacking. At least the baby was still strong inside.

Another few days passed, and we were edging toward three weeks late. Pam was getting nervous and checking on the baby and me multiple times during the day. We were doing all the tricks in her midwife book, and still no labor.

The Korean acupuncturist's words kept ringing in my ears. *The body is not strong enough to give birth.*

We went to the Thai hospital across town for an ultrasound to check fluids and talk to the doctors there. The hospital was empty and stark. We got in quickly, and the ultrasound showed a healthy baby with plenty of fluids, but they were concerned.

"We need to do a C-section immediately. You are too late and too high risk," said a young Thai doctor who looked like he was fresh out of medical school.

"Can we try to induce first?" I asked.

"No, C-section is our only recommendation."

"I want to try induction first," I stubbornly insisted as I walked out the door with Pam and John in tow. "We will try somewhere else."

We drove to Calumet, the Cambodian hospital where Khmer mothers give birth. Driving up to the front gave me chills. Mothers many months pregnant sat outside on dirty mats with their sleeping toddlers resting on their knees.

Filth and disrepair stretched from the parking lot to the reception desk. I could not imagine what lay beyond. The hospital staff said they could take us right away and give me Pitocin for the birth, but I could not take one step further.

"Not here." I turned on my heels and walked out.

We drove a few miles farther, remembering another pregnancy clinic we had heard about. Nothing materialized. The baby moved and rolled in my womb, ready to be born. But my body did not have the strength.

I felt helpless as I sat in the car and watched street after street pass by. My hand protectively shielded the baby from the potholes and ruts in the road that caused our car to careen.

I went home dejected and fearful. John and Pam talked in low tones in the hallway, glancing my way as I lay on the bed staring out my window at our bamboo trees swaying in the afternoon breeze. I knew we could not wait any longer. This baby was going to have to be born in a Cambodian hospital. I was terrified.

I remembered my first language tutor teaching me the Khmer phrase meaning "to give birth." In Khmer, it means "to cross the river." I had asked her what the connection was. She answered nonchalantly, "Most Cambodians cannot swim, so to cross the river is to risk death. Isn't that the same for people in your country? To give birth is to risk death?"

"No," I had replied curtly. But now, I was not so sure. Now I could feel that, just possibly, this river current might take me under.

THE IRON BEDSTEAD

I t was hours later that I came out of my stupor. The sun was
setting as I sat watching the waving bamboo from my bedroom
porch. I was going to have to do something I was not ready
to do.

I was going to have to put my life and the life of my baby in the
hands of the Cambodians. I did not realize until that moment how
deep my fear of releasing myself to Cambodia was. The thought sent
cold ripples down my spine, my palms growing slick with sweat
against the worn fabric of my dress. My heart pounded in my ears,
drowning out the cacophony of street vendors and motorbikes
beyond my bedroom's thin walls.

I crept downstairs, following the noises of happy dinner conversation. Walking into the room, everyone stopped talking. Their eyes
bored into me.

"Tomorrow morning, we are calling Doctor Ly Srey Vena. She will
know what to do." I sat down, grabbed a plate, loaded it with rice and
red chicken curry, and chatted with the kids about their school day.
Pam looked at me with surprise and pleasure. "After you eat, let's get
some vitals to give to Doctor Ly in the morning."

. . .

The phone rang and went to voicemail three times before Dr. Ly picked up. "*Chmumreapsua,* hello. Dr. Ly's office." Her voice was soothing.

"Dr. Ly, this is Sheryl Roberts. We came to your office in the past when my husband, John, had typhoid. I have a problem." I glanced out the window at the twins swinging on the swing set, their feet kicking in the air, their laughter pouring through the windows. "I am almost three weeks overdue with my tenth child, and I was planning a home birth. I won't go into labor. I want to try induction before a C-section."

"Yes, hi, Sheryl! Of course, why don't you come to my clinic this afternoon, and I will take a look. I will call my colleague, she is one of the best OBs in Cambodia, to meet us there."

"Okay, can my midwife come too? She has been here supporting me for three weeks."

"Of course. See you at three." I packed my bag in case I would have the baby that afternoon. Then, as if in a dream, I slung the bags over my shoulder and made my way to the car.

We backed out of the driveway in the van while the children looked at me from behind the gate, their faces pressed to the bars, concerned and forlorn. With light traffic, we made it to Ly Srey Vena's clinic before three.

I had been to her office before, a nondescript *pteya-la-veng* suitable for simple family doctor visits. The acrid smell of disinfectant mingled with the heavy, sweet scent of incense burning in a small shrine in the corner. One water jug rested on an old cooler opposite the reception desk. Austere carved furniture graced the small front room. The feeble ceiling fan pushed around the same stale air.

I could taste the metallic edge of fear on my tongue as I placed a protective hand over my swollen belly, feeling my baby shift beneath my touch. Dr. Ly met us, and after we checked in, she brought me up two flights to a simple exam room.

The room's bleak yellow walls framed a metal bed only six feet long and two feet wide, with a thin plastic mattress, and across from it, was a small, dirty chair. A small, tired orderly wheeled in a tiny bamboo bassinet and placed it under the windows facing a dilapidated building. Iron grates crisscrossed the window, casting prison bar shadows across the tiled floor.

The place was a far cry from the hospitals where I birthed my first two babies. Those were modern, American hospitals with toilet paper and feminine hygiene products for mother and baby after the birth. Meals were available whenever you needed them, and nurses checked on you hourly.

It was an even farther cry from my home births, with my warm bed, chicken soup boiling on the stove, midwives gentle and attentive, hovering like mother hens. This was cold, bare, minimalistic. No food, no baby diapers, no sheets for the bed or crib, no toilet paper, no warmth.

A doctor watched me from the doorway. The Khmer OB scanned the room as Dr. Ly filled her in on our situation. She did not smile or lay gentle hands on my belly. She turned and told the nurses to get an IV in my arm to start Pitocin. Then she sat in the adjoining room next door, which felt like miles away.

The Khmer nurses poked my arm while Pam made up the iron bedstead with the sheets brought from home. This bed gave me shivers.

It reminded me of a scene from the movie *The Killing Fields*. In the scene, the reporters walk into an evacuated Khmer hospital. Blood covered the tile floors, and filthy sheets drip from iron bedsteads standing cockeyed against the walls.

More recently, I remembered another iron bedstead in an AIDS hospital that held a dying Khmer soldier. I also remembered the room at Tuol Sleng S-21, the high school-turned-prison and torture facility during the years of the Khmer Rouge I visited once. The putrid smells and dried blood splattered in grotesque constellations about a room that smelled of rotten flesh. Tuol Sleng S-21 held another rusted iron bedstead with heavy torture devices and metal shackles attached to the legs.

I stared at my iron bedstead. This was supposed to be the bed of life, and it felt and looked like a bed of death.

Even my sheets draped over the thin mattress could not cover its iron jaws. I would labor in the chair across from the bed with my IV pole stationed next to me. Pitocin dripped into the saline and then into my arm as I stared at the bed.

The dirty yellow wall behind the bed was bare. No pictures adorned this room, only pale-yellow curtains drooped along the windows like faded plumeria petals, their once-vibrant color muted by dust and neglect. Sunlight filtered through the grime, casting a soft, diffused glow that barely illuminated the room, leaving shadows to lurk in the corners. The tiles were chipped; the grout was black with dirt. Black and dark as my mood. Chipped as my confidence.

Faded as my hope.

MALACHI'S BIRTH

T he sun was setting, and between the iron bars outside the window, I could see the rose-colored sky blink between the dingy windows of the adjacent building. Labor was not progressing. Everyone waited: John, Dr. Ly, Pam, and the OB, who sat next door and smoked cigarettes. The baby kicked and stretched. And I sat staring.

It was an hour later when the OB came in with Dr. Ly and said we'd need to discuss a C-section. John and I walked the dark halls outside my room in privacy. We were the only patients in this small clinic.

A door would creak open downstairs now and then as the clinic received a delivery, but mostly, the staff slept on cots behind the reception desk. We walked, talked, and decided to give the labor one more hour before attempting a C-section.

This was the outcome I'd dreaded and feared: major surgery in Cambodia with Khmer doctors in a clinic on the side of the road. The OB would not perform the surgery; another OB would need to be called in. We needed to call him soon before he went home, had dinner, and started drinking his evening portion of alcohol. The OB came in for one more check and found that the fetal heart tones were not consistent. I moved positions and nothing changed.

With her stethoscope draped around her neck, she looked at me seriously. "We tried. Baby might be in distress. You need a C-section. I am calling the team in." The sun sank quickly, and both the OB and Dr. Ly were on their phones calling in a team from all over Phnom Penh.

Dr. Ly sat beside me between phone calls. "Don't worry," she told me. "I know the best Khmer doctors for C-sections. You can trust them."

Trust them! I shuttered watching my OB take another puff of her cigarette and dial another number. A nurse, his hair ruffled from a nap behind the reception desk, walked into the room across from mine, a faded sign read SURGERY above the door.

The lights flickered in the cavernous room, and I knew this was where my baby would be born—not on the iron bedstead, not on my comfortable bed at home with the sheets of roses and thorns.

I could see flickering fluorescent lights and hear aluminum tables being dragged around the room. More contractions and more breathing.

Khmer, spoken too fast for me to understand, and a series of foot-steps sounded down the hall. No one stepped into the room to intro-duce themselves to me. No one shook John's hand to let them know they would be the skilled doctor who would cut me open.

Voices, footsteps, and the opening and closing of the surgery doors.

I looked at Pam. She must have seen the fear in my eyes and grabbed my head in her hands.

"Let's pray." She held me while I fought through another contraction.

"Our Father who art in heaven . . ." *Yes, a comforting prayer from my childhood.* "Hollowed be thy name. Thy Kingdom come . . ." *Yes, please, bring your kingdom to this Kingdom of Cambodia and to this small, pale-yellow room.* "Thy will be done . . ." *Your will, Lord . . . is this? Do I have to believe that? I will accept all. But this is scary.* "On earth as it is in heaven. Give us this day our daily bread . . ." *And today, Lord, can I have a healthy baby?* "And forgive us our trespasses . . ." *All the criticism and doubt and prejudice I have against Cambodians. Forgive me.* "As we forgive those who trespass against us." *Have I made amends, harmed anyone with my prejudice?* "And lead us not into temptation." *To run, scream, hide . . .* "But deliver us from evil . . ." *The iron bedstead.* "Amen." *Thy will be done. Amen.* I looked up, and Pam was smiling and looking at me.

She held my shaking hands. "I will be right here. I am not going anywhere. You can count on me."

I stood, walked to the metal gurney, and climbed on. John was there. He kissed me. "They won't let me in the surgery room. I will be out here waiting. It's you and the staff. You've got this."

A young male nurse wheeled me out of my room with the yellow-pale walls. He didn't look older than fifteen but had gentle eyes. He touched my arm and said in Khmer, "*Yueng nung tai neak laor.*" (We will take good care of you.) I wanted to believe him.

They wheeled me through the surgery doors and into a yellow room. An aluminum table. The door clanged behind us.

The nurses hoisted me up onto the surgery table and turned me on my side. A kind older man, who had probably lived through the atrocities of the Khmer Rouge, introduced himself in Khmer as the anesthesiologist.

He looked more like a kind grandfather than a doctor. I watched his hands—steady, nimble fingers that had helped deliver countless children—and felt shame wash over me. It was my prejudice deep and unexamined that had taken root long before I'd ever set foot in this country. Now it confronted me with uncomfortable clarity in this moment of vulnerability.

He explained the epidural and gently placed the large needle in my back. The lower half of my body went numb. The nurse hung a sheet between me and my belly. I could see nothing except the white sheet billowing eighteen inches away.

The anesthesiologist placed a warm blanket on my chest and tucked my arms inside gently. I heard the door open and close as the surgeon and his assistant came into the room. I never saw their faces. I heard their deep, guttural voices discussing where to cut and how deep.

I shook from the epidural. My blood felt like ice. The anesthesiologist mumbled something in Khmer and went behind the bed. I heard some water running. He came back with two plastic water bottles that he'd filled from the sink and handed them to me.

"To keep you from shaking," he said as he tucked them under my blanket. The warm bottles, the blanket, and the gentle way of the anesthesiologist calmed me. It did not feel like long before I heard a cry.

The anesthesiologist smiled. "Baby is born." *Baby is born!* I turned my head to see if anyone was there to celebrate with me. The staff became busy monitoring medications and fussing with the baby.

"Is the baby healthy?" My croaking cry surprised me.

"Oh yes, healthy," the nurse said as he handed the doctors some gauze on the other side of the sheet.

"Is the baby . . . a boy?" I asked.

"Yes, a baby boy."

A healthy baby boy. I turned my head again to see who was there. But there was no one. The door shut, and Khmer voices and my baby's cries faded into the distance. I felt the pressure of suturing. But my arms were empty.

The soft voices of the surgeons, the beeping of the machine monitoring my vital signs, the clicking of the air-conditioning unit on the wall stopped dead at my ears. All I heard was silence.

I was isolated, alone, numb.

My family, husband, newborn baby, and midwife were two doors away celebrating this new life. I was alone behind a billowing white curtain with empty arms and my shame.

BLACKOUT

Over an hour later, they grabbed the sheet underneath me and hoisted me onto the gurney. Then they wheeled me into my recovery room. My eyes searched for my baby; my body ached to hold him.

Everyone was there: John, Pam, and Malachi Peter. The nurses tenderly wrapped him in a yellow blanket I had brought from home. John turned and held him out to me.

He was beautiful! Full of life, vigor, and strength. He looked at me and then back at John. Their eyes held, locked in a knowing embrace. He did not cry; he looked and listened as John talked to him quietly.

"They've been like this for an hour," Pam whispered to me. "He was squalling when they brought him in, but as soon as he heard his dad's voice . . . well, he settled. He's so content." She patted me on the leg.

I reached for him, but they would not let me hold him. I saw round eyes, chubby cheeks, and blond, wispy hair. I gawked at my youngest son, the child of my old age, and the last baby my womb would hold. They pulled the gurney up to the iron bedstead and grabbed the sheet again, hoisting me onto the iron bed. I watched as my long legs bounced off the end of the iron bed frame.

The nurse apologized and tucked my long legs sideways and then adjusted my IV and placed pillows behind my back. I reached again for Malachi.

John handed him to me. I placed him at my breast, and he nursed. I caressed his fingers. He looked at me with his blue eyes. It was love at first sight. He stayed with me on the iron bedstead until I was too tired to hold him any longer. Then they placed him gently in the bamboo bassinet while I drifted off. Sleep swallowed me.

Like most developing world medical clinics, families take care of all the patient's needs. Food, water, sheets, and toiletries are the responsibility of the family. But John, Pam, and the kids needed to return home. They left behind a small box of diapers, menstrual pads, clean towels, and Emma.

Emma, ten years old, stayed behind to be my helper. She made herself a bed with a reed mat, blanket, and pillow on the tile floor under the bamboo bassinet. She handed Malachi to me when he needed to nurse. She helped me get off the iron bedstead without damaging my stitches. She walked me to the bathroom and back.

When the wheel on the IV pole would often fall off and roll across the room, Emma would retrieve it and place it back on the pole. She took many trips down two flights of stairs to refill my water bottle or call the nurse who napped behind the reception table.

Late that night after the birth, I awoke with a start. It was too quiet. The fan, air conditioner, and humming lights in the hallway were deadly silent. The clinic had lost electricity—another city-wide blackout.

The darkness pressed against me, suffocating in the Cambodian night. My heart pounded as I fumbled for my phone on the bedside table, knocking over a water bottle in my haste.

"Mom?" Emma's voice came small and uncertain from across the room.

"I'm here, love," I whispered, finding my Nokia and activating the flashlight. The beam cut through the darkness, illuminating Emma's worried face as she crawled toward me.

"It's so dark," she murmured, sliding under the thin sheet beside me.

Together, we directed the phone's light toward the bamboo bassinet in the corner. Malachi's tiny form lay peaceful and undisturbed, his chest rising and falling in the rhythmic pattern of newborn sleep.

"He's okay," Emma sighed, relief evident in her voice.

I stroked her hair, trying to hide my own anxiety. "He's perfect."

We sat in silence, the heat building minute by minute without the air-conditioning or a fan. Sweat beaded on my forehead and trickled down my back. The surgical incision across my abdomen began to throb as my hospital gown stuck to my skin.

"How long will it be off?" Emma asked, wiping her forehead with the edge of the sheet.

"I don't know, honey. Could be minutes, could be hours."

The room grew more stifling with each passing moment. I found myself counting Malachi's breaths, worrying about the heat's effect on his tiny body. Twenty minutes later, the lights flickered, and the blessed hum of electricity returned. The air conditioner sputtered to life, pushing cool air into our sweltering room.

"Thank God," I whispered, sinking back against the pillows.

A nurse appeared in the doorway, looking slightly disheveled. "*Neak Srey sok sbey te?*" (Are you okay?)

"*Sok Sbey* (We're fine)," I assured him.

He nodded, checking Malachi briefly before turning to leave.

"Good thing this didn't happen during your C-section earlier," Emma whispered.

The thought sent a chill through me. "Yes," I agreed quietly. "Very good thing."

I lay awake, listening to the precious sounds of electricity—the whir of the fan and the cycling of the air conditioner. In Cambodia, even the most basic comforts couldn't be taken for granted. I gazed at my newborn son and my daughter curled beside me and wondered what other challenges this country would throw at us before we were through.

In the morning, John and the kids brought me a meal from a food cart outside the clinic. Emma ran down two flights of stairs to fill my water bottle in the reception room from the old cooler. I ate, drank, and slept while the loving siblings passed Malachi around. When they all left, I placed him in the bamboo bassinet to sleep.

After two days, we checked out. But not before a nurse came upstairs with one last dose of medication. She leaned over to inject a very large vial of bright orange liquid into my arm. I tried to hold her back and asked what she was trying to give me.

She tilted her head and answered in Khmer, *"Twer sokapheap la-or!* Going to give you good health." Then she injected me. I do not know what was in that vile, but I recovered quickly and had very little pain, so maybe it was some kind of magic Khmer serum.

We left early and went home. I slept in my own bed with Malachi next to me in his bassinet. It was time to turn my attention to leaving Cambodia for seven months, something that was going to be difficult to pull off with a newborn, a healing C-section, and nine other children.

On June 8, one month and two days after Malachi's birth, twelve of us lined up to board our flight to America. It was the last time John and I would live in Cambodia with all ten of our children. We would start leaving some behind. And no more babies would come. My tired womb had done her work. Our family was complete in that one last moment on the hot, sticky Cambodian tarmac.

By the end of July, almost two months after we arrived back in America, ten-week-old Malachi Peter had traveled through three countries and fifteen states. After arriving in America, the twelve of us packed into a twelve-passenger van for a road trip to Annapolis, Maryland, to drop Joe off for Induction Day at the United States Naval Academy.

The trip was pleasant and uneventful, except for traveling with nine children and a newborn. But we stayed with family and friends, visited Washington, DC, and cried as we hugged Joe on Stribling Walk, the last time we would see him for months.

We stayed in America for seven months, from June 2008 to January 2009, moving between my parents' lake house and John's mom's house. The older boys attended a local public school while I continued to homeschool the younger children. John worked for his brother-in-law, drumming up contracts for his landscaping business. The youngest children experienced snow for the first time, watched fall colors, and celebrated a magical Christmas with the extended family.

It was like a storybook. The familiar scents of home-cooked meals and freshly baked cookies filled the air, mingling with the crisp autumn breezes and the unmistakable aroma of pine trees decorated for Christmas. The sound of joyful chatter and children's laughter, footsteps crunching on leaves and snow, the lawn sugared with ice, and the distant hum of Mark's guitar in the family room filled us with joy.

Joe returned for Thanksgiving and Christmas. We said our last goodbye a week after New Year's Day when we boarded the plane to Asia once again. This time, my oldest son waved us off from the bottom of the escalator. I turned and buried my face into Malachi's fluffy blue coat, kissed my youngest son, and wished well to my oldest. This was the beginning of the send-offs. Eventually, they would all leave, one by one. Each exit as painful as the first.

Upon our return to Cambodia in January, there was a noticeable difference. As we stepped into the Sage House after seven long months in America, I immediately caught the familiar scent of dust and mildew, mixed with the aromatic smells of lemongrass and fish sauce.

I took a deep breath and felt a sense of contentment wash over me; this was my home. This was where my children were growing up, where I had given birth to my youngest child, where I had loved and lost my unborn babies. Here were the people who had become our friends, who had cared for us during times of need and witnessed the birth of my baby. In this land, I had experienced both loss and new life. My heart was deeply rooted here. Cambodia was mine.

THE SALE

C hannel Nine TV station compromised the Sage House. Channel Nine was there long before we were, but we never foresaw its intrusion. Its tall broadcast tower loomed over our home, flaunting its dominion and wealth. Every weekend, they charged up their massive generator, which spewed black exhaust into our kitchen windows and serenity garden.

They spent hours in their makeshift and not soundproof music studio, whose wall we shared, and blasted live Khmer comedy shows, open microphone karaoke, pop musicians, and the lengthy, screeching tuning of instruments and checking of microphones. The noise reached a decibel level so high that we couldn't hear each other talk.

We tried to talk to the managers. We pleaded with the owners. But instead of compromise, they threatened Ly, who delivered our petition. "If your American family doesn't stop bothering us, you better watch your back," snarled the manager behind his teak desk, reassured by the Khmer notion of kuhm.

He would be justified. In his eyes, we were trying to harm his business. Kuhm was not something we wanted to mess with. We stopped fighting. Our weekends, usually times of rest and peace, became full of horrendous, peace-stealing noise and smoke.

Cambodians, however, believed that there were different ghosts that moved about our house. One afternoon, years earlier, when we were building the Sage House, I had gone over to check on the work. I noticed drawings of Jesus and crosses covering the walls. I asked the supervisor, who was a Christian, what that was about.

He looked up at the Channel Nine tower rising one hundred and fifty feet in the air and the four-story office building with a flat roof next to it.

"They pushed her off." His eyes scanned the railing on the flat roof. "Duct-taped her hands and feet. And pushed her off." Darkness flickered in his eyes, and he looked down.

"What? Who?" I stepped back.

"Their enemies. They have many. Probably an employee. They pushed the TV station owner's wife off the roof." He cringed and then looked at the construction workers lounging in the shade on their platforms built to house them during the build. He motioned in their direction. "They are terrified of her ghost haunting this house. Your house was the last thing she would have seen. They wouldn't work unless I did something. So, we painted the crosses."

I looked again at the crude drawings sketched with charcoal from their cooking fires on the bare concrete walls. Ghosts, superstitions. We hadn't even moved in yet, and this was an inauspicious start. I shuttered when I left, trying not to look up at the flat roof that loomed ominously over our Sage House.

Four and a half years later, my discontent only grew. I could not stand the specter of Channel Nine anymore. I was convinced we were going to get lung cancer from the exhaust, or brain cancer from the radio waves zinging above our heads, or a nervous breakdown from the lack of peace. I was done. Plus, we had the ever-present threat of kuhm lingering.

It was December 2011 when my mother and father came to visit as they did every year around the holidays. I was telling my mom all the challenges of the Sage House, and why I felt like I needed to leave. We would have to sell the house, and that felt daunting.

Years earlier, my father had made friends with a French national, Claude, who lived across the street from us when we lived at the

House on 576. He and my father were both ham radio enthusiasts, and my father often liked to visit Claude. Claude, in return, loved to show off his ham radio shack, antennas, and newest gadgets. One evening in December 2011, my father asked if we could drive over to Claude's house on Street 576 and see if he was home for a visit.

I consented, and we took off in the early evening while the kids were working on homework and Maiy was cooking dinner. My mom was resting in the serenity garden's shade, listening to the water fountain flowing down the rocks along the back wall.

We arrived at Claude's house and knocked. He wasn't home, but I turned to gaze at our house with the yellow wall and green gate. Something caught my eye. I jumped out of the car to read the sign posted in Khmer. *For Rent.* I could not believe it. I wanted my old house back, flooding and all, if I could only escape the menace of Channel Nine at the Sage House.

When I got back to Sage House, I had Ly call the number. I stood beside him, rocking and wringing my hands. "What are they saying? Will they accept our rent price? When can we move in?"

Ly motioned to me with his free hand. "House is available . . . yes. They will take our rent offer . . . House is empty can move anytime ."

"What about the flooding? The sewers? The cockroaches?" I didn't know how to go on. Did I care? I needed out. Luckily, Ly translated for me that the flooding had stopped after they had cleaned out the sewer system and raised the level of the yard.

It was done. We signed a lease within a week. We were moving two weeks before Christmas, back to the House on 576.

But we needed to sell the Sage House. We found a realtor who quickly found us a buyer, a wealthy Khmer couple with two young kids. They met us at our home to look around and negotiate a price. Soon we agreed on a price and signed a contract. They said they would return within the week with the earnest money.

The next week they arrived in a black car with tinted windows and a driver, more like a guard, with a gun. The wife, Vanna, walked in with her hands bedecked with rings, immaculate fingernails, and a Gucci purse, which she hugged to her side.

"*Jumreapsua*" I said, bowing, never taking my eyes from her purse.

Was there a check in there? A bank note? There were no title companies here checking titles or holding money. This was all done between parties. In this situation, they were the powerful, and we were not.

Vanna sat down while her husband, Heng, leaned against our couch.

"We have the money. Do you want to count it?" he asked in Khmer, looking at his nails while Vanna fumbled with her purse. The guard at the door kept his hand on his side.

"Umm . . ." John and I looked at each other. "Here?"

"Sure." Vanna reached into her purse and withdrew a bundle of hundred-dollar bills. Six hundred of them, in fact. Sixty thousand dollars in cash. I watched her fan the bills, the guard watching our every move, and John swallowed behind me.

John moved slowly, looking at the guard. "I don't want to take this to the bank . . . alone." He glanced at Ly, whose eyes widened in perfect circles. "Can you drive over there with us and walk the money to the teller while she counts it and places it in our account?"

Heng looked at Vanna, and they nodded. He motioned to the guard while Vanna placed the stacks of bills back in her Gucci purse. We followed them to the bank in our van and entered with a guard close at our heels. Vanna handed me the money, which I handed to the teller, along with our bank card. The teller ran it through the counting machine two or three times. Then deposited it. Relief.

But it was not over. Weeks later, we walked into Vanna's and Heng's bank with the property deed in our hands. This was the authentic and only document of the home's ownership. We would hand it over to them once the rest of the money, numbering in the hundreds of thousands, had exchanged hands.

We all sat in a room with a banker. The dark mahogany table separated us in our own enclaves in giant leather chairs. The austerity was daunting, especially for Ly, as owner of the property, who was a village boy from the province. Vanna and Heng sauntered in, Vanna with her Gucci purse and bright-pink fingernails, and Heng in his dark suit and leather shoes. Their guard lingered behind.

"Well . . ." Heng began looking at the manila folder I held in my hands containing the only copy of the property deed, now with Heng's and Vanna's names instead of Ly's. "Shall we start?" He grabbed a seat and motioned for Vanna to sit next to him. "We have the money in the bank and can wire it to your bank. Then, before we leave here today, you can give us the property deed." He eyed the deed in my lap.

John sat back, motioning to the deed. "Yes, we have the deed, but the wire transfer won't be complete for a few more days. We won't hand over the deed until we can see the money in our account."

Heng also leaned back, as if to match John's energy. "We won't leave here without the deed. Either you trust us"—he looked at Vanna—"or we find some other way."

John placed his hand on the table. "No confirmation of funds, no deed."

"Then we will give you cash, and you can walk it down to your bank. It's only a few blocks away." Heng exhaled. His nostrils flared.

I looked out the window at the busy streets. Who in their right mind would walk down the street with $300,000 of cash in their pockets? Cambodians made an average of $150 a year. That sounded like a death wish.

Heng gestured below the second-story window, his words clipped and measured. "Then hire the guard outside. He has a gun." I thought of the slumped teenager at the front of the bank, his AK-47 resting against his bony shoulder.

John was already one step ahead. "No, we are not walking cash down the street." Silence ensued. The banker coughed. Ly shifted in his seat, clearly uncomfortable as John matched his energy with the rich and powerful.

Vanna looked at the folder in my lap. She tapped her long finger-nails on the table in front of me. "Can I see the deed, please?" I held on to it and shifted in my seat. What if they got up and left with their deed, their $300,000, and their guard with a gun? There would be nothing we could do. There would be no recourse for us. I looked at John. He nodded.

I slipped Vanna the deed as she checked that all the details were correct: address, their names, dates, new deed and not a forged one.

All checked out. She slid the deed back to me, and with a sigh of relief, I stuffed it back in the folder and placed it in my lap.

John and Heng stared at each other, and the banker cleared his throat. "I have an idea. You, Mr. Roberts, can open a bank account here at our bank, and we can do a direct transfer right now. You will see that your money is there within minutes."

"That's a great idea!" I said.

The banker continued, "All I need is confirmation of employment, your passport, and a few other documents. And the final authorization might not happen until Monday." *It's Friday*, I thought, *and we don't have any of those documents with us.*

"Not going to work," John said, though I could see his wheels turning. "But we can open an account for Ly, and you can transfer the money into that account. Then he can transfer it to our account by wire transfer next week."

Everyone agreed that this would work. Since Ly was a Khmer national, he could open an account immediately. The relief was audible, and it took another hour for the account to be set up, the money transferred, and the deed handed over.

I was shaking when we got into the car. "That was crazy!"

John laughed. "Now you know what a drug deal feels like."

"I never want to do that again. That took ten years off my life. Let's get home and get packing."

DIRECTOR OF INVESTIGATIONS

eace settled over the House on 576 once we got rehomed in December 2011. I loved being back in our first home. The landlord had upgraded the property. We now had air conditioners in the Great Room and each bedroom, wood-lined closets, and a tiled courtyard raised above the level of the road to prevent flooding. We laughed seeing a mango seed one of our kids had thrown into the garden bed years earlier now grown into a mature tree shading the whole south side of the house.

I was content but I noticed John was not.

I found him late at night in the garden. Moonlight spilled across the terra-cotta tiles and reflected in the still surface of a small pond. He sat on a bench near the water, his silhouette hunched and thoughtful.

I was content with our work, finding purpose in the small victories, the incremental changes we made in people's lives. But I had watched John's restlessness grow.

"Can't sleep?" I asked, settling beside him.

He shook his head. "Too much on my mind."

The crickets filled our silence.

"I came here to fix things," John said, his voice low. "Nine years ago, I was so certain of myself. America felt too small, too comfortable. I wanted to pour myself into something meaningful."

"And you have," I offered.

John looked at me. "Have I? Or have I been skimming the surface? Playing white savior without addressing the deeper issues?"

I didn't answer immediately. The accusation—self-directed though it was—stung. I had asked myself the same question on darker days.

"We've tried to be partners, not saviors," I said carefully. "To work alongside, not above."

"But that's the problem," John sighed. "We still frame mission through our lens, our perspective. The Ponlou Home failure taught me that. Cambodia doesn't need more well-intentioned foreigners dispensing mercy," he continued. "The vulnerable here need justice—structural change, systems that work for them rather than against them."

"Is that why you've been spending more time with Justice Mission?" I asked.

He nodded, running a hand through his hair. "They understand the difference between helping and partnering. They're supporting local leadership, building Cambodian solutions for Cambodian problems." Remembering Matt's and Jean's violation of the UN Convention on the Rights of the Child, he continued, "And they follow the international human rights norms."

"What does that mean for you?" I asked, though I suspected I already knew the answer.

"I don't know yet," he said, but his tone suggested otherwise.

Three weeks later, I wasn't surprised when he told me that the lead investigator's position with Justice Mission had opened up. His eyes had regained their focus.

"They want someone who understands both worlds," he explained over coffee. "Someone who can bridge gaps."

"And that's you?"

"I've learned enough from my mistakes to try. I'm not the naïve missionary who left America years ago. I have nine years of understanding Khmer culture, getting fluent in the language, plus my thirteen years of police work. Undercover investigative experience will certainly help me in this new job. Plus, I am done with being a professional Christian. They will pay me for actual work."

~

I watched him in the weeks that followed, how he approached his volunteer work at the Justice Mission with renewed energy. When the director formally asked him to apply, John came to me first.

John nodded slowly. "If I take this position, I'm there to support Cambodians improving their own justice systems."

"Exactly." I smiled, watching the weight lift from his shoulders.

The Justice Mission's primary project was fighting the sex-trafficking of children, which had plagued Cambodia for decades and placed it on America's Tier 3 watchlist multiple times. We knew this job would take a lot out of both of us and possibly our family as well.

The application process took months. It was an extensive undertaking with multiple layers of interviews, including a trip to Washington, DC, for a final round of interviews.

In March 2012, they offered him the job. He would lead the investigative unit, the tip of the spear, for the Justice Mission's project in Cambodia. He would work directly with the three-star general who was the head of the National Anti-Human Trafficking Police. This was a tremendous shift for our family.

John retired from teaching, from supervising the work in Som Pov Loon, and from coaching basketball at the international school. Fighting the sex trade in Cambodia was going to be a full-time job. We no longer had to raise support, worry about a sending church, or write captivating newsletters to our supporters justifying our existence.

There was freedom in this. A salary, benefits, a retirement account, an educational fund for our kids, paid travel to America for our family once a year, and a team of true professionals who were experts in their fields felt like a dream after years of struggling alone. Our whole reason for being in Cambodia was about to change.

∼

We sat in our tranquil garden one evening after he got the job offer. He spoke gravely about the task at hand. "I should be thrilled about this. And I am. But this is going to be the most demanding job I have ever taken on. I'll be diving into the depths of hell . . ." My heart sank at the thought of what he would have to endure. He possessed a deep understanding of the culture and language, and he knew the darkness that lay underneath.

John let out a deep sigh and looked away. "I spent five years as an undercover investigator in Colorado. Now I have to pretend to be a sex tourist." His words hung heavy in the air as I saw the conflict in his eyes. "Definitely the most challenging assignment yet."

The transition from missionary to Director of Investigations was difficult for our family. We had to reduce our online presence and be aware of our surroundings. John's absence during long days filled with high-stakes investigations and operations forced us to adjust to a new normal. I tried to be supportive, but I couldn't shake the worry.

Sex trafficking has a complicated history in Cambodia. In 1992, the United Nations Transitional Authority in Cambodia (UNTAC) arrived. Many considered it a beacon of hope for a country ravaged by decades of war and genocide. But the influx of foreign UN soldiers flooding into Cambodia in the 1990s had a negative impact on Cambodian society. It led to the exploitation of local women and an increase in prostitution. This also potentially contributed to the spread of HIV/AIDS as soldiers introduced the virus from other affected countries.

The number of sex workers in Cambodia skyrocketed from 6,000 in 1991 to over 20,000 after UNTAC personnel arrived in 1992. With that came the proliferation of trafficking minors into the sex industry.

By 2012, on the bustling streets of Phnom Penh, the underground industry carried on beneath the glow of neon signs advertising beer and karaoke. Women clad in shimmering, skimpy dresses sauntered around bars and nightclubs. They were fighting silent battles amidst peals of laughter and clinking glasses. But the minors were not apparent as they once had been; they were hidden away until asked for. Posing as a buyer was the only way to find them.

Months after John started working at the Justice Mission, John and I were driving home from dinner one sweltering evening. We passed a new karaoke bar that had popped up in our neighborhood in the last few weeks, most likely fronting for a sex-trafficking establishment.

Staring out the window, I mentioned it to John. "Did you see that? Another one here in Toul Kork."

He did not look away from the road. "Yeah, we knew that one was here."

Staring at the girls, looking as young as my teens waiting at home, I replied, "So have you been to this one yet?"

"Not yet," he answered.

At once, I started giggling. "What a strange question for a wife to ask her husband. If someone was overhearing, they might question what kind of marriage we had."

He thought about it and started laughing as well. "What a strange life we live." I nodded, smiling at the irony but weeping inside about the tragedy we both had to witness.

In truth, this was no laughing matter. John said that the worst part of his job was posing as a sex tourist. "Those karaokes . . ." He waved his hand outside the window. "The pimps know they can't hold underage girls at their establishments. They go get them when you ask."

"Ask?" I gazed at the girls in front of the brothels. They already looked underage, but Cambodians often look young for their age. "How do you ask?"

"You walk in, look at the girls sitting in the chairs in the front, the older ones, feign disgust, then tell the pimp, *'Jong srey kjay.'*"

"You tell them they are not fresh enough? That you want 'unripe' girls? I've only heard that term used with unripe fruit, not people." I turned again as we passed more neon lights.

"They don't consider them people." John's hands gripped the steering wheel. "They then go find them. Not sure where, somewhere in the neighborhood."

Lights were blinking on in homes behind and around the brothels. I thought about the families there. Some would sell their daughters if the price was right.

"My team and I would then go back into the furthest reaches of the bar. The private karaoke room. They bring drinks and then, a few minutes later, the girls." He choked.

"How old?" I whispered.

"Some as young as twelve, maybe thirteen. I hated it. They thought I was a monster. They did not know I was trying to save them. There was so much fear in their eyes. I could see behind the fear was hatred."

He turned down our street, dodging the ruts in the road. He passed a garment factory, closed for the night, with the guard sleeping on a cot in front of the large double doors.

"One girl, she was so scared. She would not look at me, but she was told to flirt, to 'be sexy.' Although she tried, she was only a child. I whispered to her in Khmer that I would not take her home. I only wanted to sing and share drinks with her. She would still get paid. I knew they would beat her if she didn't get money from me."

We were silent, both of us remembering another time we had to let victims believe we were the enemy. We wanted to be seen as heroes but had to be content with being seen as the bad guys.

We drove up to the gate. I looked up to see my girls sitting on the veranda, reading. So young, so innocent. At ages eleven and thirteen, they were beginning to understand the horrors their Khmer peers had to live through, but tonight they were safe behind our gates.

John continued, "Her transformation amazed me. Once she knew I would not touch her, she became like a child again. Oh, this sick place . . ." He honked and Ly opened the gate. "We'll get them." His hand rested on the horn. "We'll get those pimps."

Months later, I laid in bed waiting. The shadows were lengthening on the cement wall in the corner of my bedroom.

Why is he not returning my texts? The piercing question continued to plague me through the evening. Kids were in bed, the outside gate locked, laundry brought in from the line, but I still did not receive an answer. John had left early that morning with his undercover team to meet with the anti-human trafficking police to prepare for a rescue operation in Phnom Penh.

His mission was to disrupt a child sex-trafficking ring. We knew this would be a dangerous mission, since these establishments were owned by powerful government officials. The risk was high. This and other fears raced through my mind while checking my phone every few minutes. My unread texts traced my growing fears.

Is it going as planned?

Are you all done yet?

Is everyone safe?

In a state of emotional exhaustion, I sent up a last prayer, breathed into what peace I could find, and slept. In the wee hours of the morning, I heard my phone ping.

Startled awake, I reached anxiously for the long-awaited reply. The text read, *All is well, fifteen girls rescued, traffickers in custody. Authorities shut down the brothels. Be home later.*

I breathed a sigh of relief and drifted back to sleep. Tomorrow, fifteen girls would have a new lease on life, and my children would wake and continue the day as if nothing extraordinary had just happened. However, I would remember our tenuous hold on peace.

The following evening after the raid and rescue, John and I pondered again his work and the sacrifices it required. With a great sigh, I watched the lengthening shadows creep along the walls. The front gate clanked and clicked as Ly locked up the home for the night. Stifled laughter came from our little girls' bedroom as they settled down to sleep, and I looked at John and said, "Fifteen girls have a safe place to sleep tonight." We both breathed easier.

THE WAT

Days passed into weeks and then into months. With Maiy home to care for household responsibilities, I took the kids to the pool daily. On one hot day at the beginning of the school year, we paddled around in the small kiddie pool waiting for the school's nascent swim team to finish practice.

"Our first meet is next week, kids," the new, young teacher from America announced to the exhausted swimmers leaning on the wall. "And don't worry about doing well, or winning, or placing, just have fun!" My heart jumped.

After years of competitive swimming, I could not tolerate watching this teacher coddle the swimmers. I stood up and stopped her as she left the pool deck.

"Hello, you must be new here. I'm Sheryl." She grinned and glanced at Malachi, moving from foot to foot on the hot deck, waiting for me to finish. I continued, "I used to be a competitive swimmer. Maybe I can help you with the team." Her face instantly softened, and she breathed a sigh of relief.

"That would be great. I really don't know what I am doing. They said I needed to start this team, and I know nothing about coaching, or competitive swimming, at that rate. I am a dancer." She smiled and her face lit up. "Plus, most of these kids can barely swim. I am so afraid of the meet next week."

"I'll go talk to the principal. I am sure he will be relieved." I noticed my own children standing to the side, watching. "Kids," I asked, "who wants to join the swim team?"

~

Months later, after swim practice, Stephen bounded into the house, put his moto helmet down, grabbed some mango slices Maiy had finished cutting, and announced with a full mouth, "Ji-hoon and I are gonna go back to school to play soccer, then he's got a concert tonight."

"Ji-hoon, I haven't heard you talk about him in a while. How's it going?" I was busy gathering a load of wet towels to take upstairs to the laundry.

"Great. We're both still getting into trouble." He looked at me out of the corner of his eye. "But we were also both elected to be on student council."

I chuckled. Ji-hoon and Stephen had the strongest personalities in their class, so it made sense that they ended up being president and vice president.

"And afterwards, I'm gonna go over to his house for dinner." Stephen glanced to see if he got my approval.

"Sure, you can go. That'll be fun."

"Yeah, his mom loves me." He grabbed another mango slice.

"Really?"

"She loves me, and I love her Korean food. I can't understand a word she says. But when I gobble it up and ask her for more, she looks at me and smiles and says something in Korean, I don't know what, but Ji-hoon says she loves me."

"Well, that's sweet. I'm glad you eat up her food without blinking."

"Oh, Mom, it's the best. I'll talk to you later." He grabbed his helmet and started his motorcycle. Moments later, he was gone.

~

Months later, in 2012, the school year ended, and we all traveled back to America for Joe's graduation, his commissioning from the Naval Academy, and his wedding in Florida.

It was a whirlwind of a trip. When we first arrived at the Naval Academy four years earlier, Malachi had been a newborn baby, but not anymore. Now, he was four years old and taking in all the sights and sounds of America. After the graduation, the little kids and I drove to Florida with my parents in their camper. John and the boys, including Stephen, Joe, Tim, and Seth, had flown down and were already getting things ready for the wedding.

Halfway down the East Coast, somewhere in Georgia, my parents and I stopped at a campground for the night. Needing to get some laundry done, I grabbed my computer and full bag of dirty clothes. I slipped on my flip-flops and trudged over to the campground laundry room in the drizzling rain. It had been a couple days since I had checked the internet, so after I put in the first load of laundry and plunked in the right amount of quarters, I opened my computer, logged in, and pulled up the screen. Immediately, a call came in on Skype from Megan, John's sister, who had been working in Cambodia as a teacher.

I took a sip of my Coke and answered, "Hey, Megan, I can't believe you're calling me right now. I'm in a campground in the middle of Georgia. It's the only place I have internet."

"Sheryl, I've got to tell you something. It's about Ji-hoon."

"What about Ji-hoon?" I put down my drink, hearing the panic in Megan's voice.

"He's dead."

"What?"

"Yes, a cement truck ran over him, killing him instantly."

My heart stopped. Ji-hoon, that sweet boy with tons of energy. Ji-hoon who played his guitar with such enthusiasm and joy. Ji-hoon, who, with Stephen, was the lifeblood of the high school.

"Megan, what's going on over there?"

"It's hell over here. Everybody's going crazy." She paused. "They couldn't find his body."

"What are you talking about?"

"He was supposed to meet friends for a study session at the Shop in Toul Kork . . . He never made it. Everybody was so crazy busy with end-of-school-year things, they didn't realize that he never made it. Then at dinnertime that night, his parents realized he wasn't home, and they started calling his friends. They told them he never showed up. That is when they frantically started searching for him."

"Oh my God." My heart stopped. One of my worst nightmares was that one of my kids would get hit or run over and disappear. That's what happened to Ji-hoon. He disappeared. "How did they find him?"

"It took hours, but they found him at a wat."

"A wat?"

"Yes. Monks were about to cremate his body as an unknown victim of a moto accident."

"Cremate?"

"Yeah, they couldn't figure out who he was. They were going to burn his body, and his parents would never have known."

I gasped, realizing in that moment that this was why my throat clutched and my stomach clenched every time my children left the house. Why I could never rest until I heard the comforting clank of the gate latch, the squeaking of the hinges, and the hum of a moto ease into the courtyard.

Until then, every evening, the tightness in my gut reminded me they were not safe until behind the green gate. Now Ji-hoon was dead, killed, run over by a cement truck, and he had been found minutes before annihilation, when he would forever be a "missing child."

"And then an even worse thing . . ." Megan went on, "Somebody took pictures of the motorcycle accident. It was so gruesome . . . they printed it in the Phnom Penh newspaper."

My blood ran cold. I knew that the Khmer newspapers were uncensored. I had never allowed them in my home. They were nightmarish. But to have Ji-hoon's mutilated body plastered all over the newspapers in Cambodia, I wanted to throw up.

"Megan . . . thank you. I'm sorry you must be there to take care of this. I've got to call Stephen." Closing the computer, I took a few gulps of air and picked up my phone.

I called down to Florida.

John picked up. "What's up?" I heard pool balls rattling behind him and sounds of laughter.

"John, yeah, gotta tell you something. You've got to tell Stephen right away, before he finds out. Ji-hoon . . . he got in a moto accident. He's dead."

Silence on the other end. I could still hear exuberant shouts and the clinking of beer bottles.

I went on, "He's dead. Ji-hoon's dead . . . one of the worst parts is they couldn't find his body for hours, and they found it right before he was going to be cremated. You got to be the one to tell Stephen. He can't find this out any other way."

"Joe and Colby's wedding is in two days . . ." he said.

"I know it's heartbreaking . . . you've got to tell him."

"I will." John hung up.

Within the hour, John texted me. He and the brothers had told Stephen.

Though the wedding sparkled with celebration, grief lurked in the corners of Stephen's smile. His best friend was gone.

September's return to Cambodia felt like stepping into a room where the lights had dimmed. Ji-hoon's absence left a hole, but something more insidious—fear—was threading its way through to the deepest places in my heart. Fear, in one form or another, had been there, but tragedy had never got this close or this terrifying. It, once again, became my unwanted companion, sitting heavy on my chest as I lay awake in the dark, listening to the night sounds of a city that followed no rules.

Under the hypnotic spin of the ceiling fan, night after night, my thoughts spiraled like its blades. Each rotation asked: How much longer? How much more? The broken government systems, the media's unchecked brutality, the subpar medical systems, the casual disregard for human life—it all swirled together, chipping away at my resolve and dragging me into a current of dread.

Cambodia's chaos was no longer just a backdrop; it had become a force that threatened to sweep us away. Every day we stayed, we rolled the dice with our futures, our safety, our very lives. How many more days was I willing to gamble?

I was reading on our front veranda when John came upstairs, cracked open a can of beer, and sat down with a sigh next to me. I had been feeling feverish. Wrapped in a blanket, I shifted and put the book down. I knew he wanted to talk.

"The prevalence study is over." He looked out over the front wall, watching the sunset on the newest building in our neighborhood, a ten-story apartment only halfway finished. The workers had all but deserted it when the owners ran out of money. It stood barren and rude.

"What did your team find?" I followed John's gaze toward the yellowing sun peeking out from the blank, paneled window openings, casting eerie shadows on the floor of our veranda.

John took a long sip from his Angkor Beer. "We found that less than one percent of sex establishments in our project areas were trafficking minors under the age of fourteen. That's down from eight percent when we started working there three and a half years ago. We sent the final report to headquarters in DC."

He turned to me, his smile hiding behind the aluminum frosty with condensation.

I sat up. "This is so great! Congrats!" I noticed the sun sinking and the shadows fading into colorless movements of light. "I'm proud of you."

He smiled and rubbed his ear, looking absently into the distance. "They are going to transition the project now that we have finished this work."

"What does that mean for your job?" I never thought that this might mean the end of his work in Cambodia. But somewhere deep inside of me, something sang. *Does this mean we are free to consider leaving? Is this my exit plan? Do I even want an exit plan?* My head throbbed as I considered all the possibilities.

"Not sure . . . They talked about labor trafficking. Maybe opening an office in Thailand to fight the trafficking of men out on the fishing boats in the sea of Thailand." He paused. "They asked me if I might want to move to Kuala Lumpur and help there. Or work on labor trafficking in Thailand, but I told them we needed to talk about it."

He paused, looked at me, remembering a conversation from long ago, and he leaned his head back. "Seems I found a mission bigger than myself. And . . ." His gaze shifted to the courtyard, where the twins and Maiy were coming out from the kitchen. "I think I am also a better husband and father." He looked to me for affirmation.

Our eyes met, and I nodded and smiled. "Yes, indeed. Those both are true."

I paused and watched Mary and Christina sit on Maiy's moto as she pushed them to the gate. A part of their daily goodbye ritual when she left each evening. She hugged them, snapped on her helmet, looked up at us, and waved goodbye.

I thought about all the years that John had been able to be present to witness these small joys with me. All the years we gained back. It was true. Cambodia changed him.

Maiy's moto buzzed down the street while Ly clanked the gate shut and locked it for the night. The twins climbed up the Jambu tree near the front wall and perched there to snag a few wax apples to nibble before dinner.

I could hear their silly conversations about whether Maiy would bring them mangos tomorrow or the neighbors would hand some over the fence in the morning.

I knew that John's work was worth the struggles. In three years, his team had rescued seventy-one women and girls, arrested twenty-two perpetrators, and closed ten sex establishments.

Looking back at John, I sighed, "Malaysia, Thailand . . . By now, I could move anywhere and adjust to any culture. Learn a new language even. Our kids might even love a new adventure. But . . ." I looked at the girls still sitting in the tree. "I'm tired." I pulled the blanket a bit higher around my shoulders.

He nodded, and we both watched the sun set over Phnom Penh.

DISILLUSIONMENT

T he push and pull of the tide of life was getting exhausting. Yet even as Cambodia threatened to drown us in its complexities and dangers, we found one place where the ground remained steady beneath our feet. The Anglican church offered us steady ground.

For ten years, we had worshiped in that quiet sanctuary. We saw multiple priests from a variety of Anglican off-shoots come and go. We watched two archbishops from the Diocese of Singapore take the bishop's seat.

Singapore's Anglican Diocese, under the Southeast Asian Province, was headed by a bishop who oversaw local parishes and regional missions, including those in Cambodia. The diocese operated under the broader Anglican Communion structure while maintaining its own synod and administrative framework to govern local church affairs and ministry. The Singaporean diocesan priests and archbishop were very invested and involved in the Cambodian Anglican Mission Church but only maintained brief and frantic visits to Cambodia. Over the last ten years, we had been enveloped into their visits, sharing our insights, ideas, and dreams for the Cambodian church.

We watched many expatriates and missionaries grace the doors of our small mission church before eventually returning to their home-lands. For almost a decade, we had worshipped, labored, ministered, dreamed, and watched as the church stumbled along in a harsh spiritual landscape. We thought we had found our spiritual home. Almost.

One evening early on, a priest from Singapore came to our house for dinner. We had many questions about the Anglican tradition. We asked him to explain the Anglican understanding of knowing truth. He described a three-legged stool. Three, the number representing supreme balance. Like the Trinity or a simple barstool. The first leg, he said, was Sacred Scripture. Yes, as former evangelicals, we easily assented to this.

The second leg, he went on, is Sacred Tradition. This was new to us, but we believed the Bible had to have come from somewhere. It came from the ancient church that had a consistent and formal liturgy and tradition. We could get behind this. It made sense that the Bible could not stand alone. The third leg, he continued, was Reason. This one stopped both of us dead.

"What do you mean, reason?" we asked honestly, leaning in to hear his answer.

"Reason," he stated, "comes as the human mind tries to discern those aspects of our faith that are unchangeable doctrine. Those teachings and the practices the church has adopted that are convenient for a particular time and place . . ."

John and I looked at him, waiting for more.

I thought, *Whose reason?* With sixty-four Anglican sects and no unifying authority, there was no consensus on whose reason would prevail, even in the Anglican Church. I wondered whether Reason was the correct tool to find the truth. But who had the authority to determine the ultimate truth of a matter?

Despite our questions, our new liturgical life captivated us. We did not reflect further on the question of authority. Instead, we filed this Reason-Authority question away in a box and spent the next ten years dedicating our lives to the Anglican Church, hoping that the uncomfortable questions of authority, reason, and disunity would just end up disappearing.

Meanwhile, our children never doubted where they belonged,

what their true north was—wrapped in the companionship of Ohm, Ly, Hok, Maiy, Sothea, and our extended Khmer family. Their truth was in their beloved Cambodia.

Their memories included overnight trips to Silk Island, where they slept under silk looms and swam in the Mekong River. Their truth was bartering for fried bananas, a pair of new Chinese knock-off shoes, or an emerald ring with local Khmer merchants who would smile at their language and give them a good price.

Their truth was in the knowledge of how to hail a tuk tuk driver or moto taxi to take them to the school to swim, to the new local mall to get bubble tea with their friends, or to the newly opened movie theater for the latest American film.

They thought Cambodia and Phnom Penh were going to be home for a long time. I was still unsure, nervous, scared. My only reprieve from my unrelenting anxiety was in the Anglican Church. Even though there was peace there, and I thought I could stay there forever, buried inside, I still had deep reservations.

Early 2013, a charismatic American priest committed to make Cambodia his home and our parish his domain. Until then, John and a handful of parishioners had been the church's backbone, pouring themselves into every Sunday service. They led the music, read scripture, preached, and guided the liturgy—their faithful labor creating moments of beauty and meaning week after week.

The new priest quickly began dismantling what they'd built. He brought in his own team of missionaries from his Anglican mission, people who needed ministry assignments in Cambodia. The faithful few who'd held the church together through the lean years found themselves pushed aside, their years of service forgotten.

Our hearts cracked watching this transformation. The church sparkled with fresh energy, yes, but at what cost? We stayed, watching helplessly as each Sunday took us further from the church we'd known and loved. Then came that one Sunday morning when we couldn't deny how far our little community had strayed from its roots. It was also the day that Reason came back to haunt us.

~

One early Sunday morning in November 2014, at the 10 a.m. service, she walked up to the front of the Anglican church and leaned down next to the altar, gathering items to prepare the Eucharistic table. John and I and the six kids were sitting in the far corner of the room.

She did not look familiar, but I knew that our new priest from America occasionally invited guests from America to come and experience his Cambodian English Church. When she stood, I noticed her black shirt and white collar, which distinguished her as a priest. My heart sank, and I glanced at John. His jaw tightened, his brown eyes steeled and fixed.

I knew that the Diocese of Singapore did not ordain women, so she must have come from America, where there were more progressive Anglican communions. Her short, graying hair and tired eyes hidden behind glasses perched on her pale, pointed nose stood out from the dark hair and soft noses of the Cambodians. Her skin, unaccustomed to the relentless heat of Southeast Asia, glistened with sweat.

She moved from the table to the lectern and, in the crackle of the microphone, introduced herself. My eyes were glued to her priestly collar, the sound muffled. John grunted and stood up. I grabbed his shirt and looked up. His eyes were dim with frustration. "I'll grab a moto taxi. I'll see you at home." He left.

I watched him weave his way out of the church and push open the glass doors in the back, his black hair disappearing down the outside staircase. From my corner in the back pew, I watched the scene unfold like an inevitable rupture of our sacred bonds, our spiritual home, and years of connection and community.

I turned to the kids; they looked at me in surprise, both at their dad leaving and the woman in a priest collar in front of us. As she moved to the altar, the empty spot beside me where John should have been screamed of division. Our children fidgeted beside me, unaware of the weight pressing down on my chest.

My position felt impossible—caught between supporting my husband and maintaining stability for our children, and for myself. But I knew this was the last straw. We had been tottering on the edge for a couple of years, from John being pushed to the sidelines after years of ministry, to the doctrinal division between the Eastern and Western Anglican traditions, to the overall feeling that we did not belong here anymore.

Watching her move about our sanctuary felt like watching something foundational shift beneath my feet. There was this immediate sense of disorientation. Confusion and disappointment, not directed at her personally, but at our church for abandoning something it had held sacred for centuries.

There was also this uncomfortable internal tension. Part of me was curious about how this decision had been made and what had changed, while another part felt betrayed by the institution I had trusted to maintain the status quo. I found myself questioning whether I had misunderstood something fundamental, or whether the Anglican Church had. The consistency I had drawn so much reassurance from was now fractured leaving me feeling unmoored and uncertain about what other changes might follow.

The rest of the service was a blur. Readings, sermons, communion. Same, yet now different. When the priest gave her final blessing, I made my way around the room, greeting my friends. Smiles and hugs and then a quick retreat. I wrangled the kids and made my way out the glass doors with the hum of conversation and laughter behind me.

On the drive home, the children were quiet, and I was deep in thought. Then came a strong sense of peace. After ten years of service and friendship, I knew I was done. Not only did the progressive pastor leave us behind, but we realized that Reason was inadequate to keep a church unified. I felt like I could no longer trust a church that kept changing the rules. Someone had to have the final say in matters of church worship, governance, and doctrine. I knew in that moment —I could not deny it any longer—the Anglican Church did not have it.

CROSSING THE TIBER RIVER

H er large, brown hand waved under her white cotton sari, the three blue stripes catching the light as she moved. The traditional habit of Mother Teresa's order transformed her simple gesture into something both humble and holy, as natural to her as breathing. Her curly hair peeked out, and her eyes sparkled. Malachi waved back at her as he sat next to me, kicking his feet back and forth during the Mass readings.

I fingered the wooden rosary beads that were carved by landmine survivors in the distant provinces. Each bead a prayer and a thanksgiving for both Cambodia and the Catholic Church, my patient teachers.

We had been attending the English Mass at the Catholic church of Phnom Penh for a few months, but the Missionaries of Charity, with their kind smiles and robust laughter, made my children feel at home.

No one was more surprised than me when we found ourselves in the Catholic Church. After we left the Anglican Church that one Sunday, I knew we would never return. John and I talked at length about where we would find our true church home.

We both knew that we could not, after all we had learned over the last eleven years, return to a nondenominational, evangelical church. We believed that the Anglican Church suffered from the same struggles as the other Protestant churches: lack of unity, authority, universality. We decided we needed to investigate the Catholic Church.

Years earlier, after Michele left our home in 2005, moved back to America, and got married, I found, in her wake, a pile of devotionals —Magnificats— she left behind in her room. Full of beautiful Catholic prayers, including the Liturgy of the Mass, Liturgy of the Hours, saint stories, sacred art, and daily readings and musings by thoughtful Catholics through the ages, each volume was small enough to hold in the palm of my hand.

I loved these devotionals and devoured them until they were dog-eared. We were far from the Catholic Church in 2005, but the beauty, poetry, and transcendence of the Catholic prayers transported me to a place I had never experienced before in my spiritual life. I feasted on them. And, in this small way, God was preparing my heart.

"Let's just look. We don't have to decide about becoming Catholic or not," I mentioned one afternoon as we talked on the veranda before dinner. It had only been a week since we had walked out of the Anglican church.

John pulled out his phone. "Even after growing up Catholic, I know little about what they teach. What I know about Catholics, I was told by a Protestant. Probably not the best way to get information." He scrolled on his phone looking for Catholic churches in Phnom Penh.

"I guess it does not hurt to hear about how Catholics defend their doctrines. We did that for Anglicans. It would at least give them a fair shot," I laughed.

"There are a few English-speaking Catholic Masses," John said. "One is in Phnom Penh Thmey. Another is down by the river and the Japanese Friendship Bridge. Another meets on Saturday night; it's in downtown Phnom Penh."

I considered our options. "Next Sunday is the first Sunday of Advent. The start of the church year is a good time to begin this exploration. Let's go to the one near the Japanese Bridge. What time does it meet?"

"Nine o'clock." John put his phone down to look at me. "It will

look a lot like an Anglican service, but there are significant theological differences. We will need to do our own work to learn more."

"No bookstores here have what we are looking for." I picked up
my phone.

"We have the internet. Let's start searching." John stood up. Before
he finished speaking, I was already on Amazon looking for e-books
on Catholic theology.

∼

That first Sunday of Advent, we shuffled into the English service. A
kind priest with sparkling eyes and a lined face greeted us at the
door.

"Welcome! Are you visiting?" His kind eyes turned to look at the
six children trailing behind us. "There is a nice place to sit under the
fans over there." He motioned with his wrinkled hand to an empty
row of chairs.

We smiled and made our way over, feeling noticeably out of place.
The service was very familiar after years of Anglican services, and the
differences were barely noticeable. But I felt a real presence of God
there. Later in the Mass, when the priest, in a sea of vestments, held
up the bread in one hand and a chalice of wine in the other while
reciting the Eucharistic prayers, I gasped. *This is so beautiful. I feel the
Holy Spirit so strongly. I must be a part of this.*

"I'm going up there and taking the Eucharist." I moved to stand.
John grabbed my hand and pulled me down.

"You can't," he whispered. "You are not Catholic. They believe it
would damage your soul to receive the Eucharist and not be in full
communion with the Catholic Church. This much I remember from
my catechism classes."

I looked him straight in the eyes. "Then I want full communion." I
sat down, gazing at the line of congregants prayerfully walking up to
receive the Body and Blood of Jesus.

After the service, I made my way to the priest wishing parishioners well as they left the sanctuary. I waited for the throng to thin
and approached him.

"I want to be Catholic. How do I do that?" I grabbed Emma's hand as she stood next to me. She had been asking me the same question ever since she studied medieval history a few years earlier and went to Notre Dame Cathedral in Paris with her grandparents.

Father David laughed, and his eyes twinkled. "We started RCIA, that's Rite of Christian Initiation of Adults, last August." He looked at a calendar behind him. "It is now the first week of December. You are a bit behind."

"I have been a faithful Christian since I was fourteen years old. Confirmed in the Anglican Church, and I have studied the Bible for decades. I need to learn how Catholics interpret the scriptures." My words tumbled over each other. "I'll learn fast, I promise."

"In that case"—his mouth twitched—"come to class at the beginning of January. We meet on Friday afternoons at the rectory. I'll write down the address." He grabbed a pen and a bulletin from a table behind him and scribbled directions to the rectory.

"Can my daughter Emma come as well? She's sixteen years old." I motioned for Emma to come forward.

Father David looked at her. "Yes, she's old enough. Both of you meet with me and the other candidates on the second Friday of January." He dashed out of the sanctuary to get ready for his next Mass.

I looked at John with a smile. "I guess Emma and I are doing this thing."

He laughed. "I guess you are." I cocked my head to see what he was thinking, but he was busy thumbing through a church bulletin. He stopped at the page listing confession times. As a fallen-away, cradle Catholic, confession was his next step to coming back to the Catholic Church after almost thirty years away. I smiled. He was coming, too.

We studied for hours every day. We compared notes, talking late into the night about all we were learning. An entire library of books that we never knew existed opened to us. Emma and I attended RCIA at the rectory, Father David's home that he shared with other priests, in downtown Phnom Penh. We learned that the Rite of Christian Initiation of Adults is the Catholic Church's formal process for adults and older teens seeking to become Catholic.

Father David gently explained that RCIA involved a period of instruction, spiritual formation, and gradual introduction to the faith community. The process typically took about a year, and culminated at the Easter Vigil, where candidates received the sacraments of Baptism, Confirmation, and Eucharist, completing their full initiation into the Catholic Church.

I devoured books that explained the patterns, liturgy, dogma, and sacraments that could be traced right back to the early church fathers, the apostles, and Jesus himself. Consistent, authoritative teachings. I kept waiting for some teaching not to fit, for there to be a hole in logic, for an inconsistency to announce itself. I looked for them. They never appeared. In fact, the harder I looked, the more the Catholic Church made sense. For the first time in my life, all my theological questions were being answered.

One afternoon, I was sitting on the veranda devouring a book on the magisterium of the Catholic Church when something jumped out at me. I caught my breath and spoke out loud to no one, "The third leg of the stool!" I looked around to see if anyone heard me. "Right here, it says that the first leg was sacred scripture, the second leg was holy tradition, and the third leg was the magisterium: the teaching authority of the Church. It's not *Reason*, it's a living, breathing apostolic authority." I slumped back in my chair, grappling with how the early protesters, Protestants, and the Church of England (Anglicans) had replaced magisterium for reason. No wonder it never sat well with me. It was a facsimile, used to disarm the teaching authority of the church.

This wasn't the first nor the last moment of epiphany. My eyes were opening, and the veil lifted on several theological points that never aligned in other denominations.

While the church's dogma spoke to my intellect, it was the sacraments which spoke to my soul. They sang of mystery and belonging. Faith was no longer an abstraction, it was tangible, tactile, and present. The cool press of water on skin during baptism, bread dissolving on the tongue during communion, the warm slide of oil traced in crosses during confirmation, the kiss of matrimony. These ancient rituals translated the sacred into tangible experiences.

Each Sunday, we listened to the teaching of the Word, the Bible, and watched with prayer as the priest consecrated the Eucharist; my heart yearned and my mouth watered as I waited to partake myself, which was still months away at Easter.

On holy feast days, the clouds of frankincense and myrrh hung as visible prayers in the air. Even hours after Mass, traces of incense lingered in hair and clothing. The beeswax candles flickered and danced, casting shadows on the altar. The ordinary made holy in the sacraments.

It made perfect sense in this land, Cambodia, which also transformed the ordinary to the sacred. The chanting of the monks, the sharp smells of joss sticks, the saffron robes waving in the breeze as the monks, barefoot and humble, walked the dusty streets of Phnom Penh. There was congruence, a thread of seeing grace in the ordinary that wove between cultures, that threaded us all together.

"I can't believe it. After twelve years of living here, we finally find the one, true Church," I said to John one night as we faced each other in the dark, listening to the geckos chatter from across the wall. "It's like, this is the reason we came here . . . to become Catholic."

It had been twelve years since we'd moved to Cambodia, and there was one thing I learned: That I could live in any culture. I could learn another language; I could navigate another medical system; I could create a nurturing home; I could figure out how to keep my kids safe and have a fulfilling life. Anywhere.

The missing piece, however, was a church that could be in all those places at once, too. And here it was. The one universal Church. The same authority, pope, readings, and liturgy anywhere in the world. I had truly found home, in every sense of the word. Home as close as Jesus in the Eucharist and as far as the ends of the earth. The Catholic Church filled a hole in me that had been whistling for years. The Catholic Church was the spiritual home I had been searching for.

THE TEAK TABLE

I bustled about the serenity garden, dead-heading flowers, checking for grubs, fertilizing. I wasn't sure why I was doing all this, but since starting RCIA, I had a feeling that things were going to shift soon. I first got this feeling in November when the rains stopped and the cool winds blew down from the north.

The twelve-story monstrosity next door shaded my little garden, but I managed with the limited sunlight. I kept a beautiful little water garden in a large earthenware pot. It was rich with fragrant water lilies and waxy duckweed with its tiny leaves, which needed little sun. A few goldfish darted below the surface.

Today, I threw some fertilizer into my bird of paradise, hoping it would bloom for me. I wondered, *am I blooming?* After all these years, *was I blooming?*

I wasn't sure what was in store for us. With John's job transitioning, the Justice Mission shifting gears, and our own draw back to America—where Joe, Tim, Seth, and Stephen were now starting their own lives—I felt the call to return to my homeland.

I had mixed feelings. Cambodia had become my love in so many ways. I was in love with Cambodian food, the Khmer people, the rice fields, the monsoon rains, the simple life. But Cambodia was also a negligent lover. There is no escaping the broken systems, ingrained trauma, and the unrelenting knowledge that there were few safety nets.

It was almost Christmas on another Monday night date night. In the stillness of the serenity garden, John and I talked about my growing unease with our life in Cambodia. I sensed that the final chapters in Cambodia were about to be written. But John was not so sure. He saw my suffering, exhaustion, and growing fears since Ji-hoon's death. He could see how I missed my four adult children and new grandbaby in America. But he was in the prime of his career while I sensed it was time to leave.

John poured me another homemade margarita. I reached for it, changing the subject to our homeschool talent night and how much artistic flair we had in our group. He was not responding but stared into the night while he settled back into the papasan chair, now twelve years old, on the front veranda.

I went on, "I also got Clara's book edited and uploaded on Amazon. She is such a gifted writer. Though the subject matter is quite serious." I pondered Clara's latest book, *I Have Been Sold*, about a young Cambodian girl sold by her father into sex trafficking and then rescued. "I am grieved that our girls had to grow up faster than normal knowing even just a little bit about the work you were doing." I sighed and took a sip of the margarita. "Yum . . . so good. Did you use orange juice?"

John was still quiet as he nodded his head.

"What's up?" I was concerned. His quiet usually meant he had something important to tell me.

He leaned forward slowly. "You are right." His eyes met mine. "It's time to go home."

I blinked twice. Tears pooled in my eyes. "Really? Can we really go home?" The silence enveloped both of us as we sat in our own worlds, thinking of the places and people both here and in America. And the path that would lead us home.

~

Everyone gathered around the table with the smells of a Cambodian Christmas dinner. We blasted the air-conditioning to simulate the coolness of a Colorado evening. The Christmas tree twinkled upstairs with presents from America spilling out from under its branches. Joe and his wife, Colby, had arrived a few days earlier. They had brought our new grandbaby and the announcement of another pregnancy. Tim and his wife, Laura, brought totes of presents I had bought and sent to their home in Pennsylvania. Seth and Stephen came back from college for their winter break.

We gathered about the long, heavy teak table. I remembered the first day we sat around that table, in May 2003, when we walked into that enormous kitchen, heavy with grief, after leaving America. Sweaty, exhausted, and unfamiliar with the tastes of Cambodian food, climate, and foreignness. The road ahead had been daunting. Today, we encircled the table feeling serene and safe in our home surrounded by all ten of our children, two daughters-in-law, and our new grandson.

I dished up the steaming rice, the savory ham, and the bubbling sweet potatoes. Clara's homemade rolls circulated from hand to hand. More steaming platters of food made their clockwise march around the table. A plate of Christmas cookies baked by Emma in the tiny oven sat on the side counter waiting.

The table was bursting with laughter and stories. Then the mood turned pensive when we remembered that old farm table under the Colorado sky in 2001, when we had discussed with excitement and naiveté opening an orphanage to save Cambodia's children.

Instead of the orphanage, we gave love and a home to seven Cambodians, encouraged Khmer orphans to take pride in their language and culture, prayed with dying AIDS patients, and held malnourished babies. We taught church history; ministered in music and hospitality; rescued women and children from sex-trafficking; started an expatriate Bible study, a homeschool group, and a swim team; and made dozens of friends and a few enemies.

We hadn't accomplished the goals that our mission organization had set out for us. But the meandering road led us to find purpose and meaning in everyday things done with great love. God multiplied those in his own timing, and we were honored to be a part of it.

And, most importantly, we loved our family well. I looked around at the expanding joy around my table—a table that matured over time and made way for the next generation as I glanced at my first grandson banging his fork, calling for someone to dish him some rice, like Olivia had twelve years earlier. Olivia, twelve years old, sat next to him, cooed softly, and spooned the steaming rice into his little bowl.

When there was a break in the din, John rattled his fork, tapped his glass, and said, "We have an announcement . . ."

Everyone stilled and quieted down, looking at him, perplexed and curious. "We've decided, after twelve years living, working, loving, hating"—he grinned at me—"our life here in Cambodia . . ." He turned back to look at his children, his eyes now somber and sad. "We're going to come home."

The table irrupted with screams, laughter, hugs, and tears. I could not tell which emotion was most prevalent: sadness and confusion from our younger children, joy from the older ones who would have grandparents close at hand, or curiosity from our college students, who were not used to having us live close.

My girls looked at me curiously as tears dripped down my cheeks. They weren't sure, trying to take their cue from me, if they were supposed to be sad or happy. I wasn't sure what my tears said either. It said both those things and so much more.

John contemplated the towering palms floundering from the lack of light in the shadowed garden one date night.

"What's next?" My voice sounded hoarse and soft.

His own voice struggled to visualize living, working, thriving in a place we had left twelve years before. "Well, the Justice Mission is interested in using some of my skill set to open a new office in Thailand. They are going to work on the illegal trafficking of Cambodian and Burmese men onto the fishing boats. They got a grant from a large superstore in America who wants to make sure their fish is being humanely harvested. There's an opportunity, though, for me to work remotely for a while after we get settled back in America. I would go over there for a few weeks at a time to get it started." He looked at me cautiously.

"Sure . . ." Remote work gave us the option to live anywhere in America. "So, the plan would be, we leave for America in June? After you wrap up work here? After we come into the Catholic Church at Easter?"

"That's the plan." John's eyes drifted to the moon half hidden behind the ghostly apartment building.

"And then once in America, you stay on with the Justice Mission until the end of the year with periodic visits to Thailand. Then contract with them for another six months." My hands lit up under the full moon, looking old, haggard, yet strong and resilient. I shifted.

"We will make a home base in Colorado," John said. "We have enough money from selling the Sage House to put a down payment on a house there." A gecko cried in the dark, and one kid laughed from their bedrooms inside. "We can make it home."

Christmas season was over. The older kids left, returning to America, leaving the six youngest children. They put on smiles, but we knew they weren't happy. This was their home, and we were going to tear it from them.

I tried to soothe their fears about life in America. "We will home-school and visit with grandparents and ride grandpas' horses."

"What about friends, Mom?" Christina asked me one night as I put her to bed. "We have our best friends here."

I caressed her blonde wisps of hair. "We'll have to make new ones in America."

"But kids in America, they don't understand us. They don't want to know anything about our Cambodian home. They think America is our home. We don't know America." Her voice cracked.

"I know. We're going to have to learn all over again." I leaned in and kissed her soft forehead. She buried her head in my chest and sighed. Rocking her, she sniffled quietly while her warm tears fell across my worn hands.

As I tucked her into bed, I studied her face, watching as the Southeast Asia light played across her delicate features. Soon, it would be different light, different shadows, different dreams. We were about to become immigrants again, only this time carrying Cambodia in our hearts as we returned to a place that had become foreign.

GOODBYE, SIEM REAP

On a beautiful Easter Sunday, April 5, 2015, the Catholic Church welcomed all six of our remaining children, John, and me into her loving embrace.

Three months earlier, shortly after Emma and I started RCIA, the kids and I had found ourselves at a demurer abbey across from the local market where we'd shopped for food for the last twelve years, never knowing it existed behind those brick walls. Seven Salesian Sisters, tasked with catechizing us, the new candidates, greeted us as we stepped into their tidy courtyard.

They kindly took my children through the teachings of the church every Wednesday. One of the first afternoons, we walked reverently into their little chapel, which looked out onto a luscious garden filled with banana trees, waving palms, and bountiful bougainvillea. But they centered our attention on a candle flame flickering next to a beautiful ornate box made from mahogany wood.

"That is Jesus in there in the Eucharistic bread," Sister said as she genuflected in front of the box that held the sacred host, making the sign of the cross. We awkwardly followed her motions. "If the candle is lit, he is in the tabernacle." We nodded and stared in awe at both the candle, the ornate box, and what it held inside.

After weeks of teachings from the Sisters and reading from the simple books the Sisters could find in their paltry library, Father Isaiah met us all at the abbey for our first confession. We each took our turn to meet with him in a simple room with a single crucifix on the wall. Sitting across from him, we shared our sins, sorrows, and struggles in our either short (Malachi's seven) years or long (my forty-eight) lives. We collectively shared a sense of cleansing, relief, and joy.

Our last weeks before we left Cambodia were bittersweet and chaotic. We enjoyed our new Catholic church family, with parishioners from all over the world and several Missionaries of Charity Sisters who loved on our children. We met with our longtime Protestant missionary friends with whom we'd forged deep relationships through cultural adaptation, traumas, and joys for over a decade. We cried with our Cambodian friends with whom we'd shared life and love while they had grown from college students to married families.

We dismantled our life piece by piece, selling everything except what would fit in a shipping crate bound for America. Each item sold was another goodbye, another thread of our Cambodian life snipped away. The furniture, books, and household goods that had made this place home would now belong to others.

The ministries were harder to let go of. After years of searching for my purpose here, I'd found places where I could make a difference. Now I had to step away from those roles and hand them on to others: the homeschool group I'd built from scratch years ago, the women's Bible study that had become a lifeline for so many, and the swim team, my heart's project that I'd nurtured from its first meet.

For over twelve years, our Khmer family had slowly grown up and created lives of their own, like birds leaving the nest. Ly married and became father to twin boys. Sothea found love too, and her own set of twins arrived while she continued teaching mathematics. Hok's gentle courtship of Sambo bloomed into marriage, while Maiy married and then welcomed a daughter into the world. Ohm, after years of caring for others, found peace in retirement living near the river with her sister. Even Srey Ning stayed in our lives. We helped her welcome her second child into the world months earlier.

Though they had their own homes now, the bonds remained unbroken. We watched their children toddle and grow, these precious little ones who called us *Yeay* and *Ta*, Grandma and Grandpa. Each new life added another thread to the tapestry we'd woven together over the years. Now, facing our departure, we knew leaving them would carve a deep wound in our hearts. These weren't just people who had lived in our home—they were our children, our grandchildren, our family.

One black cat would journey to America with us, a living bridge between my daughters' two worlds. But for the others, our loyal dogs, other watchful cats, and slow, gentle tortoise, we had to find new homes. These creatures had been more than pets; they helped us survive in Cambodia. They'd stood guard against intruders, waged midnight battles against rats, and brought laughter with their antics and peace to our anxious hearts. Each played their part in making our house a home, serving us with fierce devotion.

"At least Annabelle had grandparents when we left Colorado," Olivia said quietly as we watched a local family drive away with Daisy in the back of a tuk tuk. "I hope these people are kind."

I put my arm around her shoulders, noticing how tall she'd grown in our years abroad. "They will be," I said, remembering how we'd vetted each family carefully.

In the weeks that followed, we visited all our favorite places one last time: Silk Island for bike rides on the dusty village roads, the chocolate factory for some homemade treats, the Chinese noodle house for hand-pulled noodles, a trip to Kep to our favorite resort, and another trip to Kampot with Jamie and his family.

One last swim at the pool, one last tuk tuk ride to the new air-conditioned mall, one last dinner at the Le Royal Hotel with my dear expatriate friends, one last varsity soccer game on the new fields on the south end of town, one last Khmer glamour shot sitting at the local picture studio.

It felt that we were doing all the right things to wrap up our time, but something still felt incomplete. I suggested we take one more trip to Siem Reap to say goodbye to Angkor Wat, the ancient temples that define Cambodian cultural identity. It seemed fitting.

It was only three weeks before we were to fly back to America when we settled in Siem Reap at our favorite guest house. We spent three days exploring the temples we loved, relishing in their grandeur reminiscent of the glorious days of the Khmer Empire.

We ate fried crickets and grubs bought from a wrinkled Khmer grandma who smiled at the way my children gobbled the fried insects and washed them down with a freshly picked coconut.

We ranged over the lesser-known temples, climbing through crevices and bouldering around ancient stones that had tumbled down from their grand heights. Vines and tropical plants hid the kids in their private enclaves as they played hide-and-seek with the ancient ghosts of Cambodia's past. Under the towering Bayon's eternal gaze, we offered kissy tributes to their mysterious smiles. Centuries of solemn dignity met our playful poses, the carved guardians joining our game. After hours of exploration, the children collapsed in the shade of the bas-reliefs of Apsara dancers and majestic elephants.

The sun was setting and our feet were weary when Emma suggested, "Mom, let's get our signature picture here in front of the temple." The kids struck the same pose, no matter where they stood, whether the beach, the Phnom Penh skyline, or here at the Angkor Wat temple. They lined up facing the object of interest, tallest to shortest, the taller sibling resting their arms on the shoulders of the shorter. We have many of these pictures from over the years. Now that four of the siblings had long since started their new lives in America, these six carried on the tradition.

Emma, Clara, Olivia, Mary, Christina, and Malachi lined up along the ancient pond's edge. The temple loomed in front of them, its ancient spires framing their tiny figures like a postcard come to life. In the gray-green water below, their reflections danced with the setting sun, creating twin images of childhood against the backdrop of centuries.

I snapped a few shots and directed them to move their arms or stop stepping on each other's feet.

Then, I stopped. I looked at my children—culturally Cambodian, ethnically American. Nomads, immigrants, no matter what country they would live in. They'd been small children or not even born when we first came to this distant land when I was so afraid, lost, confused. I bore their suffering being far from family and friends.

But in twelve years, we had created this life full of excitement, novelty, new friends, and new family. Now we would be leaving. I was going back to my homeland; they were going to a foreign land. They would need to start over, like I had when I came to Cambodia. They would become the ones afraid, lost, and confused in a country who thought they were American. When in fact they were hidden immigrants. I did not know at the time the suffering they would endure. They did not either.

What began as a mission to a foreign land revealed my deeper truth: identity, belonging, and home aren't fixed to one place or culture. Through years of grappling with safety concerns, from political unrest to midnight rats, we discovered that security comes not from high walls and locked gates, but from the web of relationships we wove built on mutual trust.

Our Khmer family taught us to trust. Through them we learned that belonging transcends language and culture, while our children showed us how one could inhabit multiple worlds. Our sense of mission evolved from a propositioned plan to simple hospitality and deep connection, while our understanding of home expanded beyond physical walls to encompass both our American roots and our Khmer heart. The most profound growth came from embracing the very uncertainties that once terrified us while leaving behind what no longer worked. Cambodia gave us these gifts.

As we prepared to leave, I realized my children would need to forge their own path. Each would have to wrestle with being Third Culture Kids, with straddling worlds, with the ache of leaving their Khmer home behind. Their journey to understanding who they were and where they belonged couldn't be walked by anyone else—not even their mother who had navigated these waters before them.

In the past few months, I had seen the questions in their eyes: Were they more Khmer or American? How could they leave the only life they had ever known? Where was home? Yet watching them move so naturally between worlds, hearing them switch effortlessly between languages, seeing them love so freely across cultures, I knew they would find their way. They would discover, as I had, that their strength lay not in choosing one world over another, but in the unique gift of belonging to both.

We took one last walk down the dusty path back to the van, under the ancient canopy of banana leaves, coconut palms, and the twisted roots of sprung trees. The Cambodian jungle encircled us on all sides. The chatter of birds, a howl of a monkey, the smell of brine coming from the lotus-filled ponds filled me with gratitude and grief. I grabbed Mary's hand on one side and Christina's on the other. They smiled up at me and squeezed my shaking hands.

We piled in the van after buying one last coconut to split among them. I sat in the back seat and Malachi snuggled in my lap and held my hand. He was asleep before we turned off the uneven road. I looked down and slowly opened my hand. His little fingers, grimy with coconut milk and Cambodia's red dust, pulsed with life. Closing my fingers around his, I twisted in my seat to watch the majestic temples with their reddish glow and craggy towers shaped like lotus buds disappear from my sight. The home of the gods, the "Phnom Meru," the sacred mountain, dissolved into the horizon. I closed my eyes. It is finished. I drifted off for an eternity.

When I opened my eyes again, I was watching the rugged, snowy peaks of the Rocky Mountains loom ahead. I had left home. I was home.

Our last family photo in America before leaving for Cambodia in 2003. We are full of idealism, excitement, and faith.

Goodbye, Siem Reap. A week before we fly back to America in 2015

ABOUT THE AUTHOR

 Sheryl Roberts holds a BA in English Literature and Communications from the University of Colorado and is a licensed mental health professional who has dedicated her career to supporting overseas workers and their families through her private practice. Drawing from years of personal experience as a mother and missionary coupled with professional insight, she has crafted her debut memoir from a rich tapestry of newsletters, blog posts, journals, and personal correspondence.

When she's not writing or counseling clients, Sheryl retreats with her husband, John, in their mini-camper, to the isolated beauty of the mountain wilderness to seek inspiration and renewal. A mother to ten children and devoted grandmother, she finds her greatest joy in long conversations with her family and precious moments with her grandbabies.

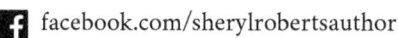

Website: Sheryl Roberts Author
https://www.robertscounseling.org/book

f facebook.com/sherylrobertsauthor

ACKNOWLEDGEMENTS

Grateful acknowledgement is made to the following for permission to reprint previously published and unpublished material:

"Song of Blessing" Words and Music by Joe Wise © 1975 GIA Publications, Inc. Used with permission. All rights reserved.

Verses 6, 7, 8 adaptations of *"Song of Blessing'* by Mark Roberts 2003. Used with permission. All rights reserved.

www.ingramcontent.com/pod-product-compliance
Lightning Source LLC
Chambersburg PA
CBHW060412130626
46555CB00005B/2036